#58/59
Summer/Fall 2023

Movement Research
Performance Journal 58/59

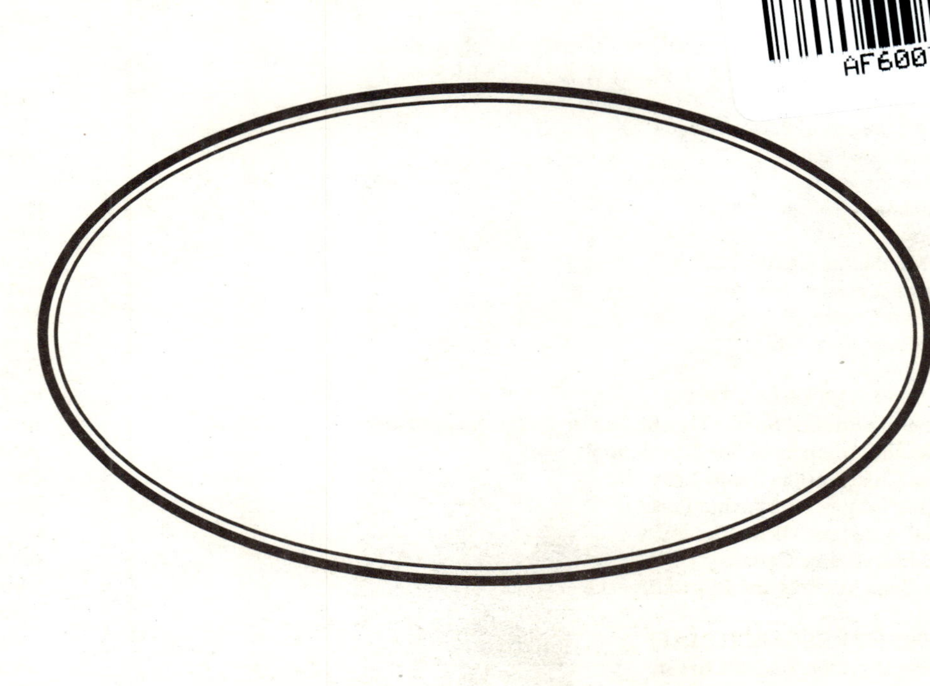

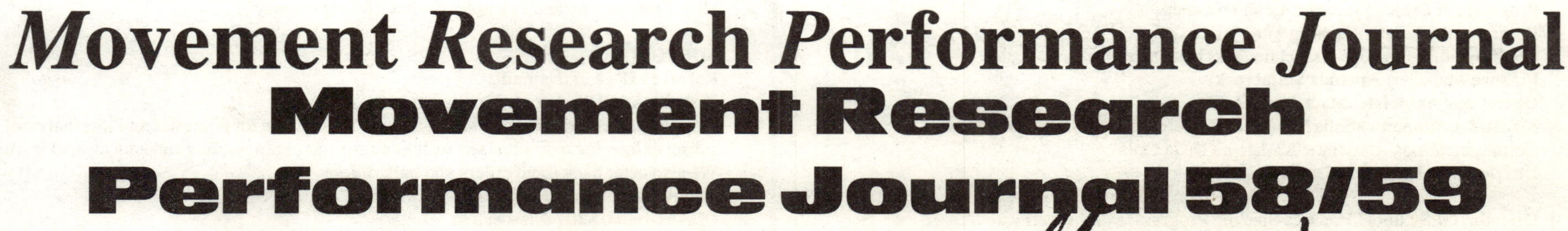

Movement Research Performance Journal

Movement Research
Performance Journal 58/59

Movement Performance Research
Journal

Movement Research
Performance Journal
#58/59, Summer/Fall 2023

Published twice annually
By Movement Research, Inc.
150 First Avenue
New York, NY 10009
212.598.0551
www.movementresearch.org
info@movementresearch.org

The Movement Research Performance Journal is deeply grateful
for the visionary support from our LEGACY PARTNERS:
Artists Space
Center for the Art of Performance UCLA
The Chocolate Factory
Danspace Project
The Kitchen
Lili Chopra
Lower Manhattan Cultural Council
Performance Space New York
Walker Art Center
The Whitney

ABOUT MOVEMENT RESEARCH
Movement Research is one of the world's leading laboratories for the investigation of dance and movement-based forms. Valuing the individual artist, their creative process and their vital role within society, Movement Research is dedicated to the creation and implementatio of free and low-cost programs that nurture and instigate discourse and experimentation. Movement Research strives to reflect the cultural, political and economic diversity of its moving community, including artists and audiences alike.

Movement Research accomplishes its mission through a range of programs including ongoin classes and workshops taught by artist educators and innovators; creative residencies offered for choreographers and movement-based artists; festivals bringing together leaders in the fiel and publications and public events providing artists with forums for discourse on a broad ran of issues. For more information, please visit www.movementresearch.org.

ACKNOWLEDGEMENTS
Movement Research gratefully acknowledges public support from the New York City Department of Cultural Affairs in partnership with the City Council; City Council Member Carlina Rivera; Manhattan Borough President Gale Brewer's Manhattan Community Award Program; Materials for the Arts (a program of NYC Department of Cultural Affairs, NYC Department of Sanitation, and NYC Department of Education); The New York State Council on the Arts with the support of the Office of the Governor and the New York State Legislatur and the National Endowment for the Arts (a federal agency).
Movement Research gratefully acknowledges the generous contributions of private support from The Andrew W. Mellon Foundation; The Blanchette Hooker Rockefeller Fund; Dance/NYC's New York City Dance Rehearsal Space Subsidy Program, an initiative made possible by The Mellon Foundation; Davis Dauray Family Fund; Harkness Foundation for Dance; Howard Gilman Foundation; James E. Robison Foundation; Jerome Foundation; Marta Hefli Foundation; Mertz Gilmore Foundation; Mid Atlantic Arts Foundation Regional Resilience Fund; NYU Community Fund; Robert Rauschenberg Foundation; Ruth Foundation for the Arts; Sustainable Arts Foundation; and Trust for Mutual Understanding. Movement Researcl is a member of Coalition of Small Arts NYC. Movement Research also acknowledges the individual donors and dear Friends of Movement Research, who contribute financial, support labor, and love.
Thanks always to the clergy and staff of Judson Memorial Church. Judson Memorial Church continues to be a beacon for free spirits in the arts and politics, and a leader among progressiv faith communities in the city and nation for over 100 years. Enormous gratitude to Frances Alenikoff (1920–2012), founder of Eden's Expressway, and to her daughter Francesca Rheanno and family, for their continuing belief in the mission of Movement Research and for keeping alive Frances' spirited example of what lifelong artistry is.

SUBSCRIBE
Receive MRPJ in the mail!
Distribute MRPJ to your Community!
Movement Research Performance Journal is available for domestic and international subscriptions for individuals as well as non-profit organizations and educational institutions. We also offer back issue orders and bulk orders.
Individual subscription rates:
USA: 2-issue: $20 / 4-issue: $36
Canada: 2-issue: $26 / 4-issue: $48
Int'l: 2-issue: $40 / 4-issue: $78
Institutional subscription rates:
USA: 2-issue: $55 / 4-issue: $95
Canada: 2-issue: $62 / 4-issue: $109
Int'l: 2-issue: $71 / 4-issue: $126
Back issue and bulk order pricing available upon request.

For more information or to subscribe online visit:
www.movementresearch.org/performance_journal/subscriptions
or mail a check to: Movement Research, 150 First Ave, New York, NY 10009

CONTRIBUTE
Movement Research, Inc. is a not-for-profit 501(c)3 tax-exempt organization. Tax deductible donations are greatly appreciated and can be made Online at www.movementresearch.org; or by Texting "GIVE2MR" to 44-321; or by Mailing a check to Movement Research, 150 First Ave, New York, NY 10009.

Movement Research Performance Journal is made possible through the generous support of MRPJ donors, advertisers and subscribers. To advertise in the MRPJ, email performancejournal@movementresearch.org

Upcoming Movement Research Performance Journals seeking dance and performance-relate topics and guest co-editors for future issues. Stay tuned for details, or contact: mrpjeditors@movementresearch.org

To contact Journal Contributors, please contact the Movement Research office or email mrpjeditors@movementresearch.org

Research Agenda

Research rarely resolves the way one expects. In the Fall of 2022, the *Movement Research Performance Journal* set out to explore the concept of "research," a word intrinsic to our name and our parent organization's long history of supporting process over product. Research is such an academic concept (less so than our initial idea of doing an issue on pedagogy), and we wanted to find a way to thread our work around the relationship dance and performance practice has to systems of "higher" education. We looked to contributing editors embedded in the university system, those parasitically attached to it, and those intentionally operating outside of codified educational systems. We wanted to leave room for some contributors to celebrate how performance upends the conventional hierarchy between teaching and learning—and for others to lambast the way dance and performance has been curtailed to a university model. We wrote to prospective writers:

> Keyword: Research
> (n.) ***studious inquiry or examination, especially: investigation or experimentation aimed at the discovery and interpretation of facts, revision of accepted theories or laws in the light of new facts, or practical application of such new or revised theories or laws.***
>
> Prompt: Movement Research was founded in 1978 as a self-described "laboratory" for investigating dance and movement. In its long history, the organization has prioritized giving space to artists for rehearsing, developing, and investigating—rather than presenting and producing—their work. The ***Movement Research Performance Journal*** can be seen as an outgrowth of this mission—extending the rehearsal studio into the space of the page. In its first issue, editor Richard Elovich describes the journal as "a new public space for the New York performance community…a slightly anarchic forum in which opposing ideas and aesthetics can be seriously developed and debated." How do we understand this mission of staying in the zone of research today? How are artists (re)building pedagogy, and processes of learning, into their practice? What contemporary or historical alternative schools, and approaches to schooling, might be seen in constellation with the founding of Movement Research? How are students of dance and performance confronting the possibility and failure of an educational system predicated on both their enrichment and indebtedness?

What we didn't expect was the almost unanimous rejection of the concept of "research" itself, as evinced in both the pointed and oblique refusals of this keyword in the pages that follow. "Research" was rejected for the way it yolked art to the measure of science. It was refused for its colonial and suprematist imperative. It was disrupted by the historic strike of the New School's Adjunct faculty. It was forgotten through a series of procrastinations that in themselves became a kind of productive avoidance, a call to de-instrumentalized ways of being and thinking in the world. Our research failed, but its failure touched on the theme that should have been ours all along about dance and performance as a way of knowing, a kind of learning that only a rehearsal space can allow. It's a topic that makes itself hard to write about, harder even to research, despite being so easily known by anyone who has been in or with its doing.

—Joshua Lubin-Levy, Editor-in-Chief

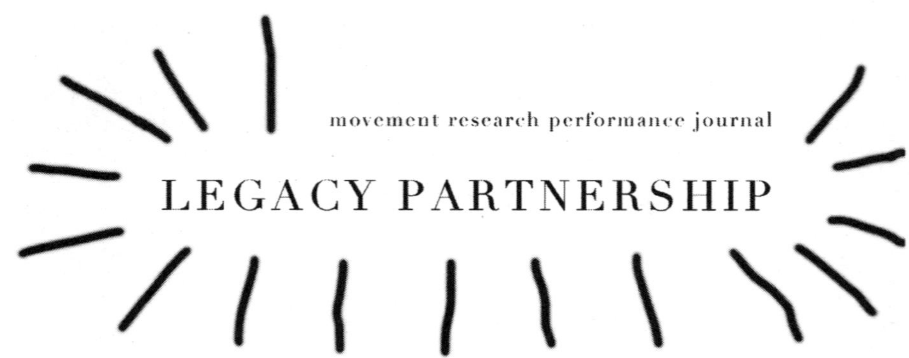

"Legacy Partners" are arts organizations that have committed to offering long term financial support to the *Movement Research Performance Journal* (MRPJ), a publication run by and for artists who work in dance and performance. These partnership suggest the fluid relation between the stage and the page (so to speak) as both should exist as venues guided by and in support of artists as they experiment with their practices.

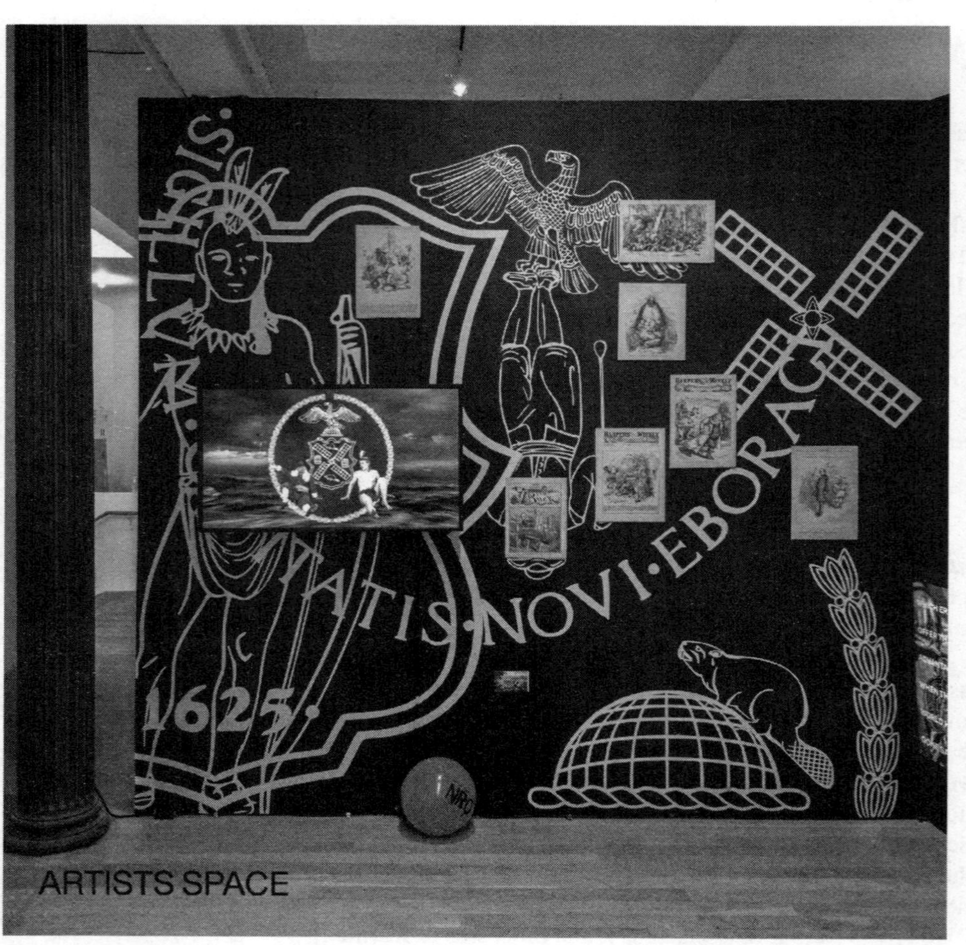

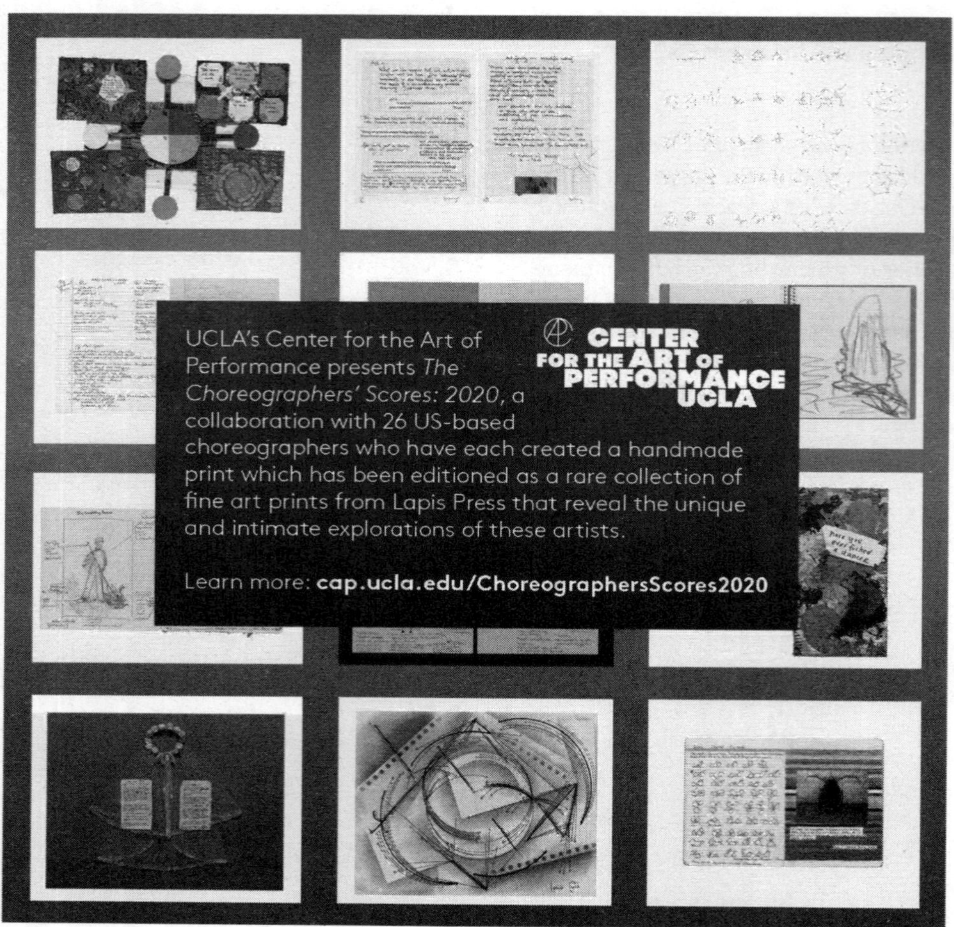

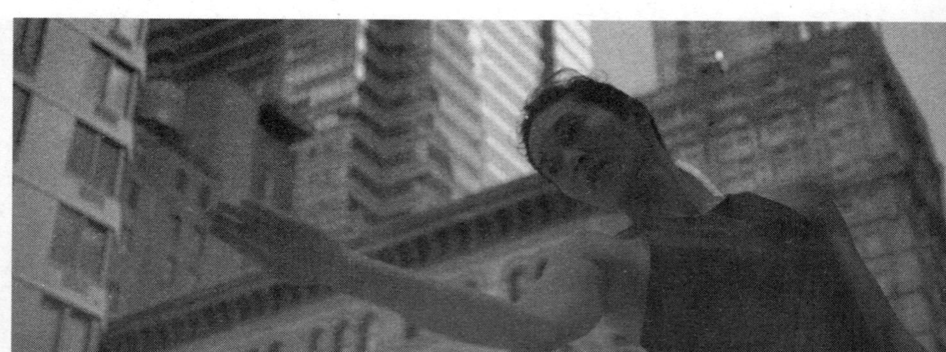

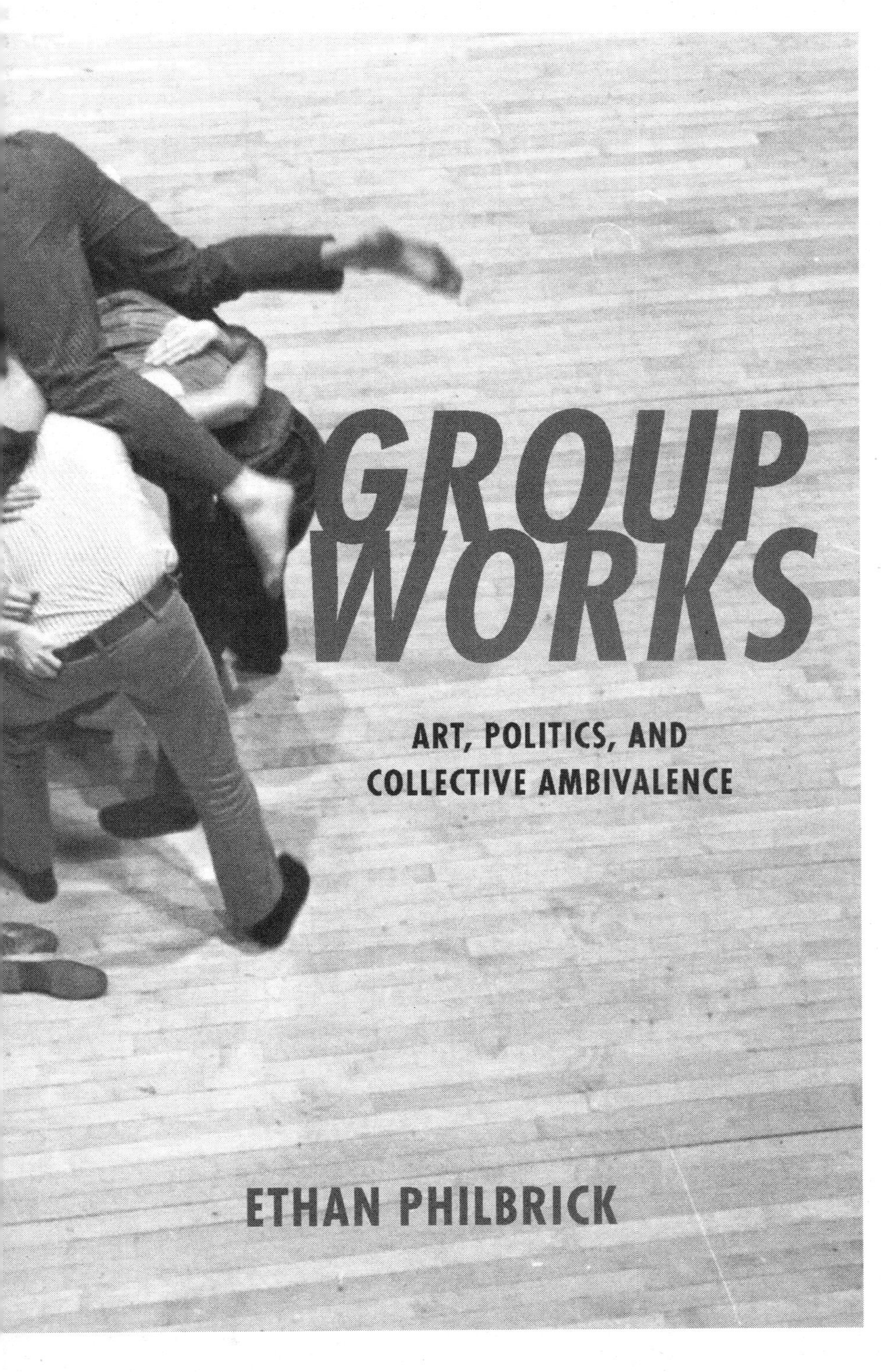

Ethan Philbrick, Group Works: Art, Politics, and Collective Ambivalence (New York, NY: Fordham University Press, 2023). Submitted on behalf of The Kitchen.

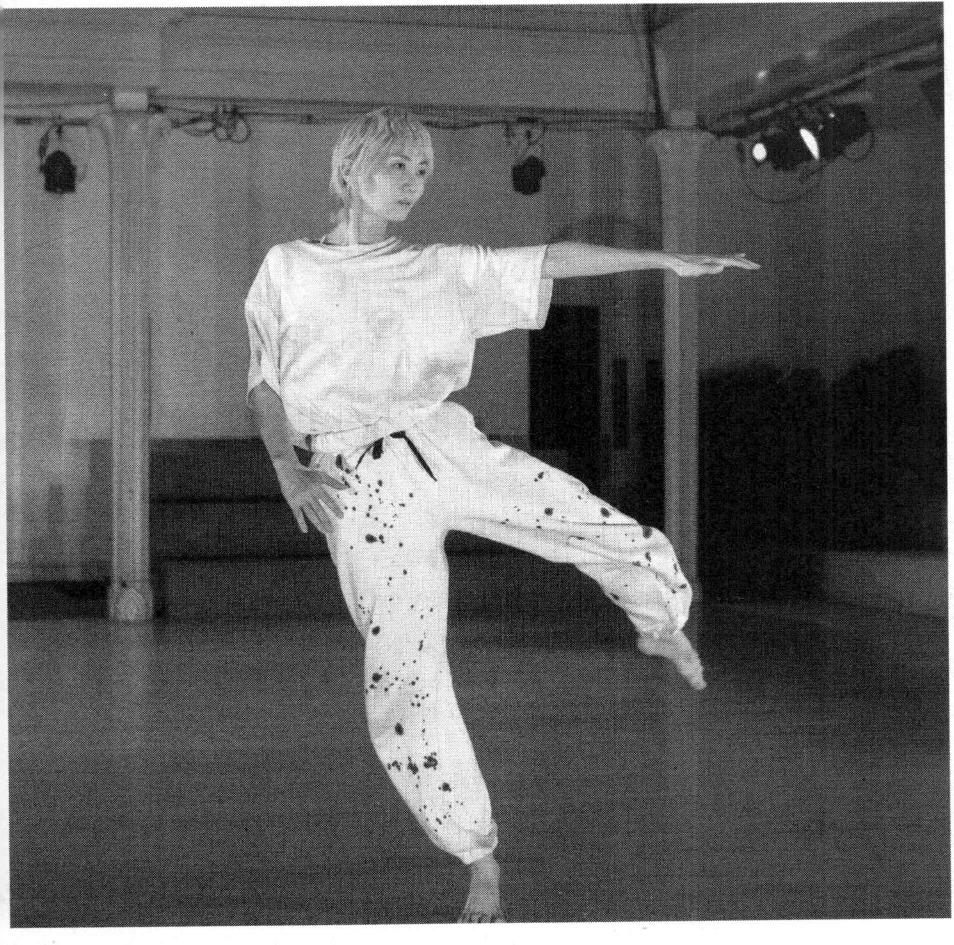

Mina Nishimura, *Mapping a Forest while Searching for an Opposite Term of Exorcist*, Danspace Project, 2022. Photo by Ian Douglas.

How is care showing up in my artistic research practice?

When I think of care I think of caring for my child. I think about ~~the~~ sensations I feel/embody while I care for her. In the moments I am exhausted, and in the moments when I am in a rush what remains is that my child needs me. ~~My work echoes~~ How I express care in my artistic process shares many attributes with my expressed care of my child. In my work, even when I am exhausted I am intentional with identifying what the work is lacking and how I can provide the necessary theme, idea, collaboration, effect, and thing that will fulfill the work to its fullest potential. ~~When I am tired, I~~ when I lack time, I never attempt to ahistoricize a work, or decontextualize a work. Instead I try to identify and name the influences that are in discourse with the work so that, again, the work can be fully actualized. Time can hold up white supremacy if we let it. Saying "There's not enough time" will allow an artist's work to become a siloed expression where the artist is the sole author, and the work is without context and ahistorical; which is not rooted in a practice of care. Care, in artmaking, is not dictated by time. Therefore care in my artistic practice is demonstrated by taking the time to situate myself and my art within a constellation of art workers and art makers.

When I talk about care, I am talking about a mindfulness around causing as little harm as possible in a particular space or practice. Colleagues, especially those of the Boomer generation, conflate my commitment to care with a (bitter) conceptualization of caregiving and caretaking, and with a throwing away of accountability. What they often miss: care shows up in everything we do—as artists, scholars, practitioners, teachers, and collaborators.

There are endless ways to define our boundaries and do it with care. There is a way into improvising (as a choreographic practice, as a survival method, as an entry point to research) with care—with an intention to not cause harm, a recognition of when we do, and what we'll do when that time comes. Why is care so important, particularly in research? The ability to center our personhoods directly reflects our willingness to push against oppressive structures, which are designed to cause harm—at the least. At worst, they kill us, the marginalized most often, but the powerholders, too, insidiously. We all have a stake in caring. Not just caring about, or caring for, but caring as a practice. As an ethic and an ethos. As something that we actively weave into the quotidian and the academic and the creative. Such a willingness must be ongoing if we, as a field of researchers and knowledge-seekers, are to move beyond surviving.

I asked my graduate school cohort—and chosen family—to chew on this idea with me. They bring to the table their unique lived experiences: Darvejon Jones (he/him) is a father and a Black dance artist and scholar. Eleanor Smith (she/her) is a Brooklyn-based choreographer and performer. I (he/him) am an NYC-based interdisciplinary artist, writer, and teacher.

–Thomas Ford

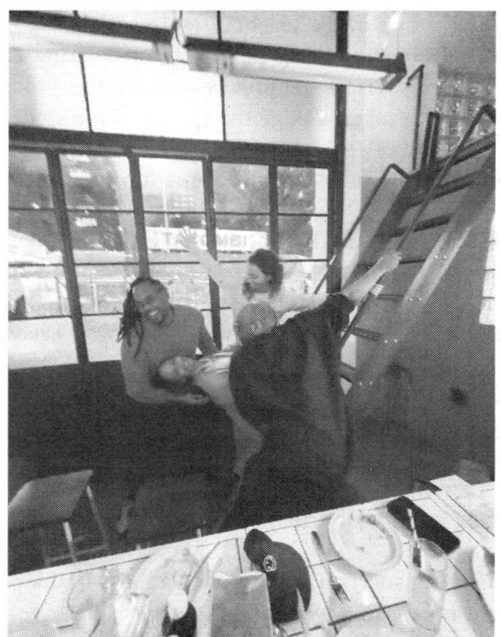

The crew (plus friend and cohort member Eto'o Tsana) in NYC after a long rehearsal day for Darvejon's *Blacklash*.

CARE AS PRACTICE

Thomas Ford in conversation with Darvejon Jones and Eleanor Smith

Thomas Ford (TF): I was just looking up the etymology of *research*. The "re" comes from the Old French, meaning "expressing intensive force." *Cerchier* means "to search." I'm going to sit in that. Do you all have any hot takes?

Darvejon Jones (DJ): I have questions around the purpose of research, and if that purpose is to own knowledge—to own the "new frontier." We actively research through a process of manifest destiny, claim this new frontier and name it. Does it belong to us now? Research in the Ivory Tower is patriarchal: you're cited using your last name, which is typically a paternal surname. I wonder if that is supposed to be the purpose of research. Is that your contribution to the field—putting your name on something?

TF: This is getting dark! *[Laughter]*

DJ: Research really starts in the body, because the first thing you do when you research something is think about what interests you. If you think about your consciousness dwelling inside of your body, then the research starts inside the body, too.

TF: That makes me think about research as a colonialist, imperialistic practice. I'm thinking about how violent colonialism is, and I'm linking that to the etymology—the "expressing intensive force." It makes me question whether or not research is inherently violent.

Eleanor Smith (ES): Or inherently colonial? I agree with you, Darvejon, that research is in the body. Taking it out of the etymology, and framing it as a practice where research is a search, and a return to the search, repeatedly, is evocative of an improvisatory practice. There's unknown, there's seeking, and there's finding—and then a "moving on" from the finding to continue to search again. And that feels like something I understand and am involved in, dancing my work with Molly Lieber. But then, coming to a graduate studies program, the idea of research begins to feel different. It feels more like what we were talking about earlier.

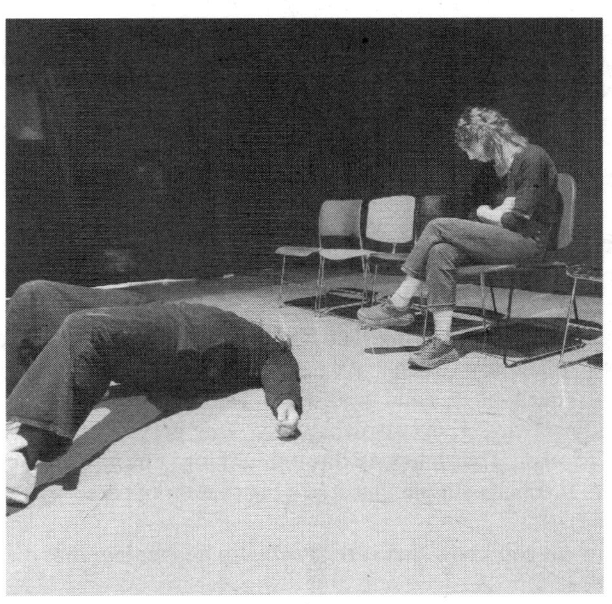

Eleanor watches Thomas during tech rehearsal for his MFA thesis, *Queering Blackness: Solo on a Theme of Reconciliation* at Hunter College.

TF: I also agree with you, Darvejon. There is an experiential component that precedes the research. I think of research as a choreographic practice as much as I do an improvisational one. I am uncomfortable with the idea of "finding," though, Eleanor. "Finding" feels like I'm landing on something, and I always intend for my research to get me to another question, rather than an answer. For me, part of researching is operating from a place of inquiry.

DJ: Research is also a seed of culture. When you uncover or discover something, there are either people who argue against your research or promote it, which creates this little world around the area of study. So in that way, research could be a mechanism for world-making—an ecosystem that things grow out of.

TF: I talk to my students about dance as a performance of culture, as an aesthetic marker and indicator of culture. I asked them, "What else is dance?" One student said, "Community." If dance is research, then research is community, too. Just look at the three of us! *[Laughter]*

DJ: I struggle with research because I feel like the primary aim of research is to name. I don't know if I want to participate in that, because the knowledge is already there—you just haven't discovered it. If my only goal in researching is to discover and name and claim, I really struggle with that.

TF: The distilling of information down to one theory is such a patriarchal, colonialist practice—in all the ways we've already discussed. As a woman [Smith], as a Black father [Jones] and as a Black, queer man [Ford], we understand those structures to be harmful because they've harmed us—violently, and they continue to. Some part of me wonders about how each of our ethics or ethos around care are grounded in those experiences. As researchers in our own iterations of praxis, we devise ways of moving toward harmlessness by *not* doing what was done to us; by doing what we wish had been done *for* us; by offering support in ways that no one cared to offer us.

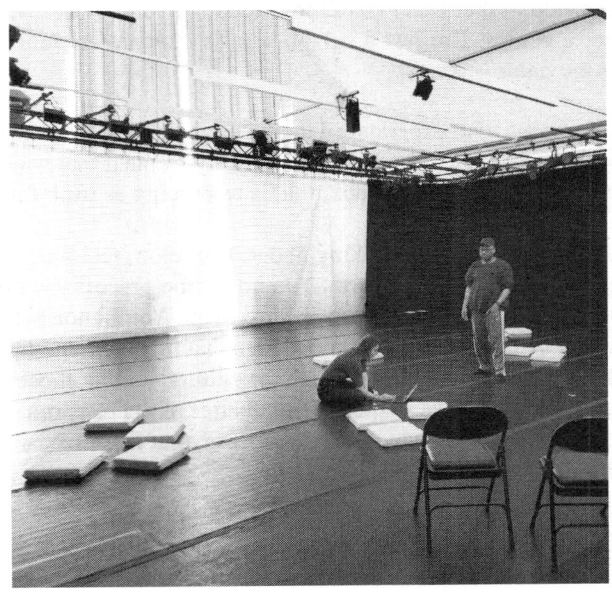

Thomas helps Eleanor prepare for her thesis—a Hunter College screening of Molly Lieber and Eleanor Smith's *gloria rehearsal (except)*, filmed at Baryshnikov Arts Center.

DJ: This is particularly true in the teaching realm. We are all teachers in academia. And, let's be clear: when we go about creating pedagogy or creating curriculum, it is a choreographic process. It is also an improvisational process—and those processes *are* research. The center of that research should be to acknowledge the sphere of the students before us.

ES: How does care show up in that specific area for you, Darvejon?

DJ: Well, if I am teaching you, Eleanor, I am going to center you by first asking you your pronouns to acknowledge how you want to be called. I am going to learn as much about you as possible so I can reach you; so I can find an entry point into your life. And you have the agency to define those things for me. I have to have an ear for it. I have to really listen.

TF: I, too, try to build structures of care and equity into my teaching. I write them into the syllabus, into my approach to pedagogy, which I think the academy has an urgent need for. Conversations around care in academia are both necessary and interesting. But, neither of you is only a teacher. I am not only a teacher. We are all doing deep research in our creative work. How is care showing up in your artistic research processes?

DJ: My research is about survival, and looking at how Black people have used dance as a mode of survival—how it is passed down and echoed. It's iterative. I can do an Orisha dance that is thousands of years old today because it was passed down. Again, it's iterative, it's reincarnated and it's coming back. And it's rooted in memory. My interest is in survival. My interest is to survive. And I take care in that by engaging in lore and legend. I also take care by taking time to really look at historical facts, so that things are not misrepresented—but in the way that oral tradition maintains a kind of effervescence. That sensational aspect of storytelling that is valuable but may not always be historically accurate.

TF: I've titled my upcoming work *Queering Blackness: Solo On a Theme of Reconciliation*. The care in my research process is as much about taking care of myself as it is about causing myself the least amount of harm. That involves reconciling with the trauma of being Black and queer in spaces where I thought I should belong and was made to feel I did not. It involves acknowledging my love for my Blackness and the violence of Black masculinity. The care is in the healing and the lengths I'll go to reclaim a sort of power in the entangling of my identity.

ES: Molly and I take care of one another—in our process and in our research.

TF: From what you've shared in our other conversations, I feel like your entire process with Molly is a practice in care.

ES: I appreciate you saying that. The systems that we have created together to research and to work are inherently systems of care, because they take into consideration each one of us as individuals — our thoughts and our bodies. We align in some ways that we want to take care of our bodies. We always give ourselves a nice, long preparatory time to come together and get attuned to one another. That happens through talking, but it also happens through a mutual warm-up practice. It sounds simple, but it is a big system of care.

TF: How do you know that care is actually happening, that it's in the room?

ES: If I walk into a space, and a choreographer or teacher or a collaborator asks how I am, in a way that makes me feel like I am actually able to answer, that feels like care is being offered. That is something I've tried to figure out how to do myself.

DJ: In order for me to know that care is present, I situate myself amongst others who have touched upon what I'm touching upon, and I really try to cite that. It is about being well-versed in the landscape that I'm situated in. Existing in a silo would be emblematic of me not caring, or of only caring about having my name on something and not recognizing the other great minds who have touched upon the same ideas. I do a lot of reading, a lot of watching, a lot of referencing, especially if I'm working with other bodies. I'll ask, "Have you guys seen this?" Or, "Have you seen this step in that Janet [Jackson] video?" I do a lot of referencing just to make it clear that I am not a genius. I'm just a person who is multi-referential. It's not about me. It's not about putting my name on it.

ES: As someone who experienced that in your process, Darvejon, what you're talking about does feel like a type of care. You didn't necessarily frame it that way in rehearsal, but now that you're saying it and I'm reflecting back, that is resonating as truth for me.

TF: All the things you are talking about, Darvejon, feel like a practice in caring for the culture and the context around the form. You honor the practitioners that came before you, those who are doing it now, and those who inspired you. You honor the people in the room by engaging them with historical artifacts—knowledge that fills the mind but also informs the body. There's a caretaking of the social, the political, the cultural—all of those forces that have been constructed by man, and which have shaped the aesthetics of the research. As someone who has also had the privilege of working in your artistic process, that labor of care gave me something to stand on, something to feel rooted in.

couch, blanket, tea, looking
at my plants. quilt on
my chair. eating. rehearsal
is research. attuning together

Care:
- deep breathing before embodied
investigation — get centered;
prepare heart for the emotional
weight of the work; get into
my body

- awaken skin by rolling on
the floor: this creates space
for meditation

- PLAYLIST ⇒ songs, songs + more
songs that hold the research
questions. Right now, that means
songs that inspire/embrace/move
towards/around/into Blackness +
gender.

- I dance under the protective eye of
my husband + artistic partner,
Steven Atwater

-TF

Thomas Ford is a New York City-based dance artist and writer. He is the founding director of companyONE. His choreographic work has appeared at venues like the Joyce Theater, Symphony Space and the Ailey Citigroup Theater. Thomas is an adjunct professor of dance and dance theory at Marymount Manhattan College and Hunter College/CUNY.

Darvejon Jones is a father, an Adjunct Assistant Professor at Hunter College, a bicoastal interdisciplinary and multidisciplinary dance artist, a performer, a performing arts writer, and a dance studies scholar. His research focuses on phenomenological hermeneutics within the genre of Black dance.

Eleanor Smith is a choreographer, freelance dancer, Authentic Movement practitioner, and teacher. She performed in the works of Ivy Baldwin Dance from 2009–2019, Molly Poerstel from 2013–2021, and Katie Workum Dance from 2013–2021. Eleanor is currently an MFA candidate in Dance at Hunter College, CUNY, where she also teaches and serves on the White Anti-Racist Caucus.

Choreography of a Strike: The New School Labor Protest

Ella Kuether

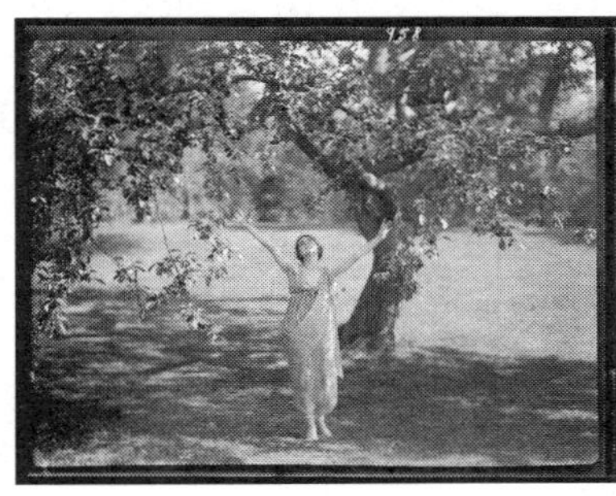
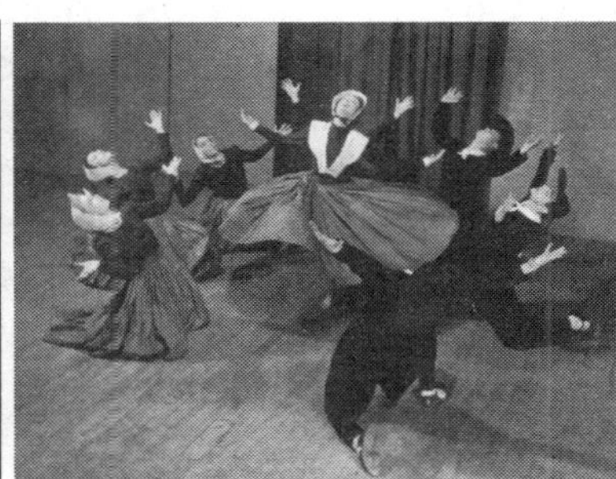

Movement has always been an artistic outlet for expression. When artists combine movement and culture, the outcomes are powerful. In 1927, Isadora Duncan used dance to celebrate American culture and to voice social protest, declaring, "I See America Dancing" in reference to Walt Whitman's poem, "I Hear America Singing." For Duncan, dance was a commanding mechanism for cultural expression. Similarly, Doris Humphrey used dance to express America's turmoil in her 1935 *The Shakers*. To this day, the Workers Dance League (founded in New York City in 1932) bears the slogan, "Dance is a weapon in the revolutionary class struggle." Dance as a form of protest has been meaningful and effective. Recently, I witnessed ACT-UAW LOCAL 7902 bring this strategy to life in their fight for employee rights during the Part-Time Faculty strike at The New School, which lasted from November 16 to December 10, 2022. The movement and imagery methods used during the rally forever changed The New School history books.

As a junior, it is safe to say my entire college experience (which has taken place during the height of the Covid-19 pandemic) has been unconventional. The New School strike was no exception. Throughout the weeks of no class, there were many moments of doubt, confusion, and restlessness. It was a time of unknowing, but in this unknowing there were lessons to be learned. These lessons posed questions that we would not find the answers to in a classroom, but rather in ourselves, in our individual and collective creativity, unity, community, and resilience. I was a part of history, a part of the longest adjunct professor strike in the U.S.

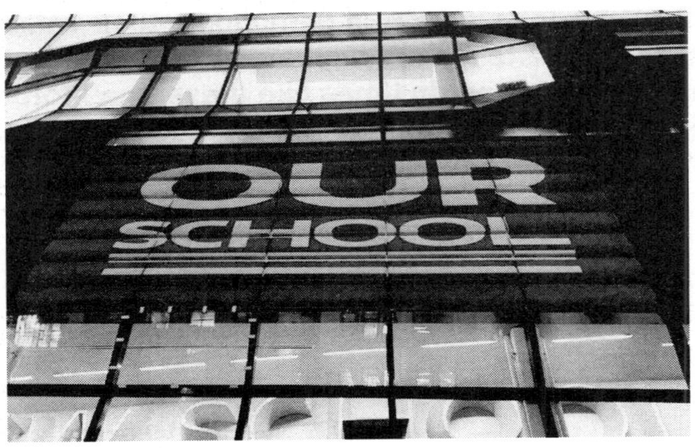

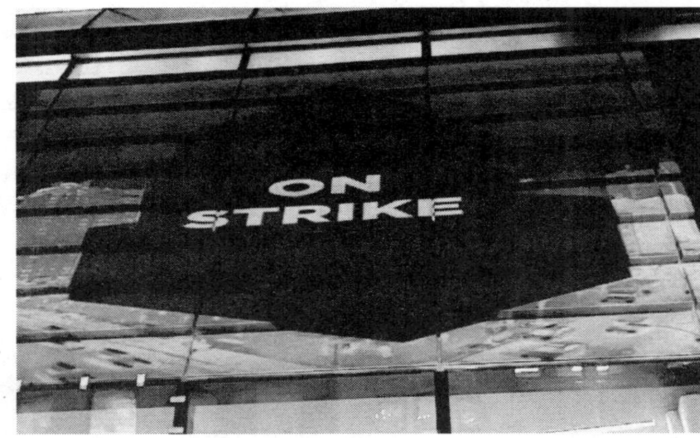

After the call to strike, I admired how quickly the students and faculty of the university adapted to the announcement of the strike. We all got to work right away. My first time visiting the picket line, I was blown away. It was the first day of the strike and the whole community showed up. Teachers and students alike gathered around the University buildings, loud and proud. We were taking a stand to make our school a better environment to learn. I hoped the administration, our audience, was watching and that they learned something from our efforts.

In the coming days, as I made my way down the street near school, I observed the many forms of protest that the staff used to gain awareness of their plight. Among them were movement and dance. The purposeful use of dance in the protest caused me to reflect upon the meaning of movement and its value in the strike. Employee voice was heard through movement and performance. They spent their days striking for better working conditions and fair compensation. Snapshots of employees on those days are etched into my mind.

The New School's location was used advantageously by protestors every day for the length of the strike. The first day of the strike was energized, and the community and student support was impressive. On that day, the bond of our community was strong and boisterous. Sounds of saxophones, bass guitars, and pots and pans echoed off of the school building. The melodies of the chants blended with music and noise to exemplify the statement of solidarity. Music encouraged the mentality that is needed to raise awareness, and momentum from the crowd cemented the allegiance to the cause. This visibility and enthusiasm grew throughout the day. The scene was an effective sight of chaos and sent a clear message. The power I felt from the community inspired me to research how dance and performance has been used as a political weapon in America.

In 1935, Anna Sokolow titled a dance *Strange American Funeral* after a worker who fell into a vat of steel. Similarly calling on a sense of loss, the staff and students staged a performance when they hosted a séance along the picket line. In this instance, a set of beliefs, rather than a worker's death, called out for collective mourning and action. The New School protesters held signs for *Justice*, *Equity* and *Sustainability*, among the University's deceased ideals. Moving ominously up and down the street, this message rang clear. A solemn tone and trudging movement mirrored the collective response to grief in the heart of Greenwich Village. Sokolow's work could be a basis for the imagery that is now burned into the history of The New School labor protest through photos, articles, live streams, social media, and the news. There was no escaping the chants reverberating from the picket lines, nor the gathering of "mourners" that lasted around the clock. If you participated in this movement, and your voice was intact at the end of the day, you were one of the few.

Channeling a popular attention-getting approach that has been used in rallies for years, another performance that animated the strike was a so-called "bucket band." Five-gallon orange buckets provided a way to make noise, but also provided a way to give tired protestors a place to sit and power up for the next round of chants. Not only were they used as a chair or platform, but they also facilitated a mean pounding. Coupled with choreography, the mood of the strike could change in a heartbeat. At times, there was a wild pounding which appeared to act as a summons for labor warriors far and wide. At different moments, the strikers offered a more subtle approach with the slow building of a quiet march. This drumming technique brought awareness even if an observer was several blocks away.

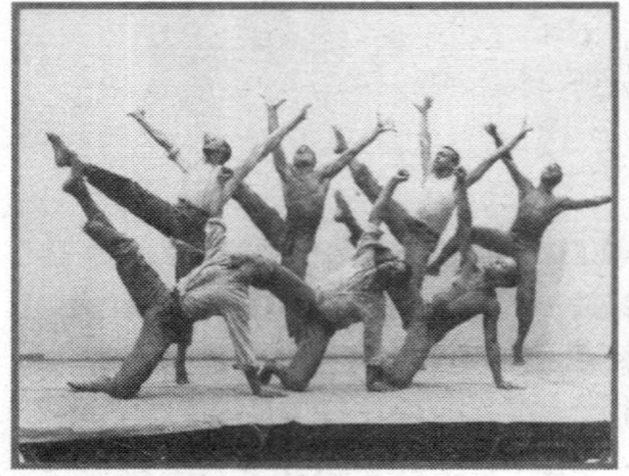

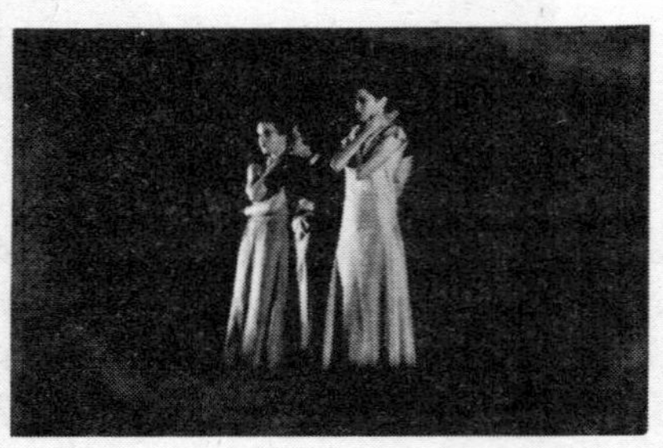

The rhythm of workers' protest echoes across dance history. In *Rainbow Round My Shoulder* (1959) Donald McKayle choreographed a work in opposition to the chain gang mentality of American labor, standing upon the bottom of buckets to represent a powerful wall of worker unity. McKayle's work might nod to Lester Horton's *The Mine* (1935), wherein oppressed workers grab their sledgehammers and pounce in unison against unfair treatment. Rhythmic and monotonous, the sounds of the drums with the steady parade of The New School protesters might make McKayle and Horton proud.

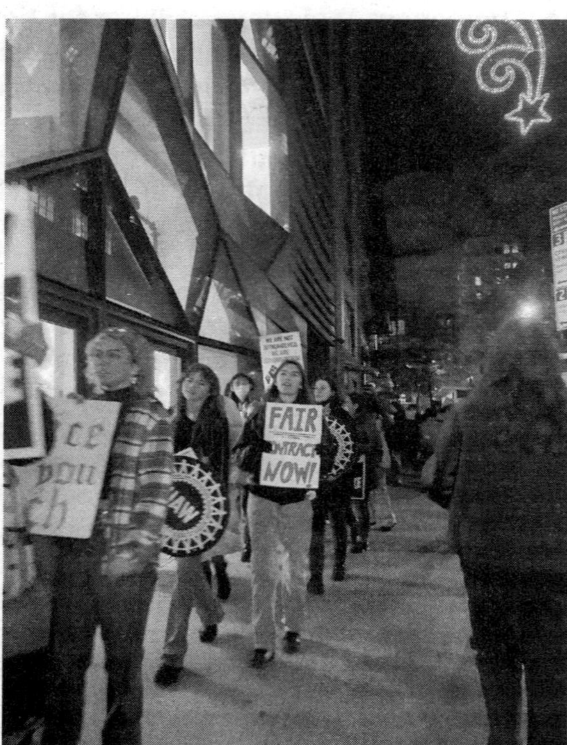

Photos of strike: Ella Kuether

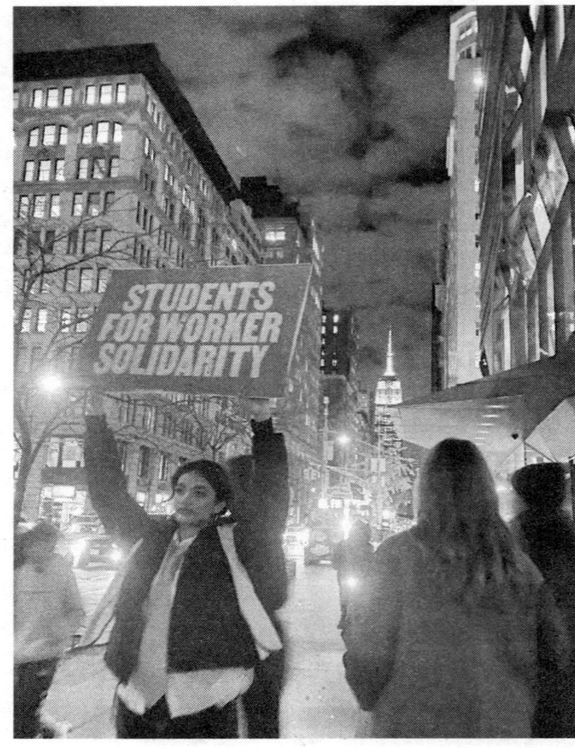

At a corner, I watched a tap dancer pound away at the pavement, sending signals of solidarity throughout the street. Clacking sounds could be heard from a block or two away, and I noticed that drivers were drawn to the cause as they awaited a green light. Propped nearby and in the hands of those marching were signs that read, "Their working conditions are our learning conditions" and "You can't put teachers first if you put students last." One thing was certain; the sound and sights displayed during the three weeks were relentless. Staff and students showed endurance, tenacity, and toughness.

As a school that is highly artistic, it was so beautiful to see how art was used to make a statement. Saxophone, bass, guitar, and the sounds of pots and pans were heard from blocks away. We had bands accompanying the chants of the hundreds of people picketing outside everyday. Creativity blossomed. People would come together to create placards to bring to the picket line — I walked around daily, admiring the handmade protest signs. It was a celebration of the people who attend and work at this school. Tables full of snacks and drinks were posted all around the university. All of us came together to get back into the classroom with our teachers.

Without its students and faculty, The New School would not exist. Tapping, drumming, chanting, and dancing were the heartbeat of The New School labor strike. Demands of healthcare and pay raises for adjunct faculty were won in the process. I feel a sense of satisfaction when I look around and realize how many dedicated and talented people I am surrounded by everyday. As a dancer, I'm struck by the way these bodies came together to make this movement — the strike wouldn't have succeeded without the participation and support of The New School community. I am taking the lessons I learned from this moment and applying them to my life as I return to a "normal" schedule.

Oppression of the worker is a theme that has a long history, and it seems it may be time to revisit it. When facing powerful employers, whether it be a steel mine, factory, Starbucks or The New School, strength in numbers and a steadfast perseverance is a strong adversary. Recent upticks in unionizing and strikes show the American worker is demanding their value be recognized. The stakes are high and workers do not appear to be deterred. In times like these, the footprints of activists and artists can be potent, guiding forces — and alter the course of history.

Ella Kuether is a multidisciplinary artist based in New York City. She is studying Contemporary Dance and Media at The New School. Her work focuses on the expression, connection, and community art gives us.

This, Our Hallowed Solidarity

Cassandra Brey

December 11, 2022 marked twenty-five days of the strike On this day, faculty, staff, students, and family members of The New School gathered as performers and audience at Judson Memorial Church. We had endured the past month with grace and strength. Part-time faculty had been fighting for a better contract and picket lines were attended day in and day out.

This was a hallowed space, a space of change. A place familiar to the artistic inspiration and movement being presented on that wintry day.

I attended the event expecting to only watch singers, actors, and speakers performed their works and discussed what the strike had meant to them. Instead, I was invited by my professor, Juliette Mapp, to take part in an improvisation with other dance faculty present during one of the open mic slots.

A spontaneous improvisation session in Judson is something I never thought I'd get the opportunity to do, but given the church's importance in the world of dance it hardly came as a surprise. Even before entering the building I was aware I was stepping into a place that knew what a movement looked like, what a movement could do. Robert Dunn and his protégés who had founded the Judson Dance Theater left an indelible mark on much of the dance faculty at the very school I attend.

Just as the Judson movement created discussion around, engaging the ephemerality of dance, we were continuing. Having been on strike for twenty-five days, we were displaying the desire for change by moving our bodies. Bodies are the most important thing for a movement to proceed: we had brought ourselves to the pickets those four weeks in solidarity. Now a few of us were choosing to bring our bodies in a different movement pattern, in a new space, to continue that sentiment.

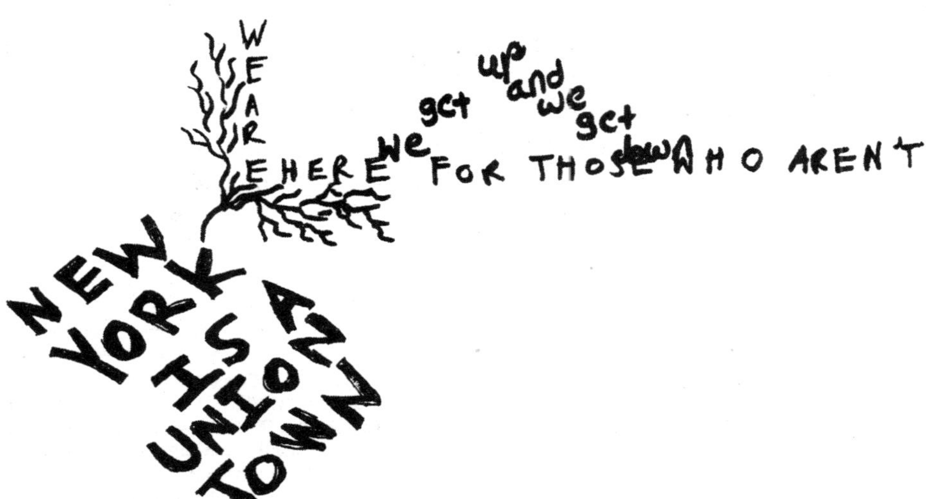

Drawings: Cassandra Brey

When I finally stepped onto the dance floor, I was flooded with an acute awareness of the history of this space and what our moment in time meant.

I was joined by two fellow dance students, Keb Barshack and Sophie Barreto, along with Professors Katy Pyle, Nami Yamamoto, and Mapp. In the five minutes that followed, we partook in an improvisation, stirring and expressing our elation and grief.

At first I started out alone, moving in solitude to the piano and making eye contact with the audience, with the high ceiling, with the ground. Gradually, I fell into contact improvisation with all of the other dancers present. I'll admit, I usually experience a form of blackout when improvising. By the end I cannot tell you what I did nor with whom; only glimpses of the experience remain.

There was something comforting about the contact we made (masks on). I let my hand trail across Keb; let myself collapse to the floor and was stepped over by Sophie; at one point all three professors present had their hands on my body as I sank to the ground in a lunge. I marveled at our closeness, partially because of the ongoing pandemic, partially because of my fear of authority figures in the dance world. I'd never gotten quite this physically close to instructors while moving. Moving with them broke a hierarchical teacher/student barrier, even if it was only for that moment in time. I'd catch the eyes of the audience and try to express that this was about solidarity. For dancers like myself, the strike had created a grief similar to that of the quarantine period of the Covid-19 pandemic.

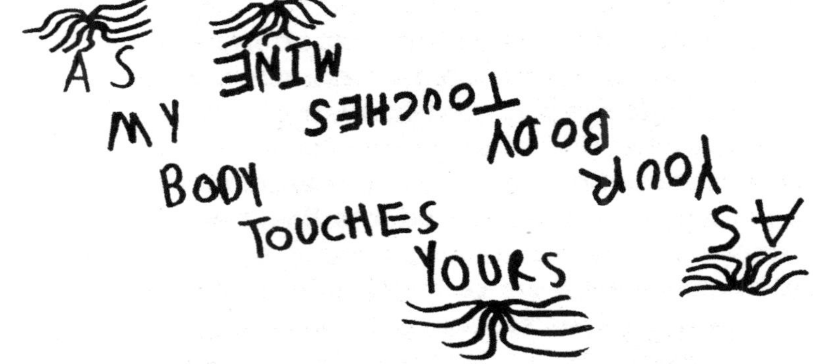

In the spring of 2020, I was permanently stuck in my house, and any interactions with dance teachers and other dancers happened over Zoom. This fall as the strike raged on, I spent most of my free time when not on the picket line in my dorm room, and any interaction with fellow dancers became restricted to the Zoom calls one professor held for weekly catch-ups. It felt as if all face-to-face interaction was truly lost again. With this emptiness in mind, it was a joy to dance again, but it was also a dance of grief. The pianist's voice held that space appropriately: what we could not say aloud was held by the music.

I moved to the altar before everyone else, and smelled the evergreen that lay there, as it was decorated for Christmas. We'd agreed this was how we would end the piece — everyone at the altar. I found myself holding onto it like a drowning man, moving around on the platform with likely less grace than I felt. On that altar, I felt my grief turn to those who weren't present as dancing bodies, those with whom we missed dancing, and with whom we would never again be in a studio, as classmates, as we'd been.

When the notes of the piano faded into the ether, we stood and bowed, applause filling the vaulted, cathedratic space. I looked over and saw tears on Nami's face; and later, she'd admit that was the moment she knew we weren't going to perform the piece she had choreographed with our class. Juliette offered yet another hug to me before I went to pull my boots back on, thanking me for participating, whispering how great that'd been for us all. In those moments as I walked back to my chair, I could still feel the presence of all that movement. There remained an echo, surrounded by other moving bodies, a feeling I'd longed for since classes abruptly ended.

Dance is an ephemera. The ontology of dance is something we discuss frequently as dance majors at Lang College: how to write about it, how to describe it, how to capture it in the moment. I do not know if this is an accurate depiction of this moment, nor do I know if it's appropriate, but it is what I recall feeling. Improv is always fleeting — I will never again do the same movements in that same order with those people in that space. The lack of photo and video documentation of this moment in the gathering makes the emotions all the stronger.

Perhaps if I had known that day twenty-five would be the final day of the strike, I would have embodied a different tone. Maybe I would've felt more hope than grief. Maybe our dancing would have taken on a different emotion, one of a future guaranteed instead of a gaping unknown.

I do know that the future, both that afternoon and hours later at 10 PM, when the union announced that a contract had been tentatively agreed upon, held a promise of solidarity far beyond what we had known before. Whether or not the audience was physically capable of dancing with us, they had been invited into the space and into our dance with welcome arms, as a way to say that it is okay to grieve what we've lost. It was a way to prove that in the future, as students, faculty, and staff, we will all be dancing together again, as the very foundation of the university itself.

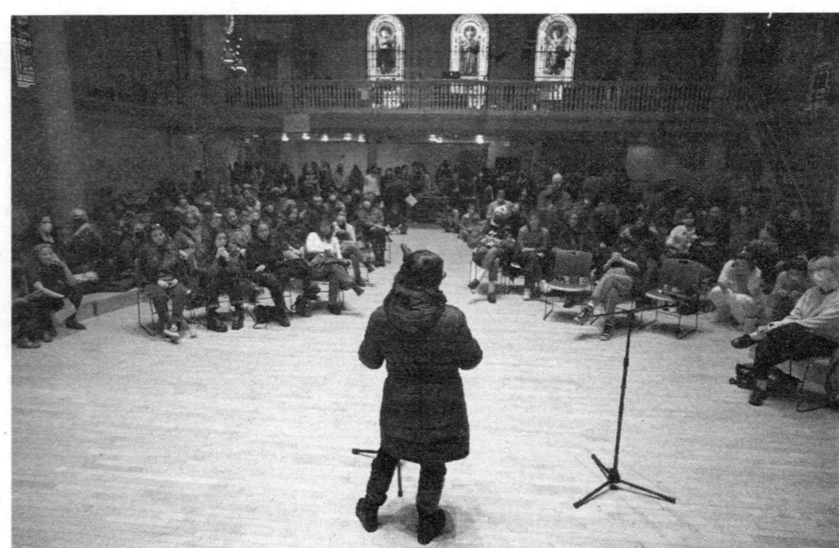

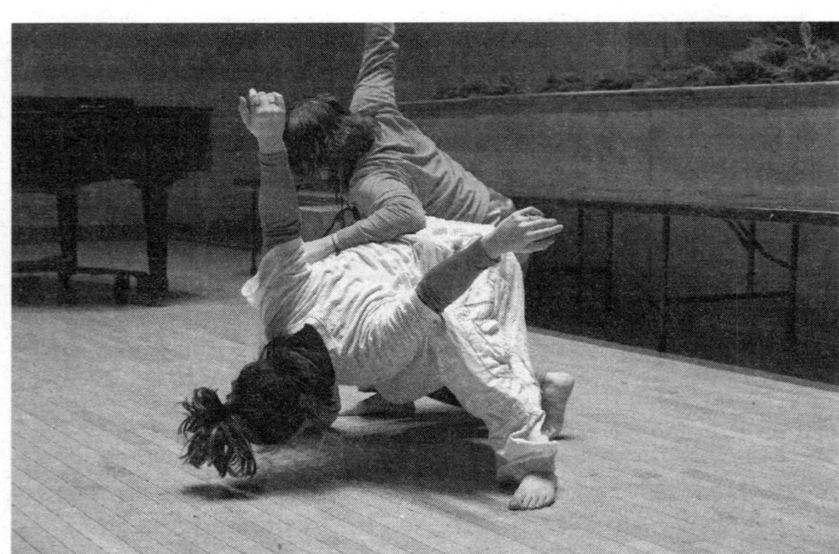

Photos: Allison Schuettinger
Dancers: Keb Barshack and Sophie Barreto

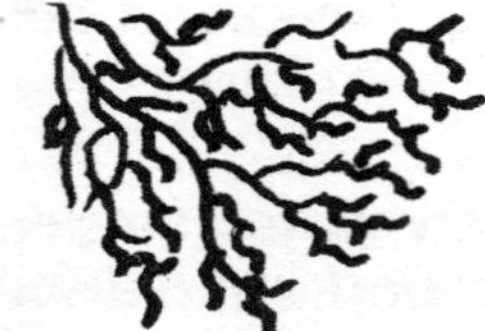

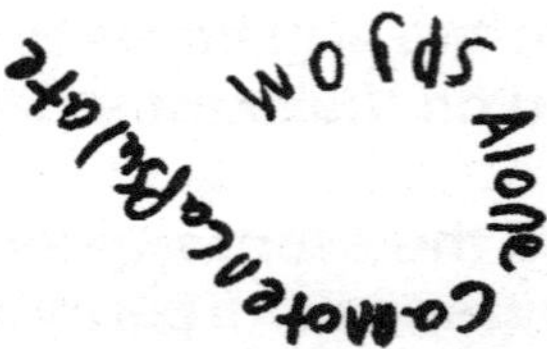

Cassandra Brey is a third-year Arts in Context major at The New School Eugene Lang. Previously published works of hers can be found in the The New School Free Press and the Pace Press. Past performance experiences include The Kansas City Ballet's Nutcracker at the Kennedy Center, the 2018 Joffrey Spectrum Summer Intensive Showcase, and several collaborative works with choreographers at The New School.

Our score took care of us

Mariana Valencia and Rachel Valinsky

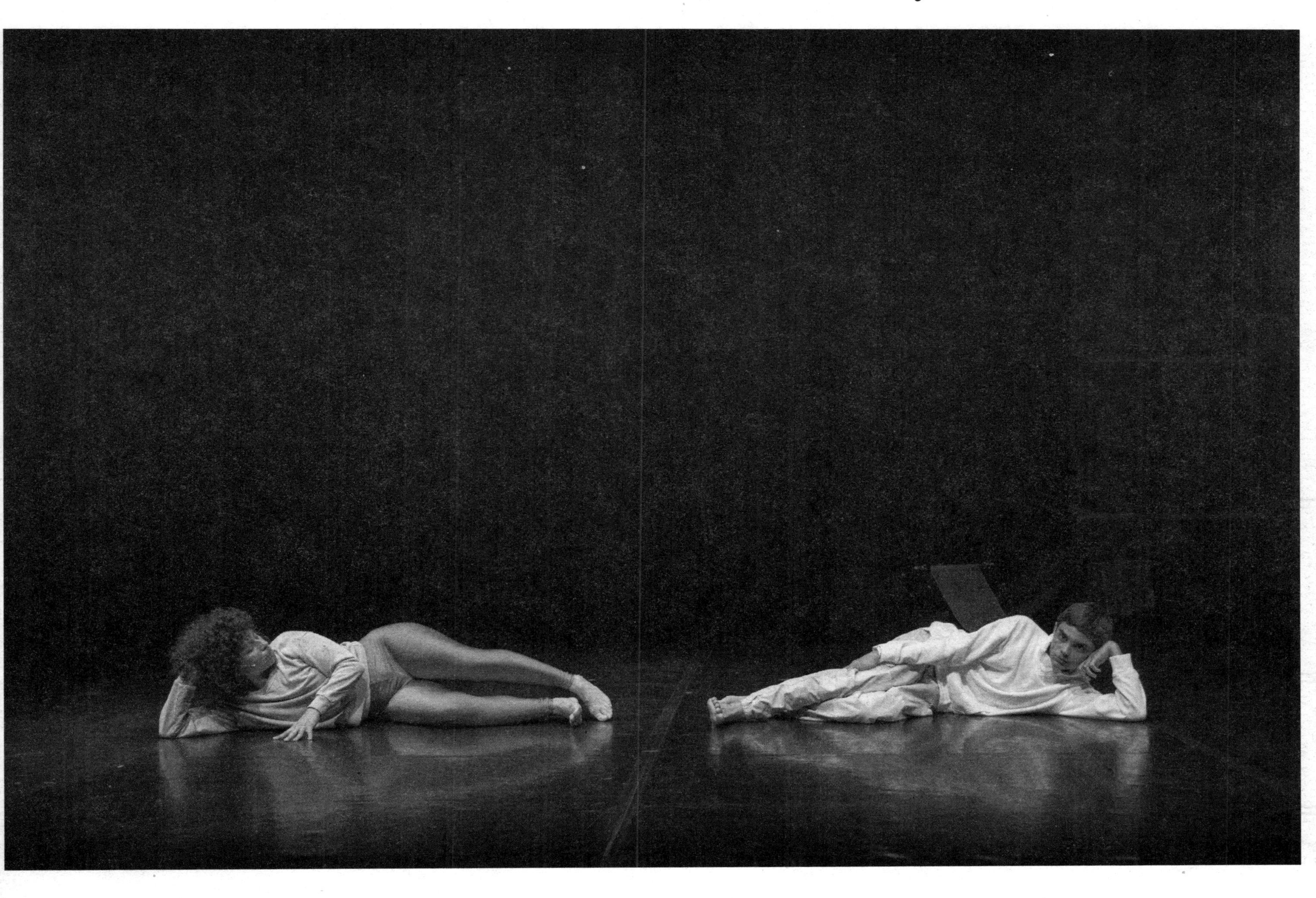

Rachel Valinsky (RV): We're going to talk about improvisation and scores and teaching and pedagogy here. One place to start might be around a particular function of the score as instruction. While we could point to a long genealogy for this, I'm thinking specifically about how, in a pedagogical context, the score might come into play. How does it relate to a lesson plan or a syllabus, for instance? The last work of yours I saw performed was *Heera*, at Abrons Art Center, in Summer 2022: you worked closely with a teenager on developing a performance together through one-on-one classes and collaboration. And then, it so happened that the following fall, we were both teaching courses in the same dance program at the New School, where the "score" of the semester broke down, in a sense, halfway through, with the strike for part-time faculty contract negotiations lasting several weeks.

Mariana Valencia (MV): Score-making guided me in teaching my student Heera how to approach our *Heera* performance, which was a score for improvisation through prompts. We were strangers at the top of the process, and it was through a score of improvisatory games that we learned about each other's limits and desires. Our score took care of us, which allowed for looseness and precision of form. Heera was nurtured by the liveness of our work, exploring himself as a performer both safely and publicly.

RV: For *Heera*, it seemed to me that while phrases you both spoke were improvised to some degree, drawing on a repertoire of possible answers, there were prompts—often a question posed that both had to answer or a conversation topic to reorient toward. Scripted prompts primed you to improvise around "sets" or "series" of answers, and also offered very clear transitions for movement, blocking, and thinking and speaking live, from one discrete scene/sequence to the next. I don't know if we've ever talked about improvisation in your work.

MV: There are scores, scripts, and prompts. A score encompasses overall form and direction. In *Heera* there were prompts in the score that accented the form. I'd often ask Heera if there was anything he desired more of. One day he said, "I want to do a scene." So I wrote a scene at the end of the performance (a script) that showcased his ability to dive right into "real acting" after improvising.

RV: In the book we collaborated on, *Album* (published by Wendy's Subway in 2019), which came out of your solo performance of the same name, we also explored these questions: how to render both the scripted monologue and the score more broadly as it relates to movement and style, and the elements of the performance that might be more improvised or intuitive: affect, humor, audience interaction...

MV: I use the audience as my partner in my scored and scripted solos. I take my lines and movement delivery off of them. There are sections that I'm very in control of, but moments land or don't land depending on the audience. In 2019, I toured the UK with my performance, *Album*. At the show in Brighton, there was a Black Studies conference nearby that populated the audience with mostly POC. Until then, I hadn't yet performed for such a diverse audience, especially not in the silos of experimental dance in New York. I was far from home, yet I felt at home with this audience. There's a line in the performance that's always received with laughter: "This is what I look like when I pose like a monkey emoji." But in Brighton, no one laughed at the line. The monkey emoji, a subversive symbol, finally landed as it was intended. I'm saying: "This is how easy it is for me to look like a monkey to you." The moment is political, references my brown body and how I'm experienced by whiteness. In Brighton, no one laughed because as POC, we had a shared understanding of this concept. That's what happens when you take a score, repeat it, and then see how it lands in different situations.

RV: With the script, the score, the prompt, you outline different ways of building knowledge around, learning from, and engaging with your work, too, and with each other—whether as audience members, readers, or collaborators. I'm thinking about this in the context of a classroom, too. In writing-related courses, like yours and mine from this past year, the prompt is as a directive or a generator for something I can't anticipate the outcome of in the slightest ("write 500 words on/around..."). It's open (Merriam-Webster reminds me the word "prompt" relates both to a readily performed action, and to the cause inciting that action); while a script is more prescriptive and relates more closely to my lesson plan, the roadmap I've set out for myself and for us — so I build more predictability into it. A score, to me, better describes the conditions under which all of these things happen or are possible: it's the structure that holds.

MV: It's helpful to hear you make these distinctions. In *Heera*, there's a section where we go back and forth with a prompt "I love ________."

RV: The prompt is, "Say what you love; what do you love?"

MV: Yes. Or another prompt for the score was "feet only." You can't really dance with just your feet. But the idea of making your mind think that only your feet are moving —that's a prompt that details the movement score.

RV: Your prompt points to a frequency, a movement, a possibility, a set of conditions, a limit, but what emerges from it doesn't have a prescribed form.

MV: In class we read Ross Gay's *Be Holding*, which is a book-long poem. He wrote a poem just the way he needed to—book-long. Or, he wrote a book as he needed to—as a poem. When I'm making a dance, I think, no one said I couldn't use words, further blurring the lines between genre and form.

RV: And in doing that, you allude to genre-specific forms or conventions but never let them be still or staid; we sit with their undoing but still see their edges. There's no one way to write a novel. There's no one way to write a score.

MV: When you're thinking about making books out of performances, what's your prompt? What carries over, what is shared, and what is simply just unique to the form?

RV: The prompt at its most elementary is a question: "What could this *be* like on the page?" And then there are a whole set of other questions that emerge very quickly: What can be transferred or translated into this other form (the book)? How does time come into it? Materiality? Movement? What about speech and sound? What about structure, modes, strategies? And what, as I often ask students when they are workshopping each other's writing, is a center of gravity in the work—whether manifest or latent—or something on the edge of it, that we can orient ourselves toward in responding to the piece and transforming it. As in, what is informing this work, or part of it, in ways that we don't necessarily have access to—be it research, annotations, routines, conversations with friends, attunements, affects, atmospherics—and how can we (if we arrive at this determination), surface it? Publishing can be a kind of re-visioning. Adrienne Rich writes about re-visioning as "the act of looking back, of seeing with fresh eyes, of entering an old text from a new critical direction" that is ultimately a political "act of survival."

Take for instance the composer JJJJJerome Ellis's book, *The Clearing*. He created an orthographic system for notating his stutter, his glottal block, so the extension of the word over time, either in the repetition or prolongation of a sound, can be visualized on the page. The experience of language becomes a decidedly temporal one. The page needs to function according to a system that can hold this understanding—teach the reader how to read it. So, like sheet music, each page has a timestamp: it stands for one minute of recorded audio time corresponding to Ellis's album of the same title, and from which the book is transcribed. But ultimately the system breaks down, letters occupy the page freely, the lineation is no longer structurally determining. Dysfluency, music, Blackness—in Ellis's work, these interrupt the experience of time as linear flow, and open it up to other forces and durations. So the "prompt" is to generate questions around a kind of translation and how you take strategies and modes that are in the work and think about them within another set of parameters.

With *Album*, I remember thinking about spacing and layout as blocking, with pages intentionally indicating what was happening onstage at that moment, or what kinds of hierarchies or spatializations you were playing with onstage during that scene.

MV: That's what performance is, too — mapping time. Space and time can hang out.

RV: One thing I love about your book *Album* and its "twin" *Bouquet* is how they mirror the scene-by-scene quality of your performances: the storytelling or monologue is sequential, sure, and sometimes progresses linearly, but more often than not segues into other things. There are deepenings and shifting intensities from page to page or section to section, and those correspondences are felt across the book and in the live performance. Nothing new here—that the linear and nonlinear coexist as much onstage as they do in life and in reading—but it's been rewarding to think about this through publishing, with artists who are so often attempting to disrupt this dynamic, or play with it as a material. What does that actually look like? How do you actually engage with the page, which is a rather intractable thing, and disrupt the linearity of a reading experience? Conversations around this question are instructive and push the work in ways that open up different experiences...

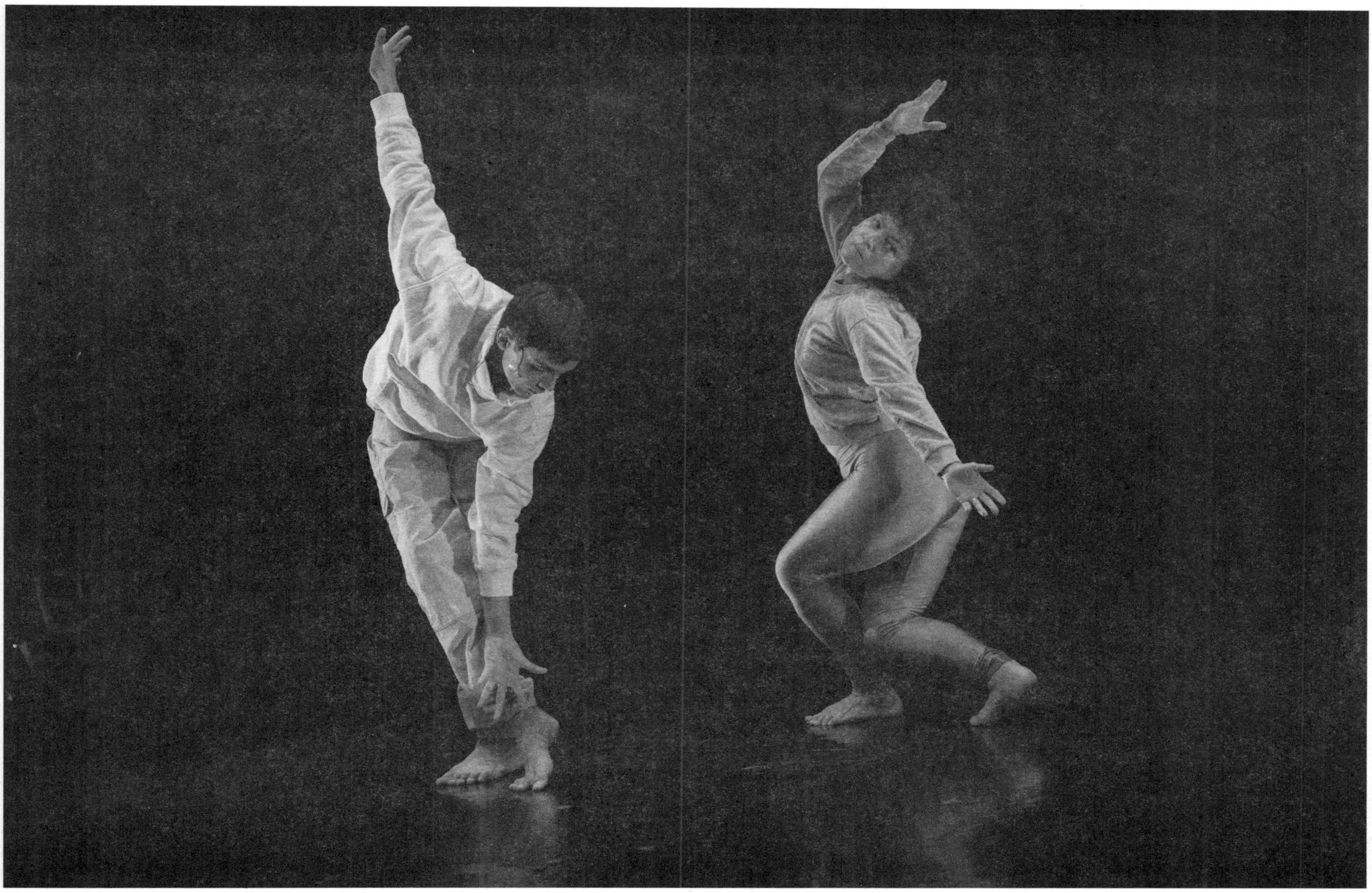

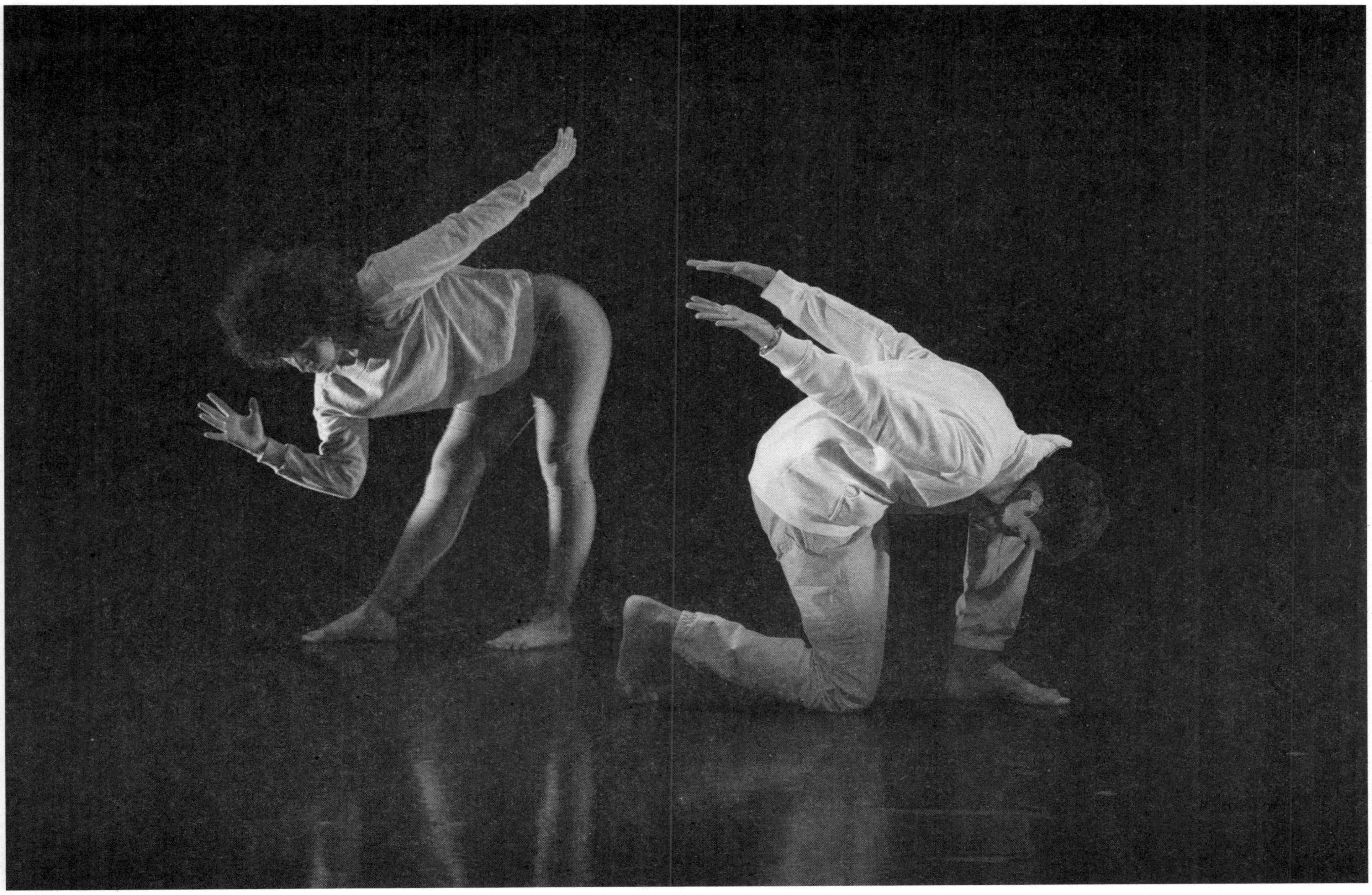

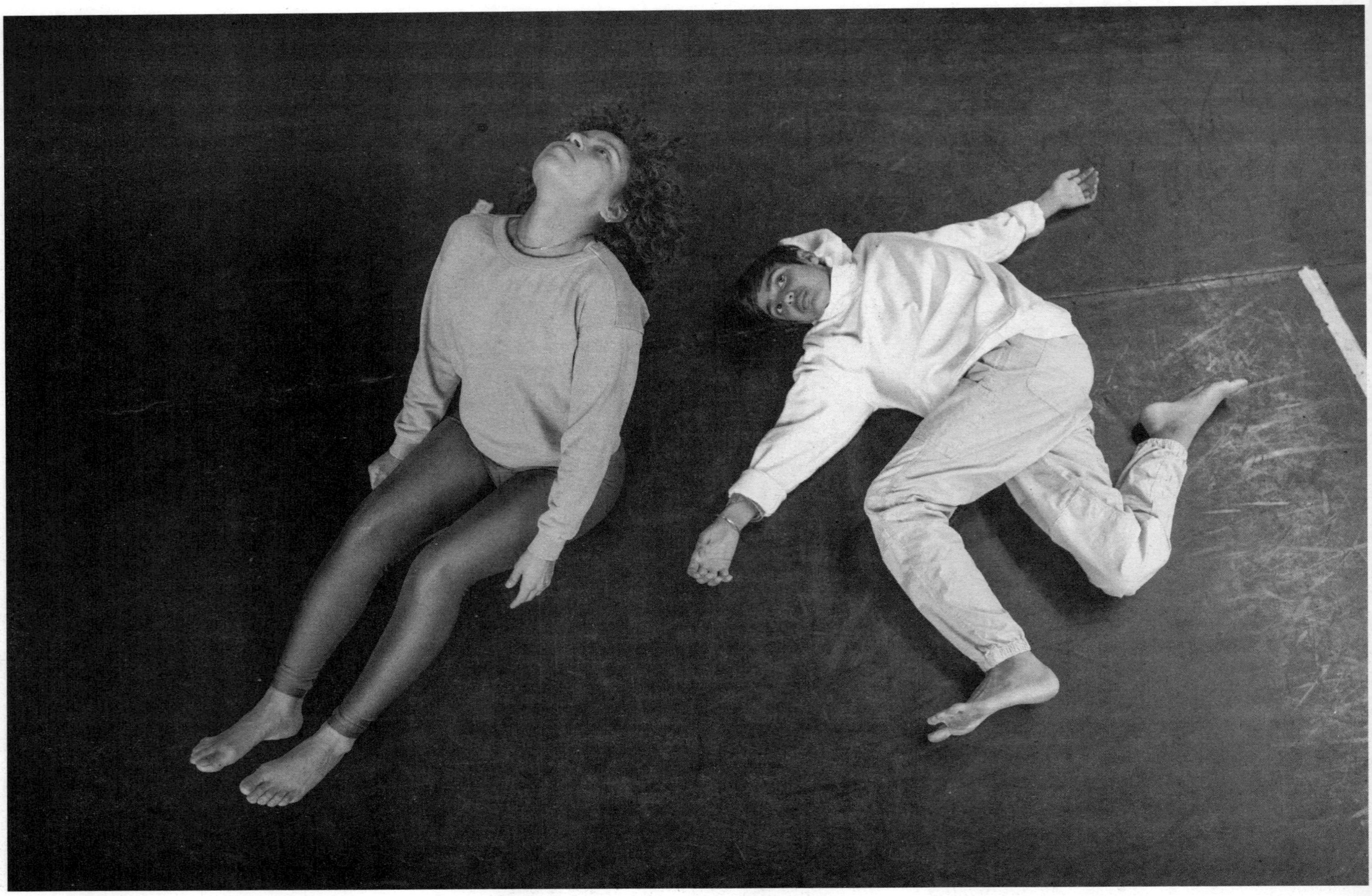

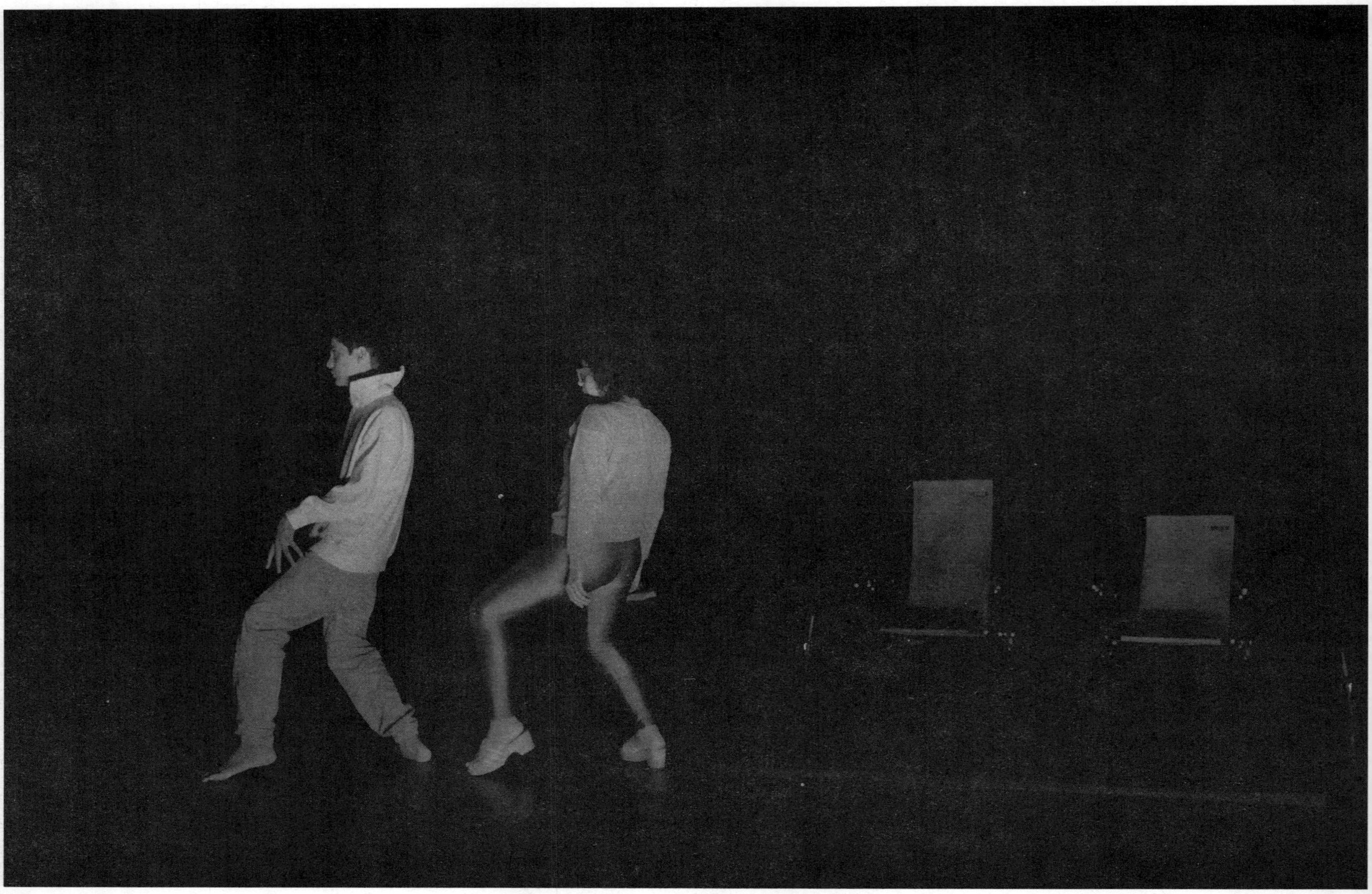

Photos: Mariana Baranova

MV: My work, whether in book or performance form, is not 100% graspable. I expect the audience to space out during a performance. People go on their own journeys and the form inspires time travel. Time travel! The nonlinear approach to my book invites the reader to choose their path. People will do whatever they want with the work. What I'm doing in my mind and through my body is simply putting what's in my notebook on the stage (or a page in a book) with clarity. Language has helped me to make a body of movement through each of my works. I'm often told by audiences that they've learned something after seeing my work. So I'm a teacher, I guess, by making what's visible to me apparent to others. What's visible to me is popular and personal. The popular is penetrable, and the personal can be aligned with.

RV: Your movement vocabulary and syntax offer pathways or modes into both of those registers, so we're also seeing—in the same way you're saying we see your notes presented—a thought process in a distilled, clarified form, and how you enter a subject as someone with a spirit of inquiry, someone with a stake in it, but also someone with a genuine, playful curiosity around things. And having the tools available to you, personal and otherwise, you show us how to bring them to bear on a question, how you elaborate on it from there, and embody that question in different ways. The performance is not synthetic at all, but clarifying. And the process of thinking or researching becomes more precise through its performance.

MV: Someone once said to me that as choreographers, we keep making the same dance. I've heard this a lot about other forms of making—many writers say the same about their work. They keep writing the same story but it's not the same book, or they keep writing the same book but through different stories. Artists keep looking at the same stuff but from different perspectives. Before I started making solos, my dances lived in silos and were very quiet. I used a lot of gesture and geometry, but nothing was being said—a muted postmodernism. Once language came out in my work, without the traditional obfuscation of postmodernism, the audience was allowed in. The practice of looking at myself again and again, from the notebook to the people, stayed active and that's what's kept on happening in my work. Looking back, *Yugoslavia*, which was a very tight dance, begins the momentum for my area of study. A string of dances followed: *Album*, *Bouquet*, *Futurity*, *AIR*, then *Heera*. Through the dances there's a progression of what I know, and how I chose to identify through my work. In *Yugoslavia*, I was mapping time through collage, and in my current work with musician Jazzy Romero, I'm just *in* time improvising with the map in my pocket. What I know is still what I want to talk about, and my new work is about exercising a practice that embraces all that I know through improvisation.

RV: That sounds so much like a kind of pedagogy. Obviously, teaching is, to some degree, a performance. In the classroom, where you are sharing space and collaborating and thinking together, how do these ideas around audience manifest? When you are teaching, do you find you are code-switching? Are you embodying similar directives as in performance?

MV: For me, what ends up happening in class is a conversation, which without the syllabus, we wouldn't have. The students do the work, and we talk through it, and the learning that happens through our conversation is half of the coursework. It allows me to use the syllabus as an adaptable path toward the next subject we're looking at together. Conversation helps us see what's coming up as a group. So again, that's like listening to the audience and shifting the performance from what the audience offers. It's a listening practice. Half the teaching situation is listening to what the students want. And that's not what we've always considered the teaching model to be. Same with performance. It doesn't have to be narrative simply because I'm using language; time isn't linear, we just keep insisting it is. Time is experience which is loaded with feeling and feeling states are non-linear. I'm not rebellious or trying to be shifty, time just doesn't go straight for me. This view helps with my teaching model because I'm allowing the students to self-orient and guide.

RV: It's interesting to think about the performance space and the classroom as two different ways of figuring a public that both have overlaps and also radically different contexts and frames.

MV: And purposes?

RV: Thinking them together, and alongside other forms of social assembly, allows for those frames and purposes to become more flexible all of a sudden. Not to equate them or say they're the same but to ask, "Why is this different than being on a picket line? Why is this different from being in an amphitheater? Why is this different from being in a black box?"

MV: Teaching is leading through example. Hopefully we can allow for people to show up as they are, but you also have to operate in a conscientious way and be intentional about what you're exposing them to.
The same with *Heera*. I looked back at when I was in the student position and thought about what I liked and didn't like back then. I didn't like being talked down to or being smashed into a mold. When I met Heera and saw how much he enjoyed learning, I knew that I was not going to "shape him," as dance often does. I was not going to put him into some kind of mold, but rather, let his body be as full as it needed to be each day. It was the opposite of containing what was good and about letting him grow.

RV: And making that intelligence visible to him, too.

MV: Sometimes all it takes is practice, a certain familiarity to the self. Embodied repetition was a practice for Heera to learn about himself again and again and again. Embodied repetition has taught me how to make my dances.

RV: You mentioned earlier that your work is about learning; with pieces like *Futurity* or *AIR*, you're dealing so specifically with lineage and thinking about how you have learned from and sought out elders to inform the popular, the political, and the cultural history you research and work through. In those two works in particular, you're staging encounters with those historical narratives and stories as occasions for learning and as pedagogic encounters for yourself and others—elucidating something of your own "journey" as a way for the audience to learn, too. You move through this research and model the kind of study that informs it.

MV: It is about study. It's "my stance on dance," my practice. In *Heera*, I was the elder for the first time and I was encountering intergenerationally from a new perspective. In my previous work, I'd always been the younger one to the elders. In *Heera*, I got to be the elder gay.

RV: In *Heera*, you materialize intergenerationally as a space of dialogue, where you're both earnestly testing a range of elements that might form the basis of identification and disidentification. In doing this, you produce shared images and movements, and these end up, too, forming new points of connection on your respective timelines—lifetimes really. The test is repeatable, scalable, and iterative, and there's no right answer, just lots of questions—what mentorship should really look like.

MV: And we both passed. It was a pass-fail course.

Rachel Valinsky is a writer, editor, and translator based in New York. Her writing on performance, dance, and moving image work has appeared in *Artforum*, *PAJ: Performance Art Journal*, *e-flux criticism*, *Art in America*, *Frieze*, and elsewhere. She has curated exhibitions, performances, and publication programs at The Kitchen, The Queens Museums, and BAM, among others. Rachel is also co-founder and Artistic Director of Wendy's Subway, a library, writing space, and independent publisher in Brooklyn, and Managing Editor at the Center for Art, Research and Alliances (CARA) in New York.

Mariana Valencia works through dance. Her work has been presented nationally and toured internationally in Norway, the Balkans, and the UK. She's received awards for her choreography, most notably, a Creative Capital Award (2023), an LMCC Extended Life grant (2019–21), a Bessie Award for Outstanding "Breakout" Choreographer (2018), a Foundation for Contemporary Arts Award to Artists grant (2018), and a Jerome Travel and Study Grant (2015–16). Valencia was a Whitney Biennial artist (2019), a founding member of the No Total reading group, and she has been the co-editor of Movement Research's Critical Correspondence.

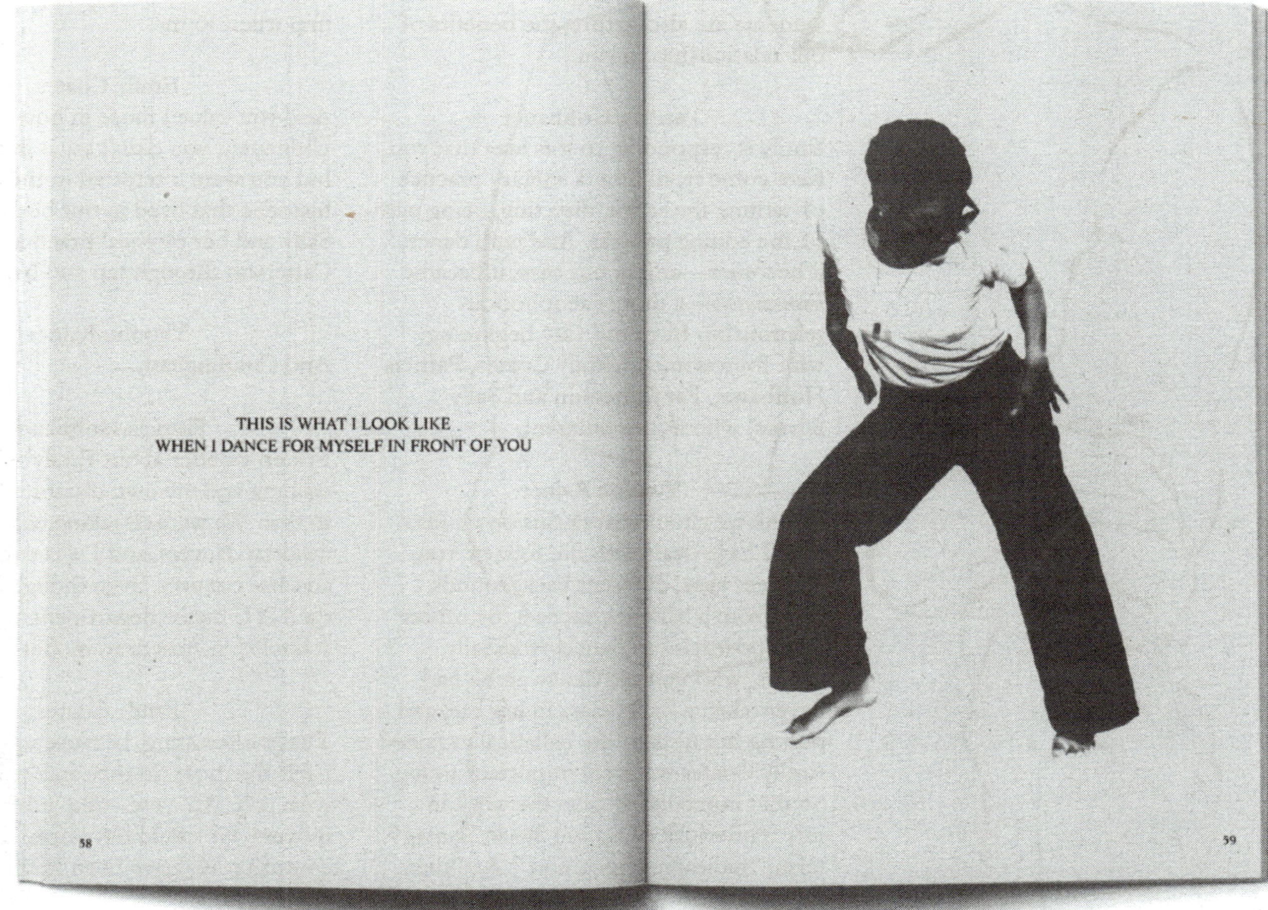

Mariana Valencia, *Album*, published by Wendy's Subway, 2018. Courtesy of the artist and Wendy's Subway.

Thursday, March 9, 2023:

A Conversation With

Yvonne Rainer, Emily Coates, and Patricia Hoffbauer

SUMMARY KEYWORDS:
dance
ballet
Yvonne
piece
movement
dancer
Emily
Pat
Sally
Performa
thought
Keith
company
choreographer
Trisha
questioned
interested
training
influence
ideas

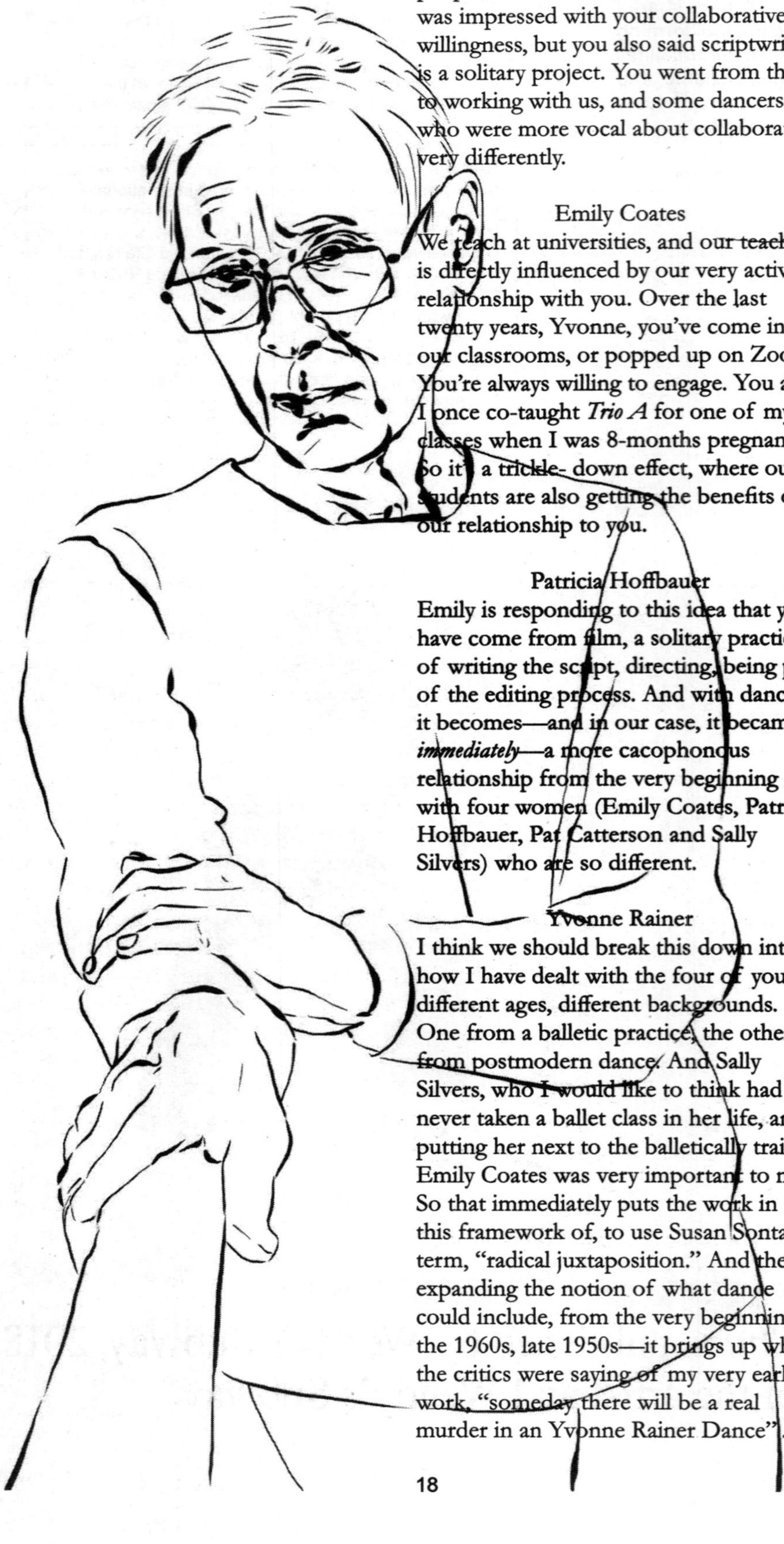

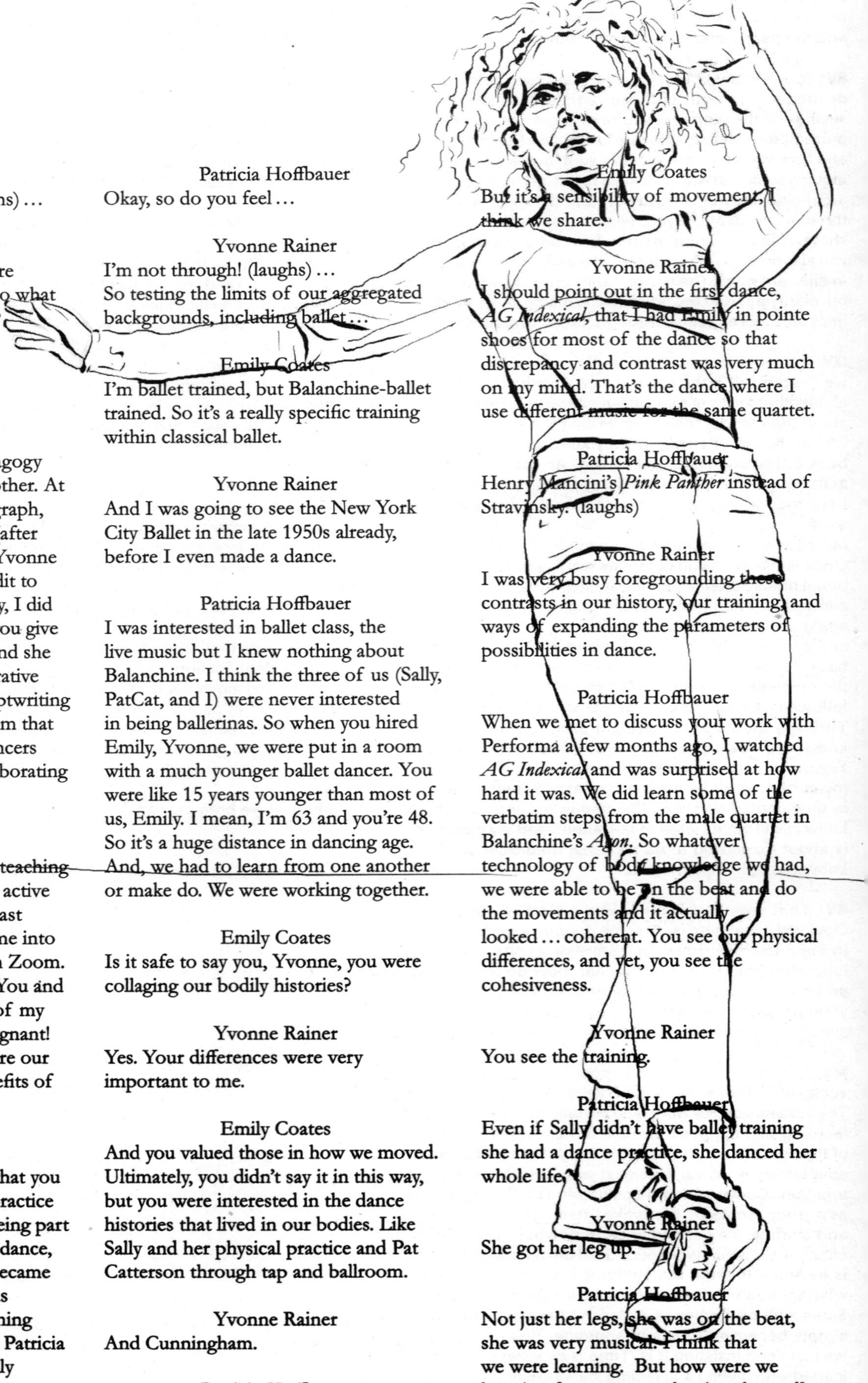

Yvonne Rainer
So, what you wanna know? (laughs) …

Patricia Hoffbauer
Well, Yvonne, you have been more interviewed than Frank Sinatra, so what would you like to talk about? Us?

Yvonne Rainer
OK.

Patricia Hoffbauer
What we have done and the pedagogy of learning and teaching one another. At your film retrospective at Metrograph, a young woman in the audience (after the screening of *Privilege*) said, "Yvonne you are so inclusive, you give credit to everyone" and you said, "basically, I did it all myself." In the film credits you give people a lot of authorial credit, and she was impressed with your collaborative willingness, but you also said scriptwriting is a solitary project. You went from that to working with us, and some dancers who were more vocal about collaborating very differently.

Emily Coates
We teach at universities, and our teaching is directly influenced by our very active relationship with you. Over the last twenty years, Yvonne, you've come into our classrooms, or popped up on Zoom. You're always willing to engage. You and I once co-taught *Trio A* for one of my classes when I was 8-months pregnant! So it's a trickle- down effect, where our students are also getting the benefits of our relationship to you.

Patricia Hoffbauer
Emily is responding to this idea that you have come from film, a solitary practice of writing the script, directing, being part of the editing process. And with dance, it becomes—and in our case, it became *immediately*—a more cacophonous relationship from the very beginning with four women (Emily Coates, Patricia Hoffbauer, Pat Catterson and Sally Silvers) who are so different.

Yvonne Rainer
I think we should break this down into how I have dealt with the four of you, different ages, different backgrounds. One from a balletic practice, the others from postmodern dance. And Sally Silvers, who I would like to think had never taken a ballet class in her life, and putting her next to the balletically trained Emily Coates was very important to me. So that immediately puts the work in this framework of, to use Susan Sontag's term, "radical juxtaposition." And then expanding the notion of what dance could include, from the very beginning—the 1960s, late 1950s—it brings up what the critics were saying of my very earliest work, "someday there will be a real murder in an Yvonne Rainer Dance" …

Patricia Hoffbauer
Okay, so do you feel …

Yvonne Rainer
I'm not through! (laughs) …
So testing the limits of our aggregated backgrounds, including ballet …

Emily Coates
I'm ballet trained, but Balanchine-ballet trained. So it's a really specific training within classical ballet.

Yvonne Rainer
And I was going to see the New York City Ballet in the late 1950s already, before I even made a dance.

Patricia Hoffbauer
I was interested in ballet class, the live music but I knew nothing about Balanchine. I think the three of us (Sally, PatCat, and I) were never interested in being ballerinas. So when you hired Emily, Yvonne, we were put in a room with a much younger ballet dancer. You were like 15 years younger than most of us, Emily. I mean, I'm 63 and you're 48. So it's a huge distance in dancing age. And, we had to learn from one another or make do. We were working together.

Emily Coates
Is it safe to say you, Yvonne, you were collaging our bodily histories?

Yvonne Rainer
Yes. Your differences were very important to me.

Emily Coates
And you valued those in how we moved. Ultimately, you didn't say it in this way, but you were interested in the dance histories that lived in our bodies. Like Sally and her physical practice and Pat Catterson through tap and ballroom.

Yvonne Rainer
And Cunningham.

Patricia Hoffbauer
I often wonder about Emily's Balanchine training and my own distant relationship to that. We were all taking ballet class for modern dancers, and I was coming from another country. Even though I went to the NYU dance department and was very schooled in American modern dance.

Emily Coates
That's interesting, because in that group I felt the most on the same page moving with you. We were compatible as movers. We could have been in the same company. We have been in the same company!

Patricia Hoffbauer
We have been in Yvonne's company! But I was never going to be in New York City Ballet. (laughs)

Emily Coates
But it's a sensibility of movement, I think we share.

Yvonne Rainer
I should point out in the first dance, *AG Indexical*, that I had Emily in pointe shoes for most of the dance so that discrepancy and contrast was very much on my mind. That's the dance where I use different music for the same quartet.

Patricia Hoffbauer
Henry Mancini's *Pink Panther* instead of Stravinsky. (laughs)

Yvonne Rainer
I was very busy foregrounding these contrasts in our history, our training, and ways of expanding the parameters of possibilities in dance.

Patricia Hoffbauer
When we met to discuss your work with Performa a few months ago, I watched *AG Indexical* and was surprised at how hard it was. We did learn some of the verbatim steps from the male quartet in Balanchine's *Agon*. So whatever technology of body knowledge we had, we were able to be on the beat and do the movements and it actually looked … coherent. You see our physical differences, and yet, you see the cohesiveness.

Yvonne Rainer
You see the training.

Patricia Hoffbauer
Even if Sally didn't have ballet training she had a dance practice, she danced her whole life.

Yvonne Rainer
She got her leg up.

Patricia Hoffbauer
Not just her legs, she was on the beat, she was very musical. I think that we were learning. But how were we learning from one another in rehearsal? I remember when Manou (Phuon, a French-Cambodian American dancer who danced with White Oak), and Keith (Sabado, one of Mark Morris's original dancers), came to work with you they were shocked at how much we talked. (laughs)

Yvonne Rainer
Oh, how so?

Patricia Hoffbauer
We talked all the time to you, we discussed the piece, we discussed the politics …

Yvonne Rainer
Oh, they were used to just following orders.

Emily Coates
Yes, and White Oak was a less vocal group in the sense of we weren't speaking up so much and debating, we were taking direction from whoever was the choreographer.

Yvonne Rainer
That's interesting because you did take directions from me…

Emily Coates
…but we talked about it. I remember feeling very happy and relieved that this group felt better and made more sense to me in my 30s, as an adult dancer, than the companies I had come from in my 20s.

Patricia Hoffbauer
We could really challenge Yvonne and say "why the hell are we doing this here?" You were not… what's the word?

Yvonne Rainer
Dictatorial? It's funny being the 'boss,' and yet I was always glad to talk about the ideas and have them questioned. I still am, I think.

Patricia Hoffbauer
Do you feel those conversations ever swayed you to change something? I know in *Hellzappopin,* conversations with David Thompson changed the piece drastically. And when we were making *Assisted Living: Where's The Money* and we were doing "Laurel and Hardy," mimicking them from looking at their films, and there was a moment that PatCat and I kissed and we were questioning your choices, saying "why are we doing this?" You would say "okay, if you don't want to do something."

Emily Coates
…the one who questioned the most just got moved to do different material. (laughs)

Yvonne Rainer
…I've forgotten a lot of this…

Patricia Hoffbauer
You were not threatened by your dancers. We did not always love what you were doing. Sometimes we loved it, sometimes we didn't. But it's like that devotion to the choreographer…

Yvonne Rainer
Yeah, I didn't demand that, I never did. I thought of you as friends, also. I could never hire anyone that I didn't already like as a person. I remember going to a rehearsal of Trisha Brown's, and at one point, I leaned over and remarked on a performer I hadn't seen before; he was new to the company. And she leans over and whispers in my ear, "he's an asshole." I was astounded. I mean, if I thought of someone like that, I couldn't work with him.

Patricia Hoffbauer
You made a different choice in terms of life and dance. You didn't ever want to have a kind of traditional dance company like Trisha's.

Emily Coates
Trisha's company was one of the last of those in the 20th century… now it's too expensive to run a full-time company.

Patricia Hoffbauer
And she was successful, they traveled! Trisha worked hard to sustain that company structure. We, you, never wanted to do that kind of thing.

Yvonne Rainer
Well, I didn't expect you to depend on me economically, and you didn't expect that from me.

Patricia Hoffbauer
It goes back to what Emily was saying, from the beginning we were all artists, or intellectuals, or teachers or community members in our own right. And I had a life of making work. Sally, the same, and so did PatCat. We came in with this baggage of having done things. We also felt that we were your collaborators, not out of an audacity, but just from life experience.

Emily Coates
And interestingly—and this is where the kind of feedback loop comes in—you were all makers, and your making was very influenced by Yvonne.

Patricia Hoffbauer
Even if I really didn't know Yvonne before that. We came to dance in many ways because of the possibilities you proposed, Yvonne. Whereas you, Emily, met Yvonne and then started to make your own work. How has your choreographic experience of making movement influenced you out of ballet?

Emily Coates
I know it's weird because everyone thinks of me as a ballet dancer, in the modern/postmodern dance world, but I have been a postmodern dancer for far longer—twenty years. Meeting Yvonne made me feel I could be a maker.

Patricia Hoffbauer
It's like the thing that formed you perhaps stays…

Emily Coates
But for you Yvonne, you keep having new ideas.

Yvonne Rainer
Or recombining old and new ideas. If you think about that program at New York Live Arts with the 2002 film and the 2022 dance, and the way you have to communicate verbally during the performance in order to engage in those tasks. To be working things out onstage, incorporates every idea I have ever had. And the kind of technical training is very important to do what seems like pedestrian movement. So it's a constantly recombining that brought me into choreography, the possibility for incorporating pedestrian interactions and technical training.

Emily Coates
It does seem like you've become more and more enthralled with training in the last five years.

Patricia Hoffbauer
Maybe in the 60s you were interested in difficult, physically demanding choreography, and now you are again? In your last piece, *Hellzapoppin*, we were tasked with observing majestic dancers performing movements that we couldn't execute verbatim because we did not have their training, skills, speed, or for some of us, the age, and create a sequence using four dancers instead of two, the way it is in the film. And that was physically hard for us. So in this way of working together, we have become a traditional modern dance company: Performa takes care of the financial/administrative structure, you are the artistic director, we are the members of the company, and you choose who comes in…

Yvonne Rainer
…and who goes out…

Emily Coates
Yeah, it's crazy, you have a non-Company company, Yvonne.

Yvonne Rainer
I didn't audition people. Baryshnikov invited me back into dance, and you, Emily, Manou and Keith were from White Oak.

Patricia Hoffbauer
What about *The Concept of Dust*? I love that piece. It contains some very structured movement material that we're supposed to accomplish, and then there is the freedom of choosing on the spot what you want to do.

Yvonne Rainer
And there also is unison movement.

Patricia Hoffbauer
Whenever we're going to start the unison is up to whoever…

Yvonne Rainer
Anyone can initiate it.

Patricia Hoffbauer
But in that process, when you directed us to make our solos, you actually made movement and we mimicked you. You danced around and we followed you and picked up steps.

Emily Coates
This makes me think about your younger following, Yvonne: the students we teach, and also the younger people you interact with, like when you visited Marta Kuzma's class "The Artist as Curator" at Yale last month. Younger artists are still drawn to your work. Do you feel you can relate?

Yvonne Rainer
Well, I answer their questions. I don't know, you tell me?

Emily Coates
It's hard to say, because at this point, you've influenced so many generations!

Yvonne Rainer
Well, they bring up very familiar questions about process and the origin of ideas and breadth of ideas, and it's about making art, you know. From my answers, they can probably adapt to their own interests. I don't find their questions outlandish, or very far from what they're seeing in the work. They're able to relate to it, which is gratifying, of course, to me. And, let's see, in Washington, DC I addressed the audience after the film screening. They were relating to what they had just looked at. I think this work is still pertinent in a lot of ways, which of course is very gratifying. It isn't like the early 60s when my generation was shocking, and seeming to destroy our precedents: Graham, Humphrey, Limon. Of course we were challenging them. But now I don't see the younger generation challenging me in such extreme ways.

Emily Coates
Right. You and your peers mainly seem to have worshipful acolytes; there is a difference.

Patricia Hoffbauer
There are some younger artists who have criticized the Judson artists for being

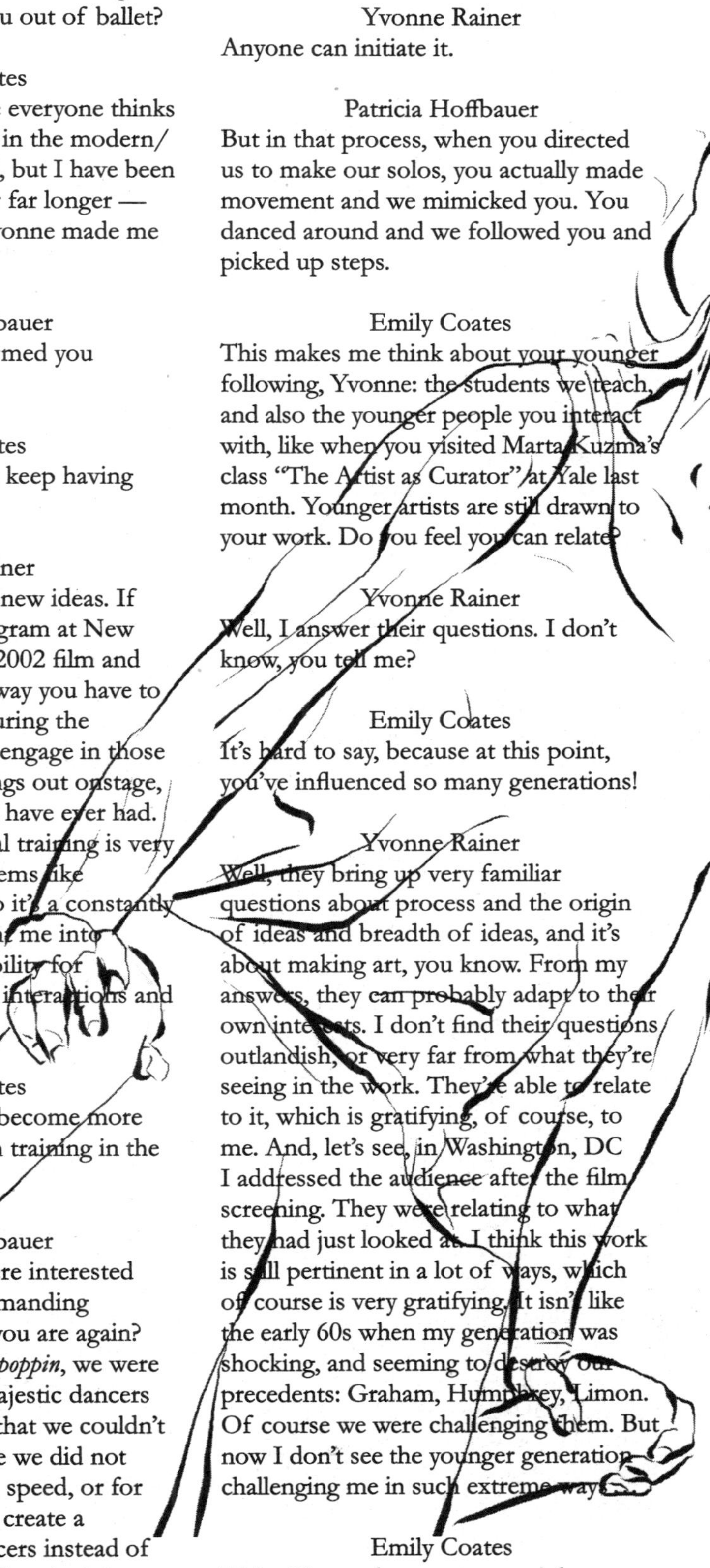

Drawings: Jesse Zaritt
Based on photos by Maria Baranova, Courtesy New York Live Arts & Performa, Yvonne Rainer. *HELLZAPOPPIN': What about the bees?*, October 5–8, 2022.

exclusive, but they also have different questions and it is not so much about challenging you specifically …

Yvonne Rainer
In the early 60s, the so-called dance authorities didn't just ask questions about our work, they were *offended.* It is interesting the way criticism has changed. Even the most advanced, avant-garde, sympathetic critics who reviewed our presentations in the 60s were critical, but now they're …

Patricia Hoffbauer
Disappointed?

Emily Coates
The most sustained challenge you've gotten, Yvonne, is the critique of the whiteness of Judson.

Yvonne Rainer
And that's justified in a way. I've tried to deal with it in a rational way and not be too defensive—the workshops that produced those Judson performances were open to anyone who came, at least that's how I remember them.

Patricia Hoffbauer
There didn't have to be a policy of exclusion for there to be a culture of exclusivity; Judson didn't say "yes" to some people and "no" to others. Which is interesting, because you're an artist associated with that word—"No." But you have gone back on your own words, as we've talked about, you have said "yes" to a kind of dramatic emotionality or to other ways of doing things that you had said no to earlier. It's like what Emily said earlier, she danced ballet for six years and has been a postmodern dancer for twenty but she's remembered for those six years. The same with you, Yvonne. But you are remembered for that restrictive kind of prescribed set of instructions, which is what I think people have reacted to, "How could you?" You have said yes to many more things in your life than you have said no to.

Yvonne Rainer
But getting back to the racial issue, as a white feminist artist whose career began within the 60's 'personal is political' credo, my need to use language for political issues is what pushed me into filmmaking. And it wasn't until my latest dance *Hellzapoppin: What about the bees*? that I felt enabled to deal specifically with racism. In this recent dance I projected the original *Hellzapoppin* dancers and the dream scene from *Zero for Conduct* (one of my favorite films) on a loop at the top of the show. Both film extracts register a subversive behavior that challenges authority: the virtuosic capacity of the black dancers in *Hellzapoppin*, whose beautiful athleticism speaks volumes about their power beyond their subservient costumes, plus the transgressive behavior of the students in the catholic school dorms in the Jean Vigo film. Those images contain a physical resistance I wanted to explore with my dancers. Concepts of resistance and transgression have been recombined in this piece as a kind of meditation on race issues in my past and present life in the U.S.

Patricia Hoffbauer
If you were to think about your next piece, let's say this was your penultima, what would you be interested in covering again, exploring anew?

Yvonne Rainer
I have two projects. One is finishing *Trio A*, deconstructing the third rendition of it, Brittany Bailey's version. Emily does the original version, Elliot Mercer does the retrograde version and Brittany Bailey does this demolishing, you might say, based on Donald O'Connor's incredible solo in *Singing in the Rain.* It's not finished.

Patricia Hoffbauer is a NY dance artist originally from Brazil. She has been produced, commissioned and presented by Danspace Project, Dance Theater Workshop, PS 122, The Whitney Museum at Phillip Morris and Gibney Dance Center, to mention a few. Hoffbauer is an Assistant Professor at Open Arts Department at NYU's Tisch, has taught at Hunter College's Dance Department, and was a lecturer at Princeton University.

Yvonne Rainer, one of the founders of the Judson Dance Theater (1962), made a transition to filmmaking following a fifteen-year career as a choreographer/dancer (1960–1975). After making seven experimental feature-length films, she returned to dance in 2000 via a commission from the Baryshnikov Dance Foundation. Her dances and films have been seen throughout the U.S., Europe, and Asia in concert halls and museum retrospectives.

A dancer, choreographer, and writer, **Emily Coates** has performed internationally with New York City Ballet, Mikhail Baryshnikov's White Oak Dance Project, Twyla Tharp, and Yvonne Rainer. Career highlights include three duets with Baryshnikov, in works by Erick Hawkins, Mark Morris, and Karole Armitage, and the span of Rainer's work, from 1961 to the present.

Jesse Zaritt is a Brooklyn–based dance artist. He is an Assistant Professor at the University of the Arts in Philadelphia, PA, having previously been the inaugural 2014–2016 Research Fellow in the University's School of Dance. Jesse has performed his solo work in Taiwan, Uruguay, Russia, Korea, Germany, New York, Japan, Mexico, Israel and throughout the United States.

Patricia Hoffbauer
I saw their performance at the Performa Gala. So you want to do that and what else?

Yvonne Rainer
I recently saw this film. I have to go to my notes. I can't remember the names anymore. It's about Wittgenstein who was heir to a fortune and gave it all away and his writing is very difficult, as the philosopher who contested language. There are some wonderful passages, which are probably quotations from his teaching and expounding on his ideas. Somehow I want to bring this language into *Hellzapoppin*, I don't know how, it's an idea. I am not finished with *Hellzapoppin.*

Emily Coates
I keep thinking about transmissions and future generations and subsequent generations. And what holds up I think, in your work over these decades, is the aspiration toward social political critique. That catches a critical theory trend, as well. But also, to your point, Pat, about so much openness, Yvonne said yes to many more things than she said no to, and what generations inherit when they inherit that collection of values, when it's so open, where do you go from there? Do you close back down? Like a pendulum effect, you open it so far that the next gesture has to be to swing back, to narrow it back in. And it's interesting to think about why your aesthetic has not been challenged so much as extended, into extreme studies of presence—it's a kind of narrowing back in.

Yvonne Rainer
I think one reason that there's been no specific revolt against Rainer ideas is that I never codified a technique the way Humphrey and Graham did, which is so specific.

Patricia Hoffbauer
There isn't any kind of a codified movement, but Yvonne, you have some ways that you work, I have some ways that I work, but we change all the time, too. That is what I was saying about *Concept of Dust,* that it was transmitted through your body, and other times we were asked to look at videos and you didn't get up from the chair. You didn't demonstrate the movement. We have been through so much in life, and somehow there's been this constant, which is to work *with* Yvonne.

Emily Coates
It has offered us an artistic home in this period of our lives.

Patricia Hoffbauer
And this bullshit about "maternity will suck you out of your possibilities of existing," maybe that's true, but we were given this opportunity to continue developing as artists, even if, as interpretive artists (laughs), collaborative artists …

Emily Coates
I just love that we couldn't have said in 2005, we would still be going in 2023.

Yvonne Rainer
I have been lucky with Performa, they look for more performing possibilities …

Patricia Hoffbauer
But MOMA wasn't luck. None of it is luck, right? Your work has been embraced.

Yvonne Rainer
Some of which is luck. I feel that I fell into a decade, the 60s decade — the end of the 50s — just at the right time, when all these ideas were swirling.

Emily Coates
You had the talent to capitalize upon it.

Patricia Hoffbauer
And you've had a commitment to stay on a path. That no matter the bad reviews, and there were many, the other kind of acclaim, the critical acclaim came from an intellectual kind of space.

Yvonne Rainer
It was an obsession, you might say.

Emily Coates
You needed to make work.

Yvonne Rainer
I still need to … (laughs)

Emily Coates
Yeah, we all need to make work and be creative artists. But how and why it manifests is different in our individual lives. At 88 I don't know if I will still be making performance work.

Yvonne Rainer
Even though I can no longer, quote unquote, dance. But I love to perform.

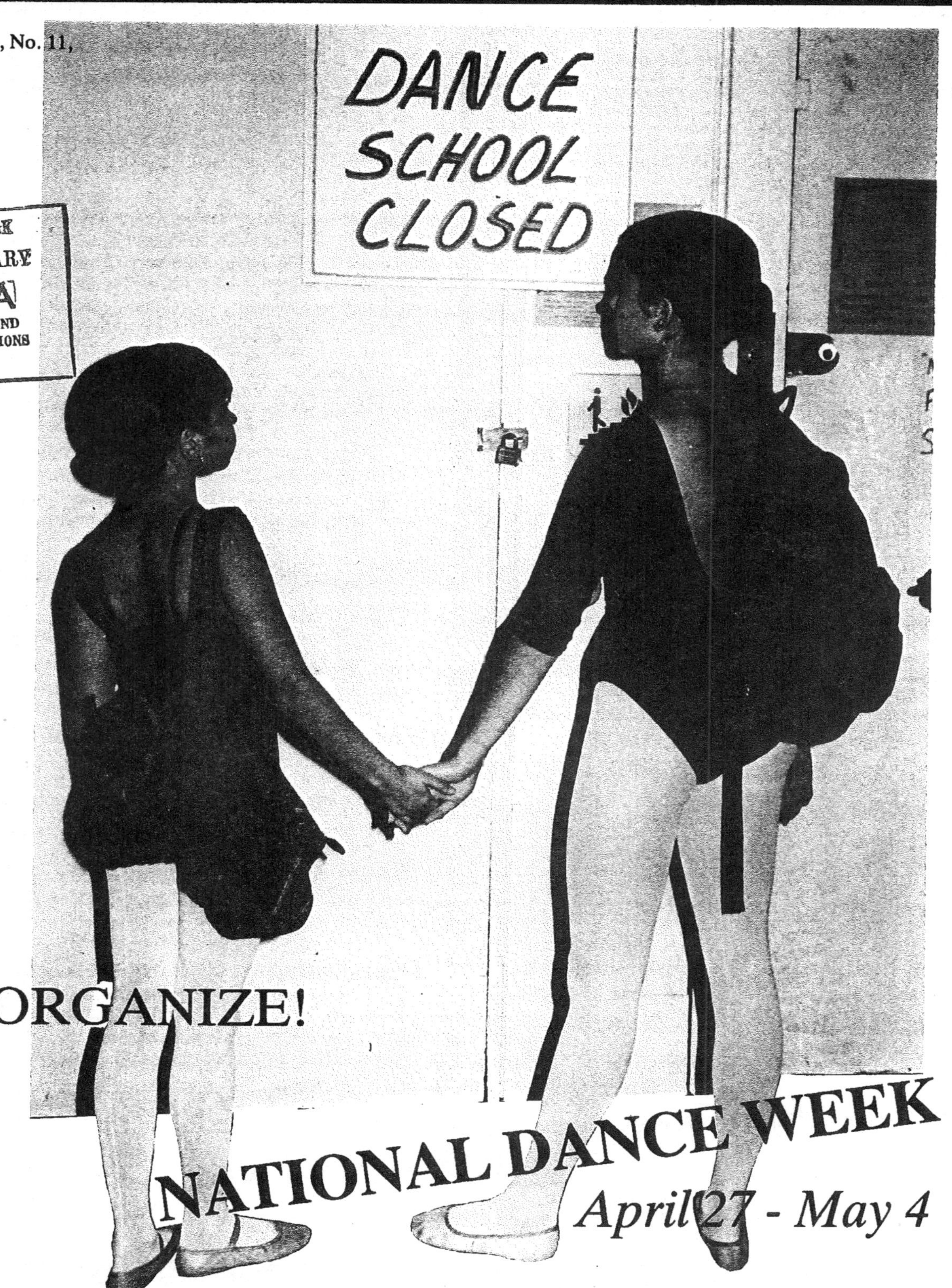

Pen to Paper... Movement in Motion

Bernadine Jennings

To talk about *Attitude: The Dancers' Magazine*, one has to discuss Dance Giant Steps, Inc. (DGS). DGS is an art service organization created to fill in missing services to artists of color especially. *Attitude Magazine* was one component that sought to document and place in context that much more than ballet and modern dance was taking place in New York City and beyond. Folkloric and ethnic dance performances and classes are viable facets of dance that receive limited coverage (if at all) in media sources. Yet ethnic and folkloric dance performances, and classes in particular, continue anchor us to our communities and heritage.

Here in New York there are countless examples of teachers and small- to medium- sized dance companies being evicted from sites they had invested in — mirrors, floors (both wooden and Marley), barres, dressing rooms, toilets, and curb appeal, and the list goes on. Increased volumes of traffic/ pedestrian took place. With constant, impossible rent increases come two options: move to another city/location or join forces with the large studios. This is an ongoing crisis.

Climbing out of invisibility status to a status of respect required *Attitude* being a reliable representation of all performing populations.

Being The Press ...

entails building relationship with several facets of *behind-the-scenes* personnel. Most people want coverage for their clients; thus, more press coming to the program is important. We do not often speak on it, but all grant applications require published press materials within one's support documents.

Ethnic and folkloric companies get limited coverage compared to ballet and modern dance. This fact reenforced for us that there was a need for our reviews and commentaries. Sure, we also provide coverage to ballet and modern dance — but we had a niche.

PRESS REPRESENTATIVES were welcoming to us, as their clients would be reviewed in a dance magazine. Audrey Ross, Jonathan Slaff, and Richard Kornfield & Associates sought us to help their clients. We still maintain ongoing relationship with them, and now one must add Michelle Tabnick with her quite full client list.

PRESENTERS like World Music Institute have always enjoyed our coverage, particularly since we have staff members with true knowledge of and experience in folkloric categories.

INSTITUTIONS like City Center, Chen & Dancers, La Mama, Symphony Space, City College, Hostos College, Henry St Settlement, Lincoln Center, among others were somewhat of a challenge, in that you had to locate the right office/person taking care of "free tickets" as they are wont to call such tickets.

MENTORS, ELDERS & PEERS
Let's now talk a bit about our community at large: Nennette Charisse, Madam Darvash and 'The Duke' V. Dukodovsky (sic), Zena Rommett, as well as the Clark Center Alumni welcomed us as individual, professional dancers in their classes. Not so for too many to name, who did not. Most of the big schools like Ailey, Steps, Broadway Dance Center, Ballet Hispanico celebrated our career transition into dance writing.

"Not having studios will kill our theater."
Gwenn Verdon

TO MAYOR EDWARD I. KOCH AND MEMBERS OF THE BOARD OF ESTIMATE:

By December 1985, seventeen schools of dance and four large rehearsal halls will have been demolished by real estate developers to produce higher income producing office buildings and luxury housing.

Theater in New York City generates $4 billion in tourist and entertainment dollars each year. The schools, rehearsal halls, and ancillary businesses form the basis of this income. Destroying places of study for young students, professional artists and others threatens the entertainment industry, the art of dance, and the position New York City holds as the mecca of dance world-wide.

I support DANSE (Dance Artists' Nationwide Space Emergency) COALITION to bring this loss to your attention; to suggest you consider restructuring tax-passalongs that burden not-for-profit schools in commercial buildings; and provide zoning laws in commercial mid-town buildings to include suitable space for the preservation and prosperity of our dance art and entertainment industry.

Tina Ramirez' Testimony for "Real Estate Crisis in the Arts"

(Monday, April 14, 1986)

GOOD Afternoon. I am Tima Ramirez, founder and artistic director of Ballet Hispanico of New York. For those of you who don't yet know us, here's the 15 second commercial. Ballet Hispanico is one of the handful of major Hispanic cultural institutions in the United States today. The New York State Council on the arts qualifies us as one of the state's primary cultural institutions. Enrollment in our school of dance, is 1,000 children. Although our home is in New York, our professional company has also performed in more than 45 other states, Europe and the Virgin Islands for enthusiastic audiences of over one million people.

At the gracious invitation of Asembly-man Nadler and his associate Marty Algaz, I've come to join with my colleagues from New York's artistic community in speaking with you today about the real estate crunch facing our institutions.

Until we moved to our present location ten years ago, we had to relocate twice—in 6 years—to have affordable, if not exactly suitable, studio space. Then in 1975, Ballet Hispanico moved into its first real home, two broken down carriage houses on West 89th Street which the city had been using for rat poison storage. But we didn't really worry about the rat poison, to us it was heaven on earth. We saw it as a new opportunity for the company and the school to reach out into a larger community.

In 1979, with help from the city, we began the long and tortuous process of purchasing and renovating our home.

Many people say Ballet Hispanico has been lucky and they're right. We were lucky. *But* we were given the opportunity to purchase our home through the West Side Urban Renewal Plan and by our community board. And my own board had the foresight and courage and daring to undertake the whole effort. With help from government, corporate, foundation and private sources, our efforts to establish our home have met to date with success. But we still must raise over half a million dollars this year in order to be able to make use of one of our buildings. At present, over 1,000 students and the professional company are cramped into only two studios while we raise the money to finish the necessary renovations.

I believe that it is extremely important for not just the City but the State to recognize that housing its arts organizations is vital to the continued health and well-being of New York. In the case of Lincoln Center, Theater Row, and the galleries of Tribeca and Soho, artistic institutions have been responsible for turning entire areas of the city around and making them ecnomically viable. It distresses me to see condominium developers list Symphony Space, Second Stage, Equity Library Theater and other arts organizations in their sales literature. Those art institutions which attract apartment buyers are at the same time threatened by the very developers who extoll their merits in sales brochures. Why not ask developers to play their Trump cards and build theaters, dance studios or galleries into those new condominiums. In return the cultural institutions will continue to contribute to increased property values.

How else can you help us? For the arts organizations who have taken the leap of faith and bought their buildings, help us to make our new homes liveable and to meet the increased operating costs generated by our new buildings. I am no longer able to worry just about my company's plies and jetes, now I must be concerned also with mega watts and leaky roofs. For those companies who are struggling to find or keep homes in New York, give them the chance to buy or rent spaces at fair prices for not-for-profit corporations. Don't take their homes away without offering them viable alternatives.

Why should you do this? People don't visit or live in New York because of the health clubs. Artistic institutions enhance the quality of live here. For years, artists have come to New York "to make it," because this city made it possible for their art to flourish—it gave us the opportunity to work and grow. We found in New York a rich and worthwhile experience. Furthermore, when a company like Ballet Hispanico dances in Paris, Madrid, San Antonio, Rochester or Albany, we represent the wonderful things our state has to offer both to residents and tourists.

We are not asking for a handout, just a helping hand. It is the best investment you can make in the future of the Empire State.

Thank you. •

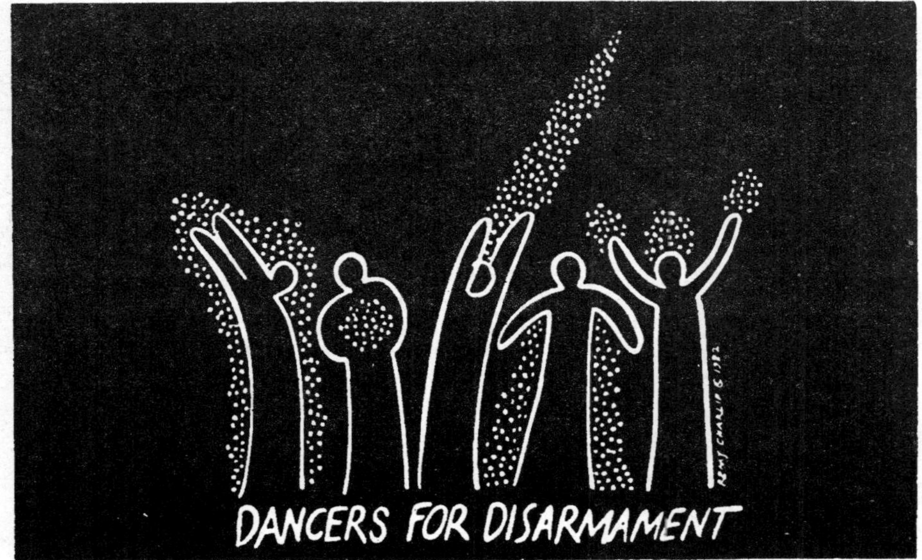

10 ATTITUDE

Perhaps you are wondering how we could afford the the printing costs, writers' honorariums (per article), layout and design fees, bulk mailing, et cetera? When we began, three of the four of us — Arthur T. Wilson, Marilyn Read, and Phillip Bond — had day jobs. Once they moved on, Expansion Arts of National Endowment for the Arts (NEA) and Special Arts Services of New York State Council on The Arts (NYSCA) provided support. Notably, Federal and New York State dance programs did not consider us worthy of support. Locally, I will not tell you about the back and forth, push/pull involved in the Department of Cultural Affairs (DCA) understanding what we were doing was unique and essential. First, during the 1990s, we were given "line item" status on their budget with the city; later after Norma Torres, Natsu Ifill, Michael Unthank, Mary Schmidt Campbell were no longer in charge, we were thrown under the bus to Brooklyn's DCA process. Dancers there decided via panels what was important to give visibility and assistance to. By their estimation, *Attitude* — and our endeavors to document New York dance citywide — was not pertinent to Brooklyn.

DANCE GIANT STEPS PRESENTS
Celebrate America: Home of World Wide Dance!
April 27 – May 4, 2003

2003

NATIONAL DANCE WEEK

For further information:
dancegiantsteps@hotmail.com
(718) 773-3046

FREE ADMISSION

website:
www.geocities.com/danceattitude

Sunday, April 27
Brooklyn,
The Clark Center Project
Charles Moore Center for Ethnic Studies;
397 Bridge St @ 4-7pm

Monday, April 28
Manhattan:
Career Transitions in Dance (*):
Lecture on Health and Wellness
Actors' Equity 165 W 46 St.
5-7pm
*not a Dance Giant Steps event.

Tuesday, April 29
International Dance Day!
Brooklyn,
Dance Quilting Bee!
St.John's Recreation center,
1251 Prospect Place
11am-2pm

Wednesday, April 30
Bronx: 5:30pm
Social Dance Marathon
The Old, the Young & the Restless can all Mambo, Lindy Hop and Boogie
The Point CDC
940 Garrison Ave
#6 Train to Hunt's Point Ave

Thursday, May 1
Staten Island:
May Day AIDS Tribute
Staten Island Ferry
Midnight, Noon, Midnight

Friday, May 2
Brooklyn,
Dance Video Production to Broadcast
The MicroMuseum 123 Smith St,
6:30-9pm

Saturday, May 3
Harlem,
Town Meeting of Dance Teachers Uptown
Hansborough Recreation Center
35 W. 134 St, 11:30-1pm

Sunday, May 4
Greenwich Village,
Liturgical Dance Tea
Judson Memorial Church,
55 Washington Sq. Park South,
2:30-5pm

State of the Arts NYSCA

All programs and artists are subject to change

The activities of Dance Giant Steps, Inc. are funded in part with public monies from New York State Council on the Arts, a state agency. They are also funded in part by City of New York Department of Cultural Affairs.

Design & illustrations Béatrice Coron http://www.beatricecoron.com

SO... we put on our *begging shoes* and sought financial coverage from non-governmental arts funders — Rudolph Nureyev Dance Foundation, Nathan Cummings, Foundation for Contemporary Arts, among others. We received great rejection letters after the application and board panels meetings' decisions, each thanking us for applying but ultimately concluding there was "no room at the inn." Capezio Dance Foundation (Ben Sommers) and Actors' Fund of America provided financial support to Dance Giant Steps, Inc. for *Attitude's* printing. Donations and subscriptions were provided as well... nominally.

Yes, we were always hand to mouth. But boy oh boy, I can tell you: *Attitude: The Dancers Magazine* has had the greatest staff and designers on board from our inception. The late activist-poet Louis Reyes Rivera typeset our layout. Late at night after the staff had gone home, we would head into the Printing Press, located at Tillary and Flatbush Avenue Extension, to get our work done. Louis did our layouts until Josh Gosciak replaced him. I need a map of the village to remember exactly where on Broadway were Josh's headquarters, I TYPE. Our final person for design and layout was Shirley Kwan from Hong Kong. She did all the layout and design for the color volume, Volumes 20 through 26.

The print industry by this time had changed. Our printer, Expedi Printing, Inc. could no longer locate ink nor paper the proper size or scale for their work, particularly newsprint for daily circulars and menus. Laying off employees was followed by fully closing their headquarters in the old meat market area on West 13th, then their Brooklyn location folded, and finally their Long Island site. Anyway, we continued in the great unknown called digital printing. Digital printing gave two options: a PDF or an actual printed copy. It also gave lots of headaches with the paperwork.

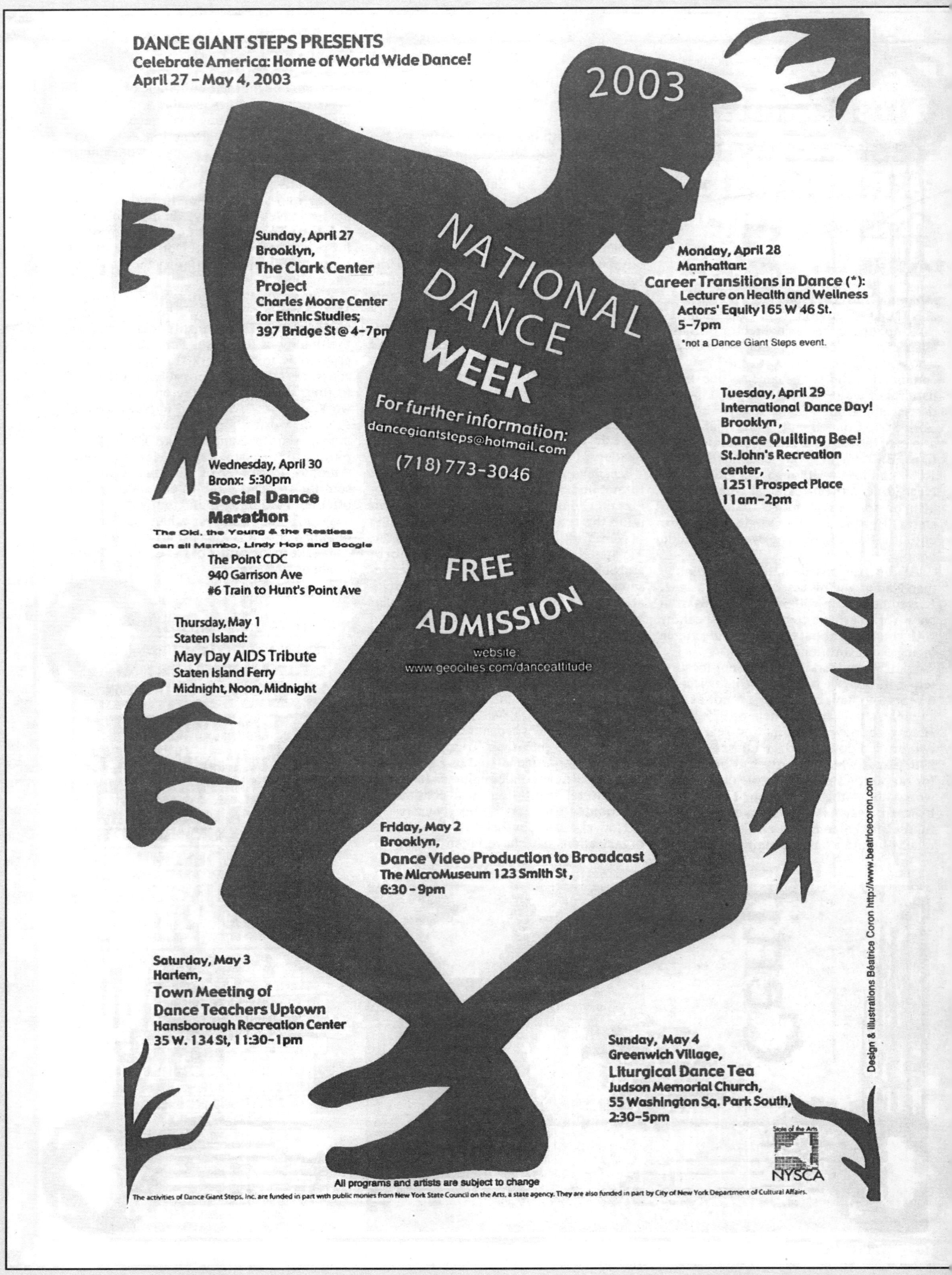

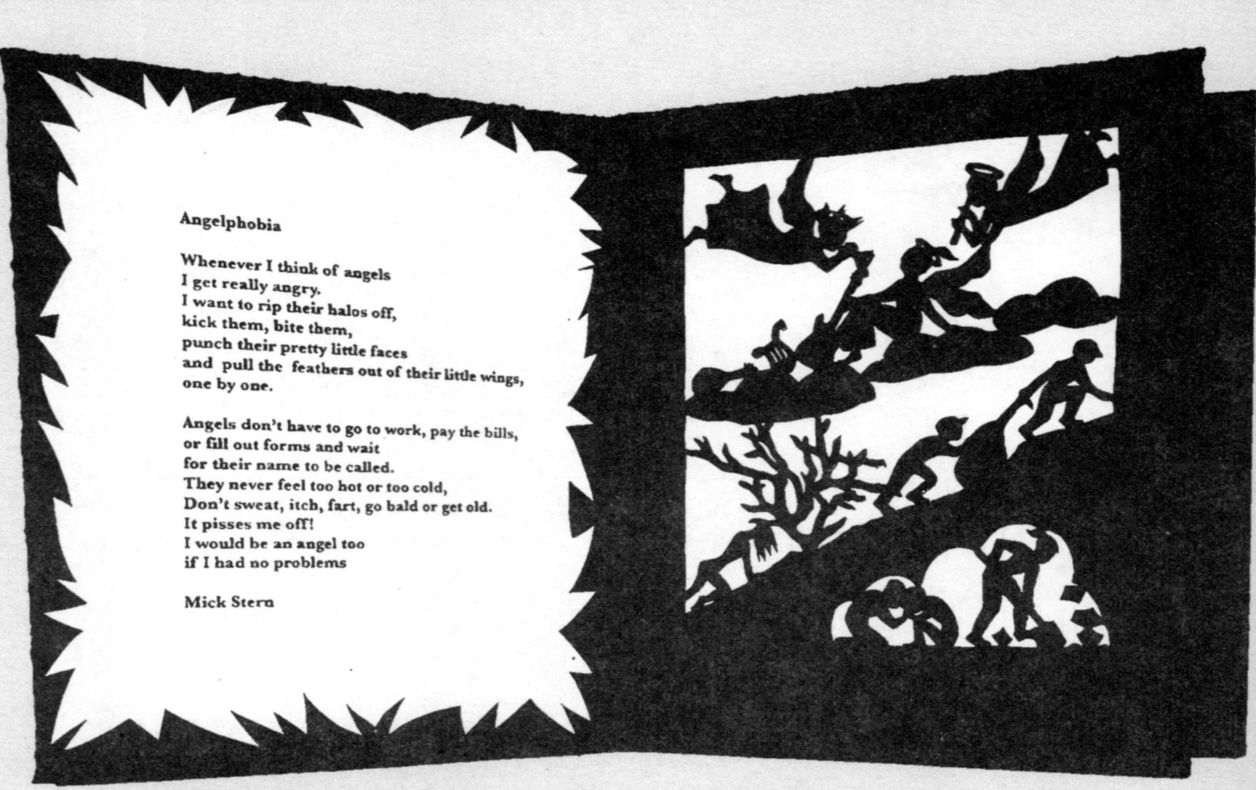

Giant Steps into another level through the deification of Clark Center is more than a noble act. It is magnanimous because it involves history that must be told. In the first paragraph I listed only a few of the things that keep me excited about living a full life. I am constantly referring to and using material/information gleaned during time spent within those walls where we had teachers/instructors/lectures who cared if we lived or died. Funding this proposal will allow Bernadine the opportunity to reach out, and reach in, to so many of us who have benefited from the energy generated during Clark Center's hey day. Many an evening our class started late because our instructors were busy answering questions and guiding many who, now, are recognized around the world for their ability to excite and, my word, "EDUTAINE".

Page two

I am where I am partly because Mama Thelma Hill, right there in Clark Center, would teach our Horton class for two hours and talk for however long afterwards as she, like all of the others, encouraged, cajoled and let us know the world of the performing arts was/is not to be taken lightly. I listened. I learned as I sat next to Marilyn Banks, Bernadine Jennings, Carla Perlo, John Parks(to name a few). Many times Alvin Ailey popped in along with Jimmy Truitt and Geoffrey Holder and encouraged us merely by their presence. Mama Thelma would insist on them giving us a word or two and we listened. And we learned. Clark Center was a haven and its legacy must be shared with today's youth who need lots of encouragement in a time when the emphasis is on profit and not progress. Many of us are ready, and willing, to assist Bernadine in her quest to share Clark Center's History through a project sponsored by Dance Giant Step that produces the 20-year-old Attitude Dance Magazine that has become a mainstay in many a studio and even more homes and backpacks.

I could go on and on. I could spend pages talking about Bernadine's abilities necessary for the completion of this project. Others will do this and her resume speaks volumes. I could speak endlessly on the necessity for such an endeavor. I won't. I will simply say, once again, please look with favor on his project and grant full funding so that the ENTIRE object can be achieved.

Please continue to walk in peace constantly surrounded with creative energy necessary to bring lots of love and prosperity for you and your loved ones.
Ase. Ase. Ase.

Please do not hesitate in contacting me if more information is required.

Peace and Love

Dr. Chuck Davis

And here, the best for last: we have had, from our inception, some of the best folks writing about dance. That is our secret: professional dance folks who do their careers and also observe, reflect, and document other performing artists in their prime, as well as those dancers and companies starting out (debuts). Most of us know the African proverb — *It takes a Village*. For what we did — all these years, from 1983 through 2010, and beyond — here is our VILLAGE! Our best writers include Jim Drobnick, Starr Siegele, Susanna Sloat, Mark Franko, Lillie Rosen, Pat Catterson, Mark Kappel, Mme. Peff Modelski, David Lipfert, Madeleine Dale, Lori Ortiz, Larry Stevens, Doris Green, Gus Solomons, Jr., Melinda Mousouris, theatre critic Gerard Raymond, Walter Rutledge, Nefretete Rasheed, S'thembele West, Ennis Smith, Annabella Lenzu, and Arthur T. Wilson. Beatrice Coron, known for her linguistic skills as well as being a Master Paper Cutter, did all of the beautiful drawings and illustrations. A few drawings were done by Gus Solomons, Jr., Queens based activist/educator/muralist Rikki Asher, and our prolific Shirley Kwan.

The most beautiful photographs were done by Professor David Fullard (SUNY Empire), South African Nan Melville, and Queens Native Son, Corky Lee. We have just lost activist Corky Lee to Covid-19 (September 5, 1947–January 27, 2021). As no other, he understood that there is a viable Asian Diaspora like there is the African Diaspora. He traveled all over the city, states, and nations to record the diverse dance activities of these populations. Throughout his life, he recorded and photographed their contrasting elements as well as their common bonds. We at *Attitude* received a legacy benefit from all his wonderful cameras.

The saga of Dance Giant Steps, Inc., as an art service organization for artists of color especially, is one of climbing out of invisibility status to a status of respect. This was due in part to our reliable representation of this performing population via *Attitude: The Dancers' Magazine*.

In closing: we celebrate ourselves with *Ethnic Dance Awards, Annual May Day!* acknowledging our losses to AIDS, *Dance Teachers' Conferences*, addressing the dance school closings from exorbitant rent increases, and on and on. This and more strengthen the resolve that We too! Sing America, We too! Make Dance in New York and the U.S. at large, the diverse variety we love to boast about. All these years later — it is nice to be recognized and remembered.

THANKS!

Attitude *THE DANCERS' MAGAZINE*

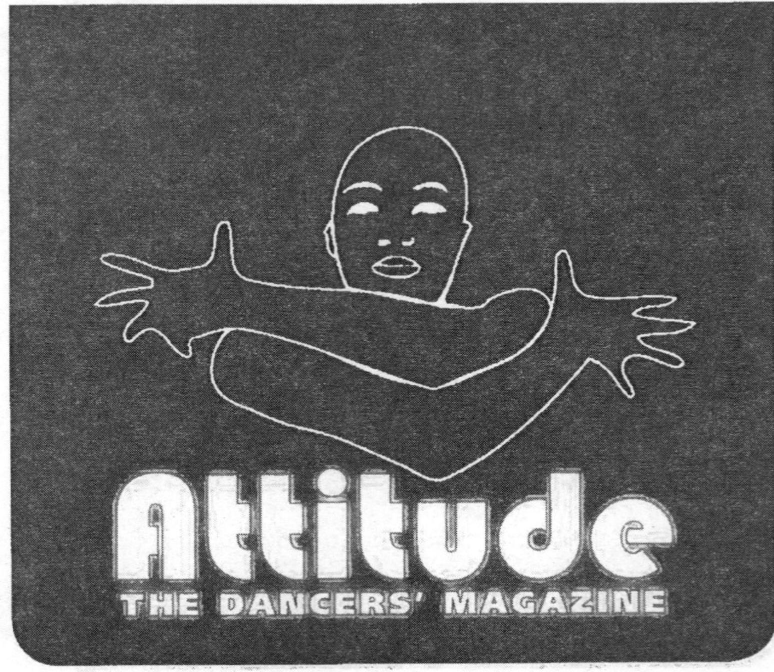

Malaika Adero
Michael Ajzenstadt
Robert Atwood
Richard Barclift
Thea Nerissa Barnes
Ann Barzel
Henry Baumgartner
Perry Bialor
Phillip Bond°
Leslie Arlette Boyce
Karen Campbell
Veve Clark
Ama A. Codjoe
Aaron Cohen°
Beatrice Coron
Madeleine Dale
Albert L. D'Angelo
Thomas DeFrantz
Fernando DeJesus
Edwin Denby°
Sonia G. Diaz
Jim Drobnick
Dorothea Edmead
Nerik Elliott
Ife Felix
Beth Anna Ferguson
Mali Fleming
Mark Franko
David Fullard
Roberto Gautier

Beth Glick
Arthur Goldberg
Jane Goldberg
Anita Gonzales
Josh Gosciak
Doris Green
Robert Greskovic
Donald Griffin
Marc Haegeman
Trajall Harrell
Robert Hicks
Millicent Hodson
Richard Holden
Kafusto Incanyesi
Bernadine Jennings
Donna Jewell
Gerald Byron Johnson
Mark Kappel
Rosamond S.King
Susan Kraft
Shirley Kwan
Kathleen Laziza
Corky Lee
Julinda Lewis
David Lipfert
Glen Loney
Vanessa Manko
Sava Martin
Mac McGill
Gayle McKinney

Darryl McKinney
Nan Melville
Mme. Peff Modelski
William Moore°
Sahyini Morningstar
Melinda Mousouris
Mami Nakae
Alice Nemecek
Kevin Ng
Donna Nowak
Alexander Oblinsky
Lori J.Ortiz
Halifu Osumare
Carl Paris
Emanhba Pedra
Richard Ploch
Melle Randall
Nefretete Rasheed
Laurence Rawlins
Gerard Raymond
Marilyn Reed
Jane Rigney
Louis Reyes Rivera
Rosa Marie Roberts
Rod Rodgers°
Elinor Rogosin
Lillie F. Rosen
Faustino Rothman
Marilyn Russo
Nkenge Scott

Ramon Segarra°
Starr Siegele
Natasha Simon
Susanna Sloat
Gus Solomons, Jr.
Ben Sommers°
Sir Warren Spears°
Julia Stalder Colson
Larry Stevens
Irene Sturla
George Edward Tait
Eric Taub
Leanna Trapedo Sims
Constance Valis Hill
Maya Wallach
Suzanne K.Walther
Monroe Warshaw
Dorothy Wasserman
Bert Wechsler°
S'thembele West
Dr. Melanye White Dixon
Sule Greg Wilson
Arthur T.Wilson
Bil Wright
Damon Wright°
Susan Yung

° = Deceased

Quiet as it is kept, Attitude: The Dancers' Magazine will be 25 years old May 5, 2007.
Here is a list of seminal participants that shared this path of dance journalism with our current staff.

We invite these folks specifically and all others (readers and dance industry folks) to submit a brief statement of the positive and negative changes within our community in the 25 years. We would also like to have a projection of Dance in America as you perceive it from your vantage point.

Please email submission to dance_giant_steps@yahoo.com from now until March 2007

64

All images courtesy of Bernadine Jennings

Bernadine Jennings is the founder and executive director of Dance Giant Steps, Inc. Founded in 1979, Dance Giant Steps is a nonprofit service organization dedicated to preserving dance history by creatin and publishing *Attitude: The Dancers' Magazine*. Launched in 1982, *Attitude* is a trade journal and audience development tool that documen diverse dance artists of regional New York and our global community

i begin with a memory
then slip into slowness.
my body is the site of radical transformation.
-

jess pretty

the breeze between the leaves
pt. 2

i'm standing in the middle of a field in the berkshires.
the land i'm on, and the house behind me, have belonged to the same
black family for four generations;
the Hart's.
the house serves as an archive of their family lineage.
the land serves as an energetic reminder of all who have passed through,
of all who survived.
behind the house is the field.
behind the field are woods.
in the woods there is a creek that i walk to every morning.
i sit on a log and meditate, listen to music, sing out loud, listen to voice memos & record new ones to be sent out.
just beyond the creek is a larger body of water.
i know this because i hear it,
not because i see it.
it stays tucked out of sight.
rushing
remembering.
back in the field, there is a bridge that crosses over a brook. it leads to
a flock of trees.
i find myself in a lot of stillness here.
listening.
remembering.
one morning i stood flush with the trees in meditation.
the sky stood proud with deep gray and white clouds
and the winds carried a steady breeze that could move you
if you let it.
my weight shifts between my feet as
i notice the trees getting carried away.
they sway back and forth in community with each other;
calling and responding.
it is playful
it is familial.
it is familiar.
a distant creaking sound comes to the forefront.
i look to the back door to see if someone else has come outside, but no one is there.
the creaking continues and is echoing louder.
i walk deeper into the
flock of trees
and at once, i understand.

this is the sound of the trees moving in the wind.
this is the sound of the trees moving in the wind.
it is siren, it is creak, it is crack, it is call.
i stand in their chorus
swayingswinginggrooving
callingandresponding

grateful to be a witness to all that can take place in
the breeze between the leaves.
-

i start a five-minute timer
and walk to lay down on the floor close to the window. i am on my right side.
i close my eyes and
imagine myself back in that field in the berkshires.
the field
the trees
the breeze
are inside me now.
this is a memory i recall in slow motion.

my left elbow slides back, dragging my left hand along the top of my leg
as my hand reaches my hip, my left shoulder backs up into the floor and
my right scapula spreads itself out onto the surface;
finding rest once my left shoulder joins it on the ground.
i keep reaching my left hand outward along the floor,
my left foot shifts back and as i continue to spill my weight toward the direction of my hand
my pelvis and left foot lay flat on the floor.
it feels like i'm here forever,
and i would be here longer
except my left arm keeps reaching
and now my knees are both falling over to the left side.
my right arm takes the long way around - my fingertips brushing a circle over my head.
eventually, my right arm arrives on the ground in front of my chest,
i press into my right palm
and as i rise up, my left forearm rotates
and my left palm now presses into the ground.
i'm rising,
my right ear leads the way.
my arms almost get to straighten
when i feel the warmth
from the sun on my face
i smile, eyes still closed.
i slide my hands across the floor towar–
the timer goes off.
i'm brought back into the room.

i've never liked moving at a fast pace.
as a child i was clumsy and fell a lot.
i would get flustered at trying to keep up with everyone else's speed to the point where i would literally trip and fall and hurt myself.
the world is such where we prioritize our work and not ourselves.

prioritizing myself and my slowness is my work.

slowness feels
indulgent, luxurious, decadent, vulnerable, tender.
when we move fast it is harder to keep track of these parts of ourselves.
which is on purpose.
moving slow forces us to look, to contend, to get familial/r with exactly
where our bodies are at.
to be present on an epic scale.
this defies
everything we've ever been taught about how to navigate this world.

slowness as a practice is
inherently black.
inherently queer
inherently feminist.
nothing will get done before we get to it.
–

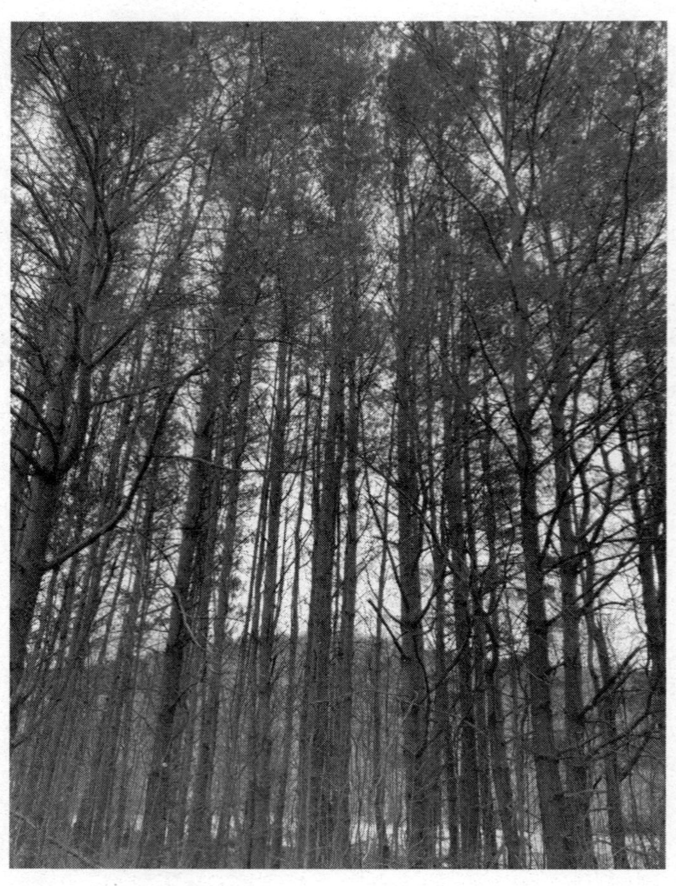

when ferguson happened, i created a class called
contemporaryTRAP
to keep me company.
being at a PWI, i either felt
invisibilized or tokenized
by my white peers/mentors/faculty.
contemporaryTRAP was a space that provided
proof of my black life
proof of my black joy
& proof of black celebration.
it was my call & response.

today,
my class still holds similar values.
but as the world turns,
so do the ways in which i approach my research and thus, my teaching.
when i think about all it took to get through the pandemic
(we still gettin through)
there was so much stagnation.
i didn't want to move inside of systems that lacked
care and consideration for my body.
and as i prepared to return to the classroom
i found myself wondering how i was gonna teach movement again
inside of a large institution that lacks
care and consideration for my body.
what was the "so what' of all of this?
why am i choosing to teach in a classroom right now,
and why are these students signing up to be in my classroom right now?

my students say:
"i wanna move fast"
"i just wanna dance"
"i don't wanna talk"
"i don't want to check in"
"i don't wanna improv"
"i don't have anything in me today"
"i just want to turn my brain off and move"
"i just wanna do moves"
"I JUST WANNA DANCE JESS"

lately,
what they struggle with is slowing down,
to notice exactly *what* they're doing and *how* it feels to do it.
i want them to integrate the things we learn in class into their everyday lives.
what do you learn by moving together in this room
& how can you carry it forward into your life once
you back outside?

adrienne maree brown says:
"there's a conversation only the people in this room can have, find it"
i emphasize two things in my classes: the community, and the self.
we must be able to find our self and our own voice
and we must work at
and wonder about how to be in relationship to each other.
how to be in community with one another;
this desire is most critical to me.
this comes from my background in house dance/music,
but it's also been forever known.
because community is how i got here.

Nia Love says "you don't take class, you make class."

when the next pandemic happens, i want us to be able to look at our neighbor and say
"neighbor,
we gon help each other make it through"
by witnessing each other, being vulnerable with one another and surrendering to slowness amidst all of the things.
we have the power to transform the shit that flings itself at us everyday.
through practicing awareness
and care
and consideration
and intention
and slowness.

it takes a village.
which we hear a lot in regards to raising a child;
but
we cant thrive as our own ecosystem.
some days i'm the root
some days i'm the trunk
some days i'm the branches
some days i'm the leaves

this body is a site of radical transformation.

this body can imagine itself as the breeze between the leaves.
and if we can imagine it, then it's real.

jess pretty (she/her/hers) received an MFA in Dance with a minor in Queer Studies from the University of Illinois at Urbana Champaign. pretty has collaborated and been a part of the works of: Will Rawls, Claudia Rankine, Kevin Beasley, Okwui Okpokwasili, Niall Jones, Jennifer Monson, and Cynthia Oliver, among others. pretty recently took over as Creative Director of AUNTS; a punk/DIY performance series that hosts events/festivals/shows to highlight the works of experimental dance makers in NYC. pretty recently relocated to Minneapolis, MN, where she is an Assistant Professor of Dance at the University of Minnesota Twin Cities.

Dearest Mother and Siblings,
Today I finally received your long-awaited letter.

Here, it is not so important whether one is trained in a certain task or not. They do not even inquire about one's background or former occupation. They only ask for one's name, which is enough for them.

hir kommt es so genau nicht darauf an ob man eine Sache ordentlich kan oder nicht. Hir fragen sie überhaupt nicht erst groß was man ist oder was man früher gemacht hat, nicht einmal nach den Namen fragen sie wen sie nur wissen wie man sich rufen läßt das ist ihnen schon genug.

One can earn a lot of money here, but one also needs a lot.

Man verdient hir viel Geld man braucht aber auch viel.

I am as free and comfortable here as I cannot be in Germany, especially in my business.

denn ich befinde mich hier so frei und wohl wie ich es in Deutschland nicht kann, speziell nicht in meinen Geschäft.

I will only come out if I do not have my own business by April 1st, 1873, or if I am not married by that time. If either of these two things happens, I cannot come. Otherwise, I will definitely come at that time.

Ich komme blos raus in diesen fällen wenn ich bis 1 April 1873 noch kein Geschäft habe und wenn ich bis zu dieser Zeit noch nicht verheiratet bin, sollte eines von diesen beiden passiren dann kann ich nicht kommen im andern fall werde ich aber ganz bestimmt um diese Zeit.

We do not belong to the place where the poetry of our lives faded away. Our true home is the place where our actions belong. We will only be satisfied to die where we have worked and accomplished things.

Nicht dem Ort, wo die Poesien unseres Lebens verblühten, gehören wir an; die Stätte ist unsere wahre Heimath, der unsere Thaten gehören; wo wir geschafft und gewirkt, nur da allein wirden wir befriedigt sterben.

Verily, no man shall be able to deny that, for whosoever must labor, America deserves the preference. However, one must be able to adapt oneself, and that proves very difficult for many who have played a role in Germany. The motto is: Eat the bird or die.

Denn kein Mensch wird es leugnen können das für jeden der Arbeiten muß Amerika der Vorzug gebührt nur muß man sich rein schicken können und das fällt so vielen welche in Deutschland eine Rolle gespielt haben sehr schwehr. Motto. Friß Vogel oder stirb.

The Irmscher tailor is already too rich, he does not associate with small people who have nothing. None of his countrymen visit him, because they only hear about how much he already has and how well up he is.

Der Irmscher Schneider ist schon zu reich der gibt sich mit so kleinen Leuten wo noch nichts haben nicht ab es besucht ihn auch keiner von seinen Lands leuten da sie jedesmal blos zu hören kriegen wie viel er schon hat und wie gut er ab ist.

We may live like in paradise here, but nobody should think that people feel happier here than in Germany. Everything is overfed here, so that in the end, everyone loses their taste. Then they cry that everything is better in Germany, but why is it better there? Because they do not have it. If one gets meat 2 or 3 times a week there, it tastes good. Here, however, everyone gets 3 meals a day with 4 or 5 different kinds of meat, so much that it becomes disgusting. And then one thinks it is not good, just because they have too much. What is thrown away here could feed many poor families. One thing is for sure, when one is doing well, they do not appreciate it, at least not here in this country. Only through the difference can one find out, but what good is preaching if no one believes it?

Wir leben zwar wie in einen Paradis, aber es braucht ja niemand zu denken das sich die Menschen hier glücklicher fühlen wie bei Euch denn hir wird alles überfüttert so das zuletzt jedes den Geschmack verliert, dan schreien sie das alles in Deutschland besser ist, aber warum ist es da besser: weil man es nicht hat, wenn man da jede woche 2 oder 3 mal Fleisch bekommt so schmeckt einen das ganz gut, hir hat aber jeder Mensch jeden Tag 3 mal 4 u. 5 verschiedene sorten Fleisch so das es einen zum Ekel wird und dan denkt man es ist nicht gut, blos weil man zu viel hat, das was bei uns fortgeschmissen wird da könnten noch viele arme Familien davon leben. Soviel ist sicher das wenn es ein Mensch gut hat so weiß er es nicht wenigstens hir in diesen Land. Blos durch den underschied kan man es ausfinden, aber was hilft alles predigen glauben thut es ja doch niemand.

Many greetings to all our friends and anyone who wants them (they are free). I send my warmest regards to all of you. Your son and brother

Viele Grüße an die Freundschaft und an alle die welche haben wollen (die kosten gar nicht) Ich grüße dich aufs herzlichste Dein Sohn und euer Bruder

Otto Quellmalz

care. of. Mr Adolph Georgi
NQ 64 Av. A betw. 4 and 5 Str.
New York Nord Amerika

On the morning of July 10th, 1866, Otto Quellmalz began his journey from Oberfrohna near Leipzig, Germany, to New York, USA. He regularly wrote to his mother about his life, the cost of everything, and his reflections on his role as an immigrant. Reading these letters helps us understand the process of assimilation. He died in 1908 in San Francisco.

This page is a collage of different letters from Otto, arranged in chronological order by visual artist Anna Schimkat, who is currently an artist in residence at ISCP (International Studio and Curatorial Project).

The collage will be published simultaneously in the summer of 2023 in Movement Research, New York, and as part of the "Dialog" program of artspace "Ideal" on a billboard in Leipzig, Germany.

Otto's voice is also included in the sound installation and live performance called "Passage," a collaboration between Anna and Felix Kindermann, who is also artist in residence at ISCP. "Passage" explores the cultural and linguistic polyphony of New York and its immigration history.

www.idealartspace.de/dialog_about/
www.annaschimkat.de
Gotha Research Library of the University of Erfurt, DABS, New Collection, Fuhrmann/Quellmalz, various letters

p. 30–31

Anna Schimkat is a visual artist who has expanded her work into sound art through installations and performances. Schimkat creates spaces that sharpen perception and force the perceiver's action. Her sound materials include self-made instruments and field recordings of her main instrument, the world around us. Anna Schimkat has exhibited work at Z.i.m.m.t., Germany; RE:FLUX 16, Festival D'Art Sonore, Canada; and Galerie für Zeitgenössische Kunst, Germany, among others.

A Lineage of Antagonism

Sam Max

When performance artist Ann Liv Young was an Artist-In-Residence at Amsterdam's School for New Dance Development (SNDO) in 2011, a clique of five undergraduate dance students attempted to abduct Young while she was performing onstage. A disoriented audience watched from their seats as the students took Young's mic, restrained her, carried her toward a table, pinned her down, and tried to tape her body to the surface. Young bucked against her students for several moments before freeing herself, ultimately scrambling away. She then tossed the table across the performance space, locked eyes with her students, and said to them with a threatening and raw resolve, "You'll not ever take me." Footage of this incident can be found thirty-one minutes into Kathryn Karwat's and George Pitts's documentary on the artist, *I Don't Exist If You Don't* (2016).[1]

The students' insurrection took place during *37 Sherrys* (2011), a performance Young staged with the undergrads who signed up for her five-week workshop. The title of the performance refers to the number of students registered for the course, as well as the moniker of Young's frequently revisited performance persona "Sherry"—a crackling, brash, uninhibited white Southern therapist-cum-antagonist known for her intense, relentless audience work, and whose pseudo-clinical practice she refers to as "Sherapy." Young's idea was to spend her five weeks training the SNDO students in the basic elements of Sherapy in order to create one giant Sherry: a super-organism that would collectively enact Young's perspective that antagonism toward the audience is the most efficient route toward revealing subtextual truths in the room.

Young, like Sherry, is an antagonist insofar as her primary tactic is to set the stage for danger to occur. She takes interest in a theater that uses artificial elements (her drag personae, among other strategies) as a mask behind which she can incite confrontational or accusatory audience interactions that tend to bewilder at worst, and drive unsuspecting audience members into frenzied states of undress at best (as was the case at 2010's Bastard Festival in Trondheim, in which a man was moved, in response to Sherry's provocations, to join the character onstage, pull down his pants, and shake his penis at her).[2] Much of these interactions begin with Sherry prodding an audience member with the therapist's own antagonistic assumptions about them, effectively putting them on the spot, and then proceeding with a dramatic line of questioning that forces the audience member to either succumb to Sherry's force or try to undermine her authority. The latter, of course, almost never successfully occurs, both because of how Young has designed the character's logic (Sherry would never claim to be wrong) and due to the fact that this is a premeditated performance, after all, wherein Young and her team physically and atmospherically control the theatrical settings in which Sherapy is conducted.

"I think at one point they said they were trying to teach Sherry about force," says Young's videographer, production assistant, and partner at the time, Michael Guerrero, regarding the students' physical attack on Young at SNDO in 2011.[3] After taking a post-attack breather offstage, Young comes back to lecture the performance students who staged the coup mid-show, shouting on the mic that she would "never ever force any of [them] to do anything, ever," which she says would be "disgusting."[4] Young grabs her things and leaves, refusing applause. The show is over. The lights stay on.

More than an amateurish assault gone wrong, the scene is emblematic of the slippery relationship between Young and her antagonistic alter-ego, as well as her students' clear inability to tell the difference between the two. That inability to decipher whether Young is Young or her characters extends to audience interactions beyond SNDO as well, as Young has been frequently physically assaulted while in character, not only as Sherry but also as the rabid Mermaid in her *Mermaid Show* (2012), a half-aquatic embodiment of chaotic evil who spits raw fish guts at the audience.

One of Sherry's mantras, invoked at many of her performances (including when she performed in blackface as "Sheriqua" at Black Dance in 2012, in an evening curated by Dean Moss) is that "I'm a character! I'm not a real person! This is theater! If you don't like it leave! Leave!"[5] Despite the fact that it's a worthy sentiment which seeks to liberate artistic antagonism from the moral codes of society, it's an unconvincing principle coming from a performance artist who creates work on and with her own body—who isn't an actor playing out someone else's script — and who also seems consistently fixated on disturbance over resolution. In the eyes of a contemporary audience, with whom artifice continues to fall increasingly out of favor, the employment of a constructed persona cannot convincingly render the artist behind the character unaccountable, nor could the character absolve the artist.

In an essay titled "Neutrality is not an option," originally featured in a publication on the Artists-in-Residence at Amsterdam University of the Arts, Ibrahim Quraishi writes that the announcement of Ann Liv Young's invitation to be in residence at SNDO in 2011 "caused a buzz of excitement in the school" and that the coup staged in *37 Sherrys* certainly lived up to the expectations around Young's invitation to campus.[6] In the piece, Quraishi interviews four students who participated in Young's workshop, one of whom was a young Florentina Holzinger, the Austrian choreographer who at the moment is continually selling out the Volksbühne in Berlin with her vivid, haunting, high-intensity, feminist work, and who—not unlike Young—has achieved in her moment a kind of celebrity status as a show pony of the European dance theater. Quoted

[1] which streams for free on Vimeo, and includes appearances from the palpably Young-obsessed *Times* critic Gia Kourlas, as well as the performance scholar Anna Watkins Fisher
[2] Kathryn Kárwat and George Pitts, *I Don't Exist If You Don't*, SEEN Documentaries, 2016. 70 minutes. https://vimeo.com/142011298. 12:30–14:13.
[3] *I Don't Exist If You Don't*, 32:40–32:50.
[4] Ibid., 33:26–33:37.
[5] Ibid., 57:31–57:45.
[6] Ibrahim Quraishi, "Neutrality is not an option," ON AIR, Issue 3 (October 2011): 12–13. https://issuu.com/bouwkunst/docs/onair3/6.

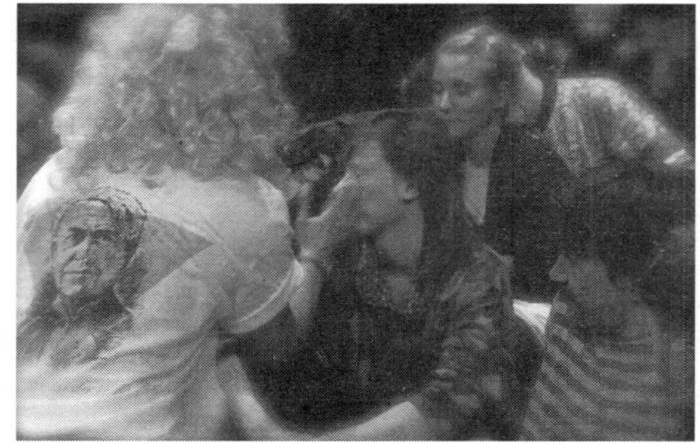
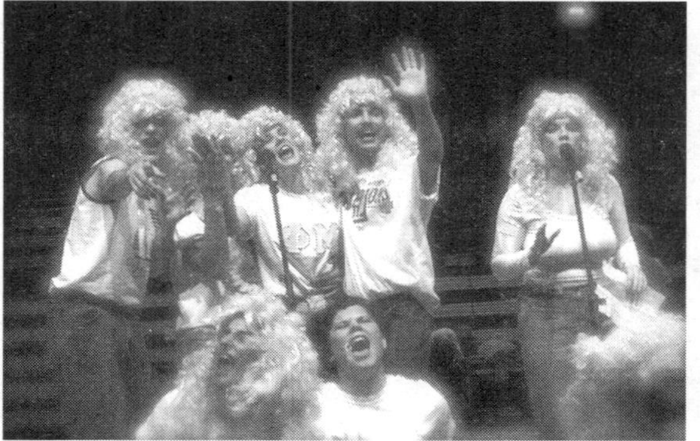
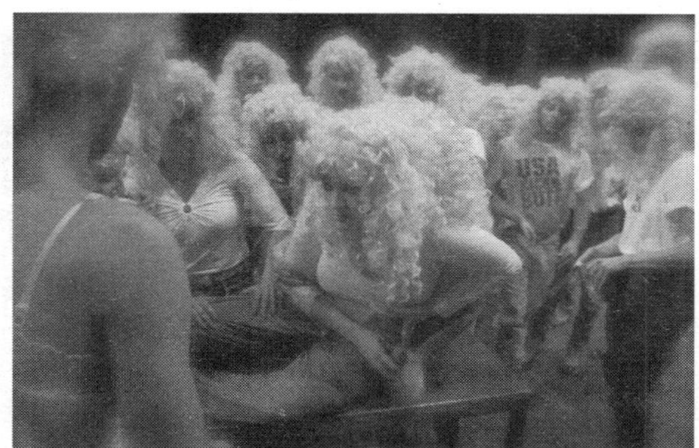

Ann Liv Young's *37 Sherrys*.

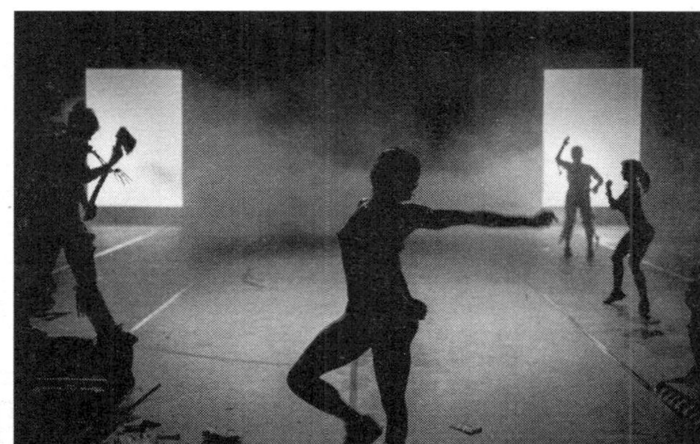
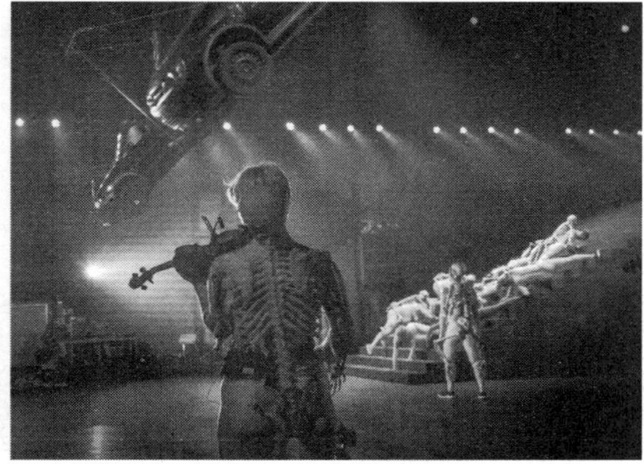

Florentina Holzinger's *A Divine Comedy*.

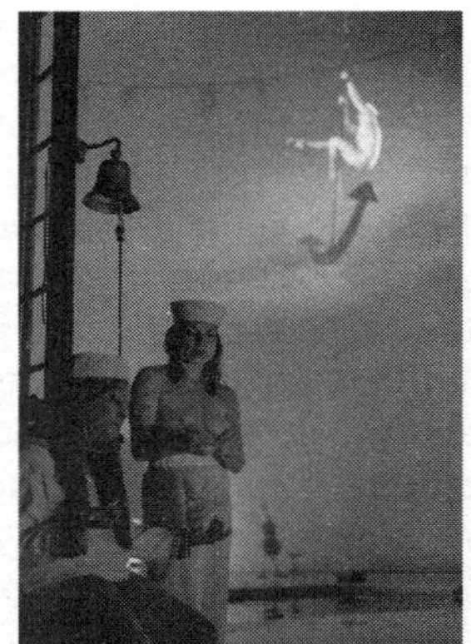
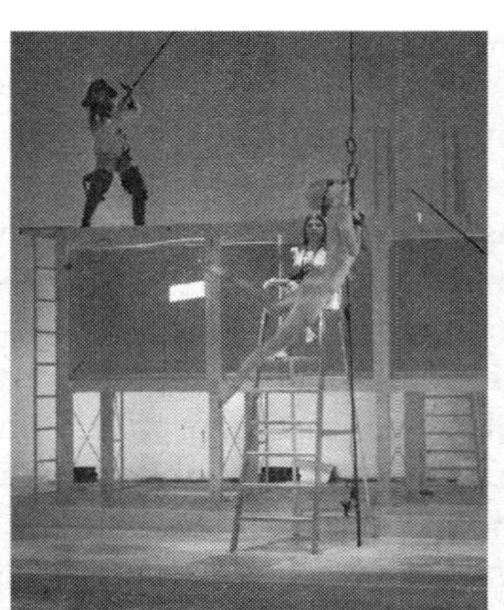
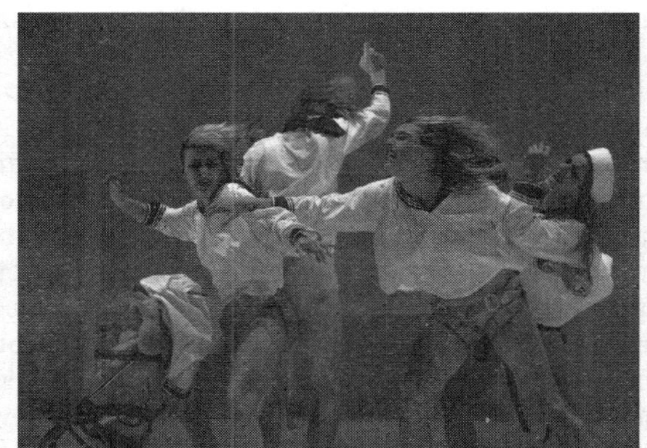
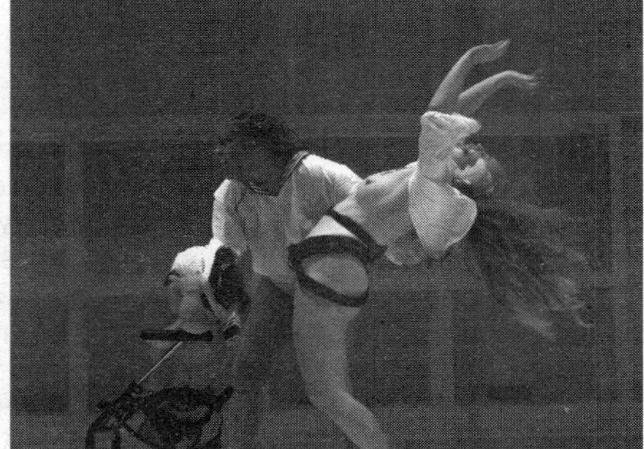

Florentina Holzinger's *Ophelia's Got Talent*.

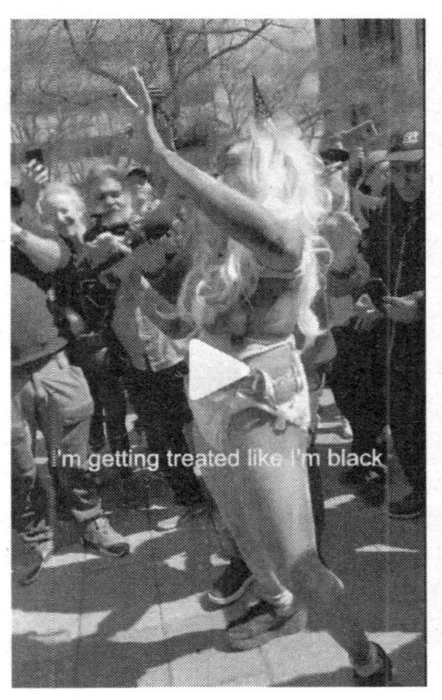

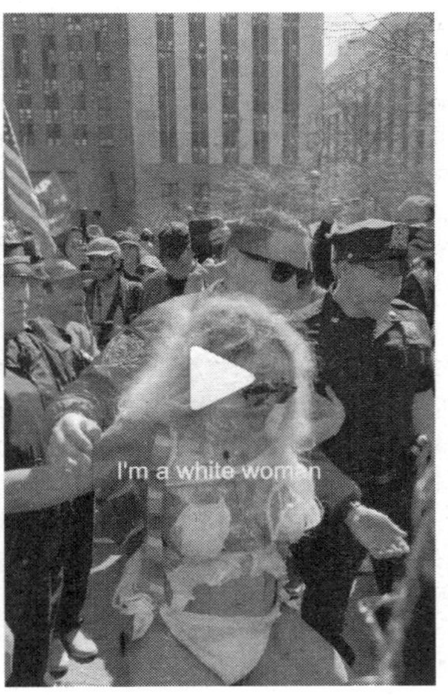

"Why are the cops asking that normal whyte lady to leave the rally?"
Crackhead Barney @crackheadbarneyandfriends IG April 7, 2023.

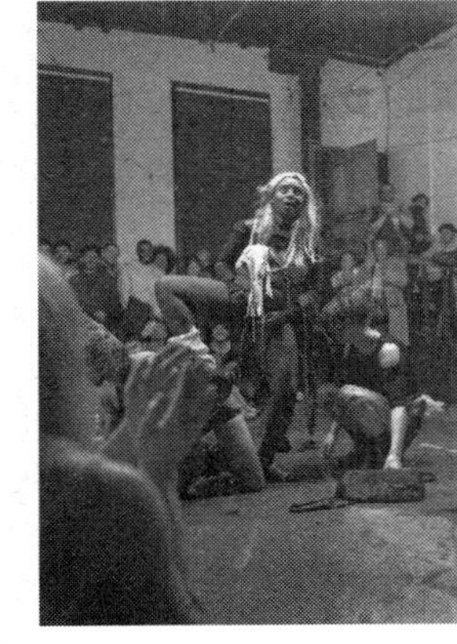
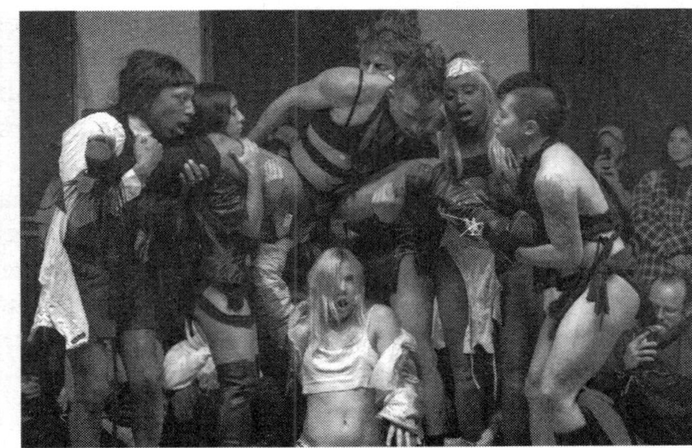
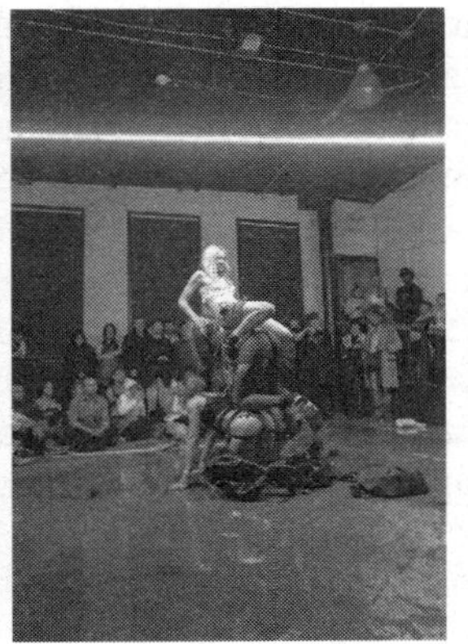

Michel Hart
Nicole Marianna Wytyczak
Nicole Marianna Wytyczak
@rabbistravinsky,
ram.com/p/CqvwVOks-1I/
Richard McDonough.
sy of OCDChinatown

Young Boy Dancing Group at OCDChinatown c/o The Firehouse.

in Quraishi's essay, Holzinger (then a fourth-year student at SNDO) recalls of Young's methodology, "the call for participation was very open," further identifying that, "[w]e were clearly put into the position of students who needed the judgment of an authority to be able to define their value."[7]

Holzinger and Young both share in a post-dramatic feminist lineage, wherein the martyrdom of self-identified female bodies comments on the complications and risks of what it might mean to do such a thing (martyr themselves) while actively doing it. In their works, the choreographers frequently grapple with the boundary of agency and complicity. Both Holzinger and Young return to the disciplinary nature of the dance studio as a textual element, meant to indicate unresolved antagonistic power relations between instructor and student. Some of Holzinger's work comments explicitly on her own experience of a dance education, wherein she constructs scenes of female instructors barking corrections at barre-bound students. Similarly, an early choreographic motif in Ann Liv Young's work (for instance, in her 2005 breakthrough dance *Michael*), features Young playing herself as a choreographer, shouting prompts like "GO!" at her dancers from the audience, while they exhaust themselves in taxing marathon sequences.[8]

Holzinger's idea of antagonizing the audience also shares Young's aesthetic interest in aggressive visual imagery, much of which features her performers in high-wire situations that seem to set the stage for actual danger to occur. Such is the case in Holzinger's *Tanz* (2019), admirably a Harley Davidson balletic freak show, and *A Divine Comedy* (2022), which (also admirably) feels like a parking garage overrun by panicked axe-wielding LARPers. In these works, women get battered around in a car suspended midair, tremoring on aircraft cable. Others hang by tight harnesses, careening around the stage, maneuvered by an unseen hand, repeatedly getting slammed into walls like retired crash dummies. Holzinger's body of work demonstrates what it would be like if Cirque du Soleil and Wes Craven were asked to collaborate on the Olympic Games opening ceremony. She makes a spectacle out of the potential for onstage danger to occur, but ultimately, the threat of danger, while pervasive, is too premeditated to feel real. While the level of artifice in her work, matched by the high production value, is awe-inspiring, it does create a kind of programmed, animatronic *Haunted Mansion* ride effect.

Holzinger's brand of antagonism importantly differs from Young's by largely removing audience participation from the equation, treating them mostly as voyeurs behind the fourth wall. Her audiences passively witness an onslaught of jarring and violent extremities that sometimes seem to include actual torture of the women who make up her ensemble. Fitting for the context of the German Stadttheater, Holzinger's antagonism is more of an intellectual approach: ideological and sensorial, but not implicating her audience in any meaningful way. Infrequently the audience might be directly addressed with a rhetorical question, but such a gesture is hardly sustained with the same intensity of Young's interrogation room. It's more like hearing your ketamine dealer wax philosophical to herself while pissing on a wall at 3 A.M.

That removal of audience interaction does a lot to shield Holzinger's antagonism from personal criticism—even in the more evolved and self-critical approach of her new piece *Ophelia's Got Talent* (just invited to the 2023 Theatertreffen). The work begins with a warped staging of a popular TV competition (*America's Got Talent*), as Holzinger's ensemble performs for the audience shocking or disgusting sideshow talents. One performer swings a five-gallon water jug from her nipple piercings, and then the judges tersely critique her. At first, *Ophelia* winks at the audience, reminding them of their entitlement in the enjoyment of an experience of aggression wherein women's bodies are physically on the line. But what feels most moving about *Ophelia* as an installment for this choreographer—who to date has made post-dramatic hostility her praxis—is actually its palpable dissatisfaction with and commentary on her past work's sense of antagonism. Once a lap pool is revealed on the Volksbühne stage, and the performers move beyond the narrative container of the competition show, one can feel Holzinger sliding back and forth between her artificial antagonism and a more personal and sensitive version of reality. What's tangible and moving is how she starts to question her role as an adversary within the context of her own show.

Following an uncharacteristically soft sequence in which the ensemble swims laps onstage—their movements gently underscored by a lifeguard performing an ASMR-style reading of cryptic lines from metaphysical texts—a floating cast member softly recites an autobiographical monologue about how all she wanted after she was raped was to walk into a bakery and get a cupcake, because while being assaulted, she thought she was going to die and never have a cupcake again. In a dreamlike sequence that immediately follows, the speaker is joined by a parallel cast of young girls dressed like pirates, who hold large circular mirrors up to the physical forms of their battered and exposed older counterparts. Framed in a more antagonistic way, the account of assault could easily create a feeling of buzzy and exploitative trauma porn, but instead the audience is braced by a tone of genuine vulnerability and grief about such a loss of innocence. *Ophelia*, undulating with these kinds of contradictions, is the work of an antagonist-choreographer who has tasked herself with holding both confrontation and reflection in the same hand. In this way, Holzinger's approach diverges from Young's tactics around making the audience vulnerable, favoring a chasm of mournful reflection over repetitive prodding.

Looking at the evolution of antagonism in Holzinger's work—tactilely manifest in lap pools and mermaids replacing chainsaws and motorbikes—one might begin to wonder about the new, subtler approaches to antagonism that have developed in recent memory. Once a perverse transgression in perhaps the mid-1900's, the bluntness of trying to take a shit onstage (a key element of Young's 2010 work *Cinderella*) today starts to feel contrived or even boring. Exposing one's own genitalia to the audience is hardly a confrontation in and of itself any longer, and most literal simulations of interpersonal assault or violence feel numbing alongside the increasingly accessible and pervasive documentation of war, hate crimes, and genocide in the media. While antagonism continues to occupy an important dramaturgical position for performance artists amidst a world that seems increasingly broken, there is also a palpable shift in the antagonist's strategies for engaging that overwhelming brokenness. Her tools may no longer be weapons of mass destruction. A new sort of antagonist begins to confront the audience with a threat of unexpected intimacy, rather than the threat of distance or alienation.

Through discombobulated scenes that depict young people engaged in intimacy to the point of probable injury, Young Boy Dancing Group exemplifies a version of antagonism toward the audience that's built on closeness rather than a sense of distancing shock. Maria Metsalu, a virtuosically embodied performer, is one of the performance art collective's leaders. Also a graduate of SNDO, her work bares traces of Holzinger's, both in her look and in her aesthetic values, which foreground intimacy and shun spectacle. In practically spare settings, Metsalu and her co-conspirators Manuel Scheiwiller and Nica Roses work with a rotating cast of local performers who are sourced from wherever the core group is currently touring. The dances they build collectively are defined by task-based prompts with a casual, nearly pedestrian sensibility, which are loosely guided by shifts in ambient techno music. These tasks are often performed with facial expressions characterized by desperation and mourning—which can make the dancers seem catatonic, tweaked, or working through a particularly strenuous comedown.

Tests around intimacy and proximity, not only among their ensemble members, but also between the performers and their audiences, comprise Young Boy Dancing Group's specific relationship to antagonism. One of the more compelling aspects of their work is how they physically implicate the audience by imposing uncomfortable

[7] Ibid., 13.
[8] David Velasco, "Performance: Ann Liv Young," *Artforum*, September 2010, https://www.artforum.com/print/201007/ann-liv-young-26143.

spatial relations between performer and audience, sometimes through the use of materials like fluids (including bodily fluids). A performance at O'Flaherty's outpost on Avenue A in New York City earlier this year focused on an unwieldy use of open flames and hot wax. On an unfussy plywood platform covered in black trash bags and an inch of murky water, one performer assumed a headstand split while Metsalu penetrated him with a phallic ready-made topped with a long rotating wire propeller, about six feet in diameter. From the propeller, the crew suspended about a dozen lit candles held in place by wire. The ignited anal sculpture helicoptered slowly, designed to careen the open flames within inches of the surrounding audience's faces, testing their resistance to the proximity of danger. It's an image that embodies the essential ultimatum of the antagonist—provoking the audience to choose whether they'll publicly endure discomfort, or retreat to some familiar version of safety.

Young Boy Dancing Group's recent New York collaboration with OCD Chinatown included the fearless New York-based performance artist Crackhead Barney, who essentially pissed all over herself and her fellow dancers during her solo, mere inches away from spectators seated on the floor. Known for her uninhibited interview performances that target anti-abortion protestors, Trump rallies, or homophobic demonstrations by Hasidic Jews, Crackhead Barney has created a body of work that solidly overlaps with Young Boy Dancing Group's confrontational sensibility, but her work departs from abstract antagonism, transgressing toward a more extreme version of antagonism rooted in reality, one that also very much puts her body entirely on the line.

Most closely approaching Ann Liv Young's interview tactics as Sherry, Crackhead Barney's method of antagonism is characterized by punchy interrogations—live broadcast or edited for consumption on her (frequently shadowbanned) Instagram account *@crackheadbarneyandfriends*—that directly confront her chosen subjects. In one particular video, she has slathered herself in white clown paint and dressed herself in a fried platinum blonde wig to attend a MAGA rally. There, she asks Trumpers why she should or shouldn't be considered a "white lady," and then later gets on the ground in front of the attendant police force and begs them to kick her.[9] They don't, which is also somehow a part of Crackhead Barney's point. Her antagonism plays on the nightmarish funhouse of racist media tropes by absurdly purging that rhetoric of its purported meaning, and baffling the right-wingers or transphobes who comprise her audience.

Her whiteface performance—Young's "Sheriqua" in relief—showcases a critical difference between Young's and Crackhead Barney's antagonists, which might also elucidate how the role of adversarial performance artist has changed through time. While Young's Sherry constructs an artificial theatrical setting wherein she can control the conditions for her personal vision of danger to occur, Crackhead Barney goes completely rogue, preferring to visit the site of literal nontheatrical danger, imposing herself on that extant reality. Her work inverts a lineage of theatrical antagonism: rather than using a fictional character to set the stage for danger, she visits the site of literal danger and allows it to set the stage for her.

Tucker Carlson, formerly of Fox News, excerpted a video of the aforementioned Crackhead Barney performance in his reporting on Trump's arraignment in April, contextualizing the clip as representative of the "scene outside the courthouse today."[10] In the video, a separate reporter from the network asks Crackhead Barney why she's "trying to instigate violence right now" to which Crackhead Barney responds with Dadaesque irony "because I'm Black and I like violence [...] I'm an animal! I'm a Black animal! Blehhhhhh!"[11] It's essential Crackhead Barney, her antagonism fueled by a mission to deflate hegemonic sentiments by knowingly and ironically beating them to the punch. Carlson smugly follows up the clip by calling Crackhead Barney "one of the few news anchors we trust in this country." While the clip was met on Instagram with excited support from Crackhead Barney stans, who were mostly just happy with Crackhead Barney's appearance on such a large platform, Carlson's removal of the work from its context, and his remark, seem like an insidious attempt on his part to undermine the artist—and her transgressive oppositional views—by flatly, smugly condoning her words. In Fox News's reframing of Crackhead Barney, suddenly she is no longer a performance artist, but rather a sensational pawn who can be used to boost the ratings of a news station that is, like Crackhead Barney, more performance art than it is actual news.

In contemporary culture's hall of distorted mirrors, wherein it feels increasingly difficult to differentiate truth from fiction, it also becomes increasingly easy to confuse an artist's antagonistic tendencies with an actual threat to public safety. Ann Liv Young seems to have fallen out of favor in the eyes of presenters for a variety of reasons that aren't worth attempting to comprehensively unpack here, but certainly a takeaway is that audiences, critics, and presenters have lost patience with the assignment of trying to parse Young as a person in contrast to her fictional characters' antics. Young's students mauling her during the performance of *37 Sherrys* feels like one example that embodies a continually ballooning public tendency to use an artwork for the purposes of assigning moral value to the personal life of its author. Seeing Young as the engineer of disturbance, confusion, and disarray, the students feel moved to teach her a lesson. They stage an insurrection that conflates Young with her Sherry character by punishing the physical body that houses both. An easy narrative is that an antagonist, no matter how purportedly fictional, deserves to be punished or shunned for the chaos they've inflicted on their audiences. Presenters, programmers, producers, and festival curators are in a position to easily dismiss many of the more prominent antagonists and provocateurs, allowing issues of institutional liability or post-pandemic financial insecurity to trump these artists' ideological or aesthetic contributions. Young will offend. Holzinger's images will corrupt the children, and it'll be harder to get money from their parents in the future. Young Boy Dancing Group is a touring fire hazard. Crackhead Barney doesn't care about the venue's sacrosanctity.

For gatekeepers, the question seems to be whether antagonists are worth the trouble they cause, when in reality their worth is—precisely—the trouble they cause. In a landscape that increasingly asks performing artists to clearly state a firm, unchanging, and acceptable moral outlook before being allowed access to an institution's resources, antagonism as a practice remains an important counterpoint to the wealth of performance work that seeks mostly to corroborate a general audience's preconceived views about society. The hope of many, understandably, is to train an audience by making them feel good about having exposed themselves to culture, but giving that sentiment too much power dismisses the potent value of performances that gravitate toward disruption.

While it may alienate audiences who prefer work that explicitly centers the trendy conceits of care and healing, antagonism can be profoundly transformative, prompting the public to engage with an experience of deep discomfort or uncertainty, framing the task of insisting on one's vulnerability in a public setting as a courageous personal practice for surviving the mess of contemporary life. In this way, antagonistic performances become like a vaccine, introducing a simulation of disruption into the bloodstream, so that one is better primed to observantly navigate the ongoing disruptions to life that one will inevitably face in the future. The experience of being publicly vulnerable in the face of an aggressor won't feel immediately good to everyone, but dealing with the antagonistic event can be personally transformative, even enlightening, in the reverberations and memories of the experience. Causing trouble is not only the antagonist's immediate point, but also her lasting power.

[9] https://www.instagram.com/p/CqvwVOks-1I/
[10] https://www.instagram.com/p/CrJfiq4OoYX/
[11] Ibid.

Sam Max is a writer, director, filmmaker, and critic working in New York and Germany. Their works for stage are represented by Suhrkamp Theater Verlag (Berlin), and they currently hold two commissions from the German State Theaters, both to premiere in 2024. Upcoming: Contributor to BOFFO's *Talking to the Sun at Fire Island Vol. 2*, Editor of a forthcoming monograph on Spiral Theory Test Kitchen, and their debut feature-length film *Baby* will be produced by Kindred Spirit.

How has the hot breath of the earth, the battering of its rain, the reprieve of its gentle snows shaped my own sinews, my gait, the ebb and flow of my own bodily humors? Duration, spread across my skin with the slow sweep of the seasons. Like these trees, we are all, each of us, weathering
–Astrida Neimanis and Rachel Loewen Walker

We Are So Close

Dages Juvelier Keates

Our bodies are weather systems – the contractions of wind in our breath, the translation of sunlight into sugar in the plants that become food, the rivers in our bladders, sluicing forth hormones and medications into wastewaters, filling future aquifers. We are made of time, from the minerals of our bones to the salinity of our teardrops. We are not merely "in" the world, in weather: we are of it, we make it. As intra-active agents,[1] ongoing, ephemeral archives of what is and what has been, we belong here.

And our belonging extends to modify, amplify, minimize our reach into the world: eyeglasses, underwater sea cables, drone bombs. We extend our affects through prostheses: fear extends through my arm to become a firearm. Desire tip taps my fingers on the keyboard, shaping the search of the algorithm that feeds that desire back into me. We are an ecology of biological and technological alterities, touching worlds in and out of existence.

---

1 Karen Michelle Barad, *Meeting the Universe Halfway: Quantum Physics and the Entanglement of Matter and Meaning* (Durham: Duke University Press, 2007).

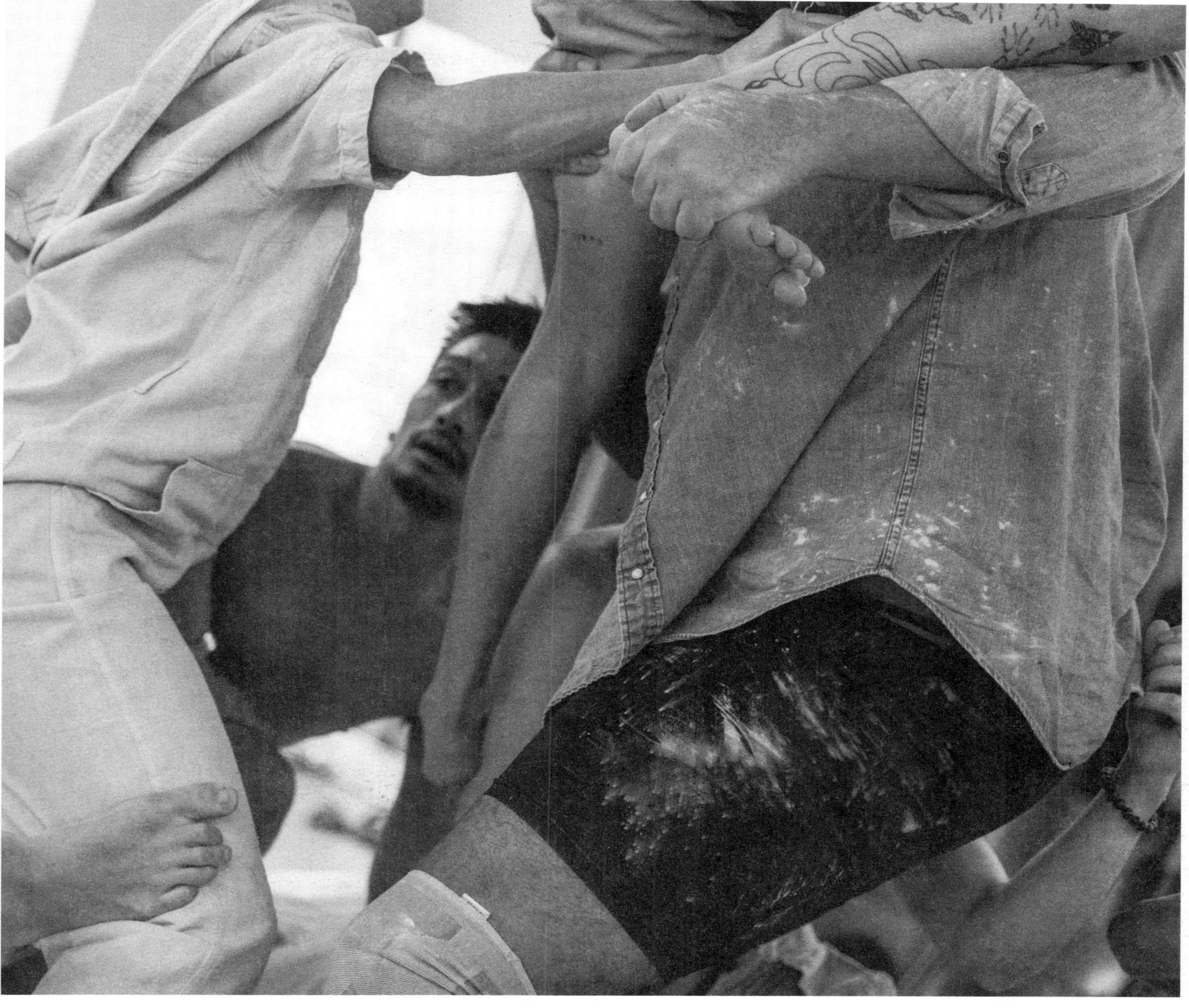

Photos: Maria Baranova

Weathering is a group work in which the space between bodies is peopled with absences. Someone else was here. The imprint of loss makes its mark: the clay-like residue of a life that has been, that has touched and been touched. A life in the shape of a body, and we can't tell where and when it begins and ends. That ambiguity can cut both ways, into presence, and into grief. Grief can also be generative in how it opens up a sixth sense, a sense of what it is to be present with what/who is no longer here. Perhaps we can grow this sixth sense to meet the moment of the sixth extinction.[2]

We are living through the collapse of the climate as we know it. This process will continue and accelerate throughout our lifetimes. It is the horizon for all thought, action and cultural production. Pandemics, ocean acidification, massive wildfires, rampant extinctions, deforestation, and crop failure are the most recent catastrophic symptoms of this collapse. Yet, why does the climate crisis feel so distant, so abstract? Is there no indication that anyone is panicking? What would it take to get us in touch with what is happening?[3]

Philosopher Timothy Morton says, "we are starting to trust that we are in a catastrophe, which literally means a space of downward-turning. It's much better to think you are in a catastrophe than to think you are in a disaster. There are no witnesses to disaster [...] Catastrophes involve you, so you can do something about them."[4] We do not stand outside, we are not passing through, nor do we control the symptoms of this downward-turning. The word "symptom" comes from the Greek roots *sin* (together) and *pipto* (I fall). Symptoms allow us to perceive where we are. A catastrophe is a disaster we can feel: we fall together as our world falls apart.

What if instead of trying to block our situation out, we let it all sink in–seep in? *Weathering* amplifies our perception of details in duration, in proximity, and in the multiple, often spongy tubes and routes of connection that bridge the distance between the abstract/far and the detailed/close. Aesthetics have a crucial role in making the slow violence of the Anthropocene visible. Through proximity to the bodies pluming on the platform, moving glacially, intricately, and all at once, we experience scale shifts that clarify the stakes of presence, palpably and tactilely.

---

2 Elizabeth Kolbert, *The Sixth Extinction: An Unnatural History* (New York: Henry Holt & Company, 2014).

3 "We know the (ecological) catastrophe is possible, probable even, yet we do not believe it will really happen." Slavoj Žižek, *Living in the End Times* (London: Verso, 2011), 328.

4 Timothy Morton, *All Art is Ecological* (United Kingdom: Penguin Books Limited, 2018).

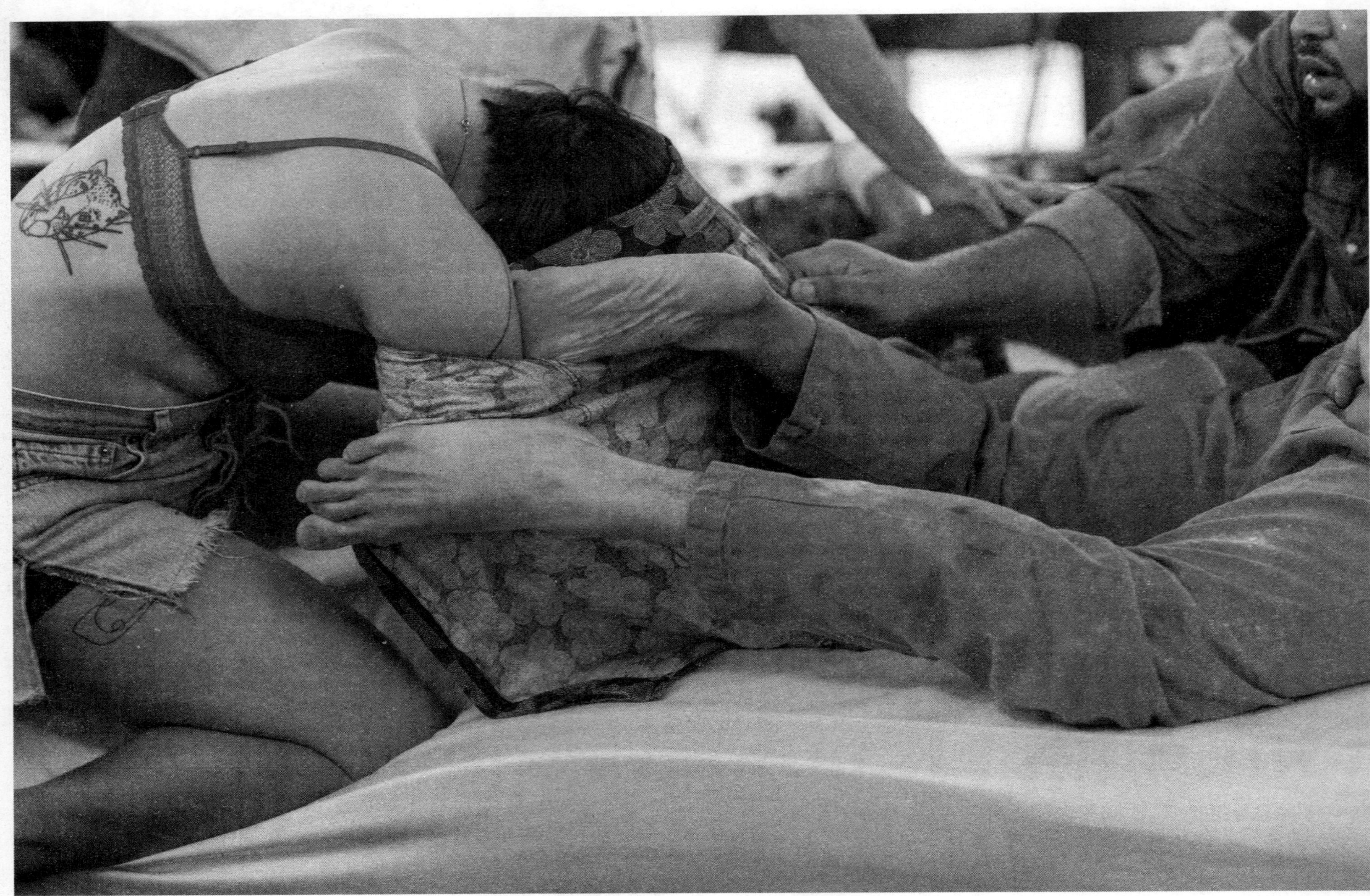

We are touched into existence. It is the bodies of others, in proximity, that define and constitute the so-called subjective site of the self. Enclosed in a permeable kinesthetic skin sac that touches both ways, we perceive the world through movement. These gestures accumulate, touch us back. As ongoing, sensate ephemeral archives, the haptic is alive all the way through, from tip to tail to nail, through fascia, neural net, memory. Our skin is guessing, like a blanket brained with microfilaments: where do I begin? Where does the other end?

Weathering lives in the questions of how we feel close enough to touch and be touched by the moment, by the momentous. Perception changes in relation to proximity: the further off a thing is perceived in time or space, the more crude and abstract our thinking about it, and the less likely it seems to happen. When we think about things right here, we use details. What is closer feels inevitable; what is further feels less likely. The immediacy of somatic sensation draws us back from the abstraction of disaster and makes it real, as catastrophe.

We can reimagine our corporeality as the locus that can draw the future to the present. The tool of our attention is the body and our bodies are made up of each other. In rehearsal, Miguel said, "the chaos in my body organizes into something harmonic and into something that is no longer me." Together, we are climate, water, soil, bones, storms. We become wind, dirt, spore, rain. The weather is humidity inflaming our joints, lightning charging the air we breathe, frost biting our skin. *Weathering* acts as a presence prosthesis for tenderizing the senses, an affect attunement portal to wet complexities. The work trains us to thicken our attention, to stay with the trouble.[5] To render the world sensible, we need to come to our senses.

---

5 Donna Jeanne Haraway, *Staying with the Trouble: Making Kin in the Chthulucene* (Durham: Duke University Press, 2016).

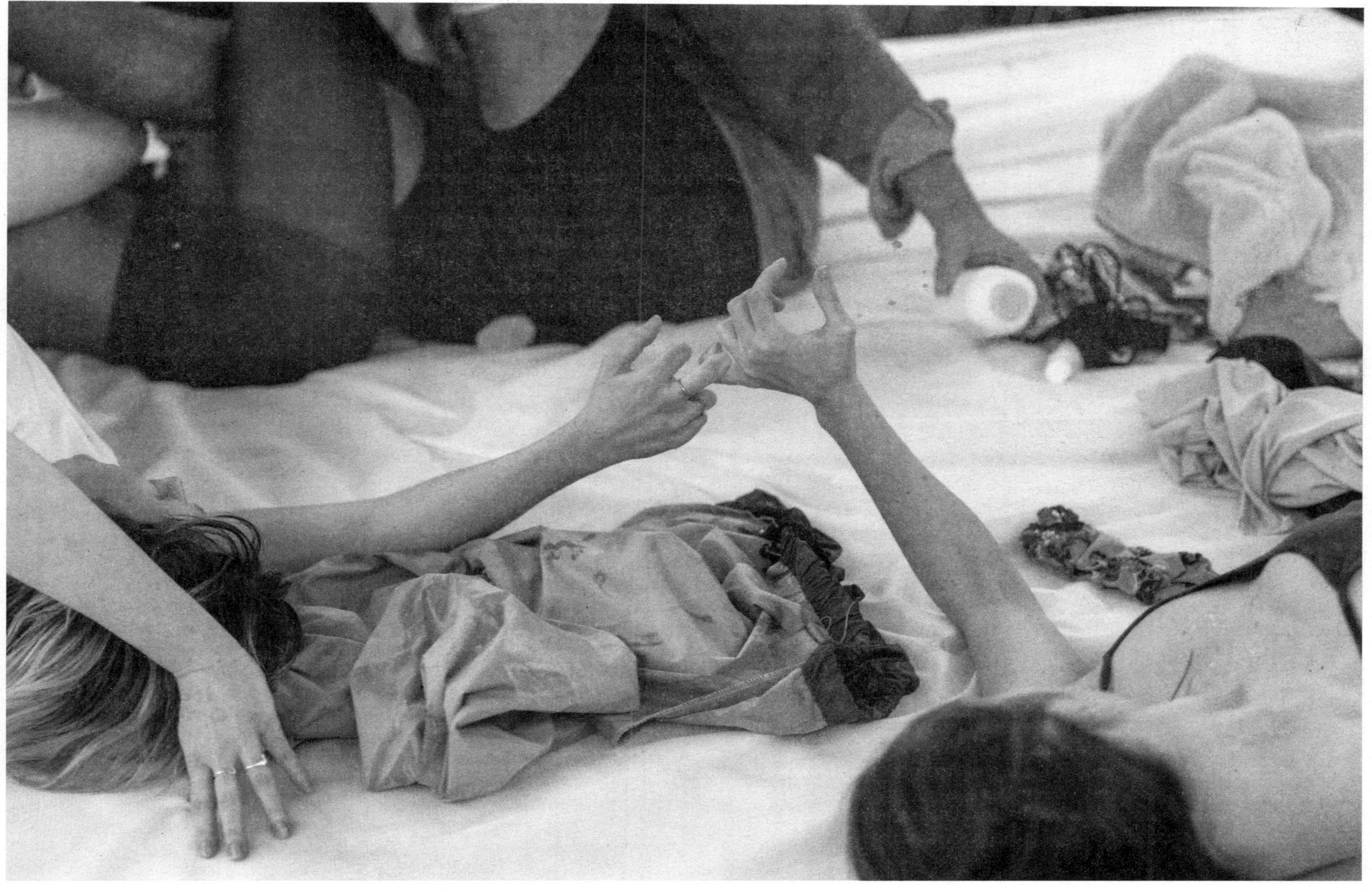

As I read *Weathering*, I am thinking about species deafness and species anosmia. I am thinking about how one of the symptoms of coronavirus (neo-plague of the Anthropocene, from the perverted sacrifice of wet markets and acid oceans, our greed for racoon dog flesh) is anosmia, or the loss of smell.

Smell literally comes into you. It is one of the two "chemical" senses that materially alter you. We feel smells enter us, impinge upon us, invade us and then do something to change us chemically. Once they land on our olfactory bulb, we have no choice but to absorb them. As such, in the hierarchy of the senses, scent gets rendered "primitive," racialized, gendered, and situated in the anatomical systems imagined most leaky: the digestive, the reproductive.

We cannot shut down our sense of smell.

It is said that smell is one of the earliest senses to develop in the womb. We smell our way out of the feeling of separation and back to the parent's body, to the milk that flows from one generation to another, to a sense of what was before the rupture. The Garden of Eden was lost when Adam and Eve used their senses of sight, sound, touch, taste to self-consciously snatch from the world. They saw, heard about, touched and tasted that forbidden fruit, but they did not smell it. Thus olfaction is considered a gateway back to the garden, a space of unbroken consciousness.[6]

---

6 "the longing to re-establish total union never quite goes away. We all share a desire to recover the lost paradise of uterine existence, when we were warmly housed inside the body of another, when there was no diffferentiation between the loved object and the self, no separation and therefore no possibility of need or loss." Olivia Laing, *Everybody: A Book About Freedom* (New York: W.W. Norton & Company, 2021).

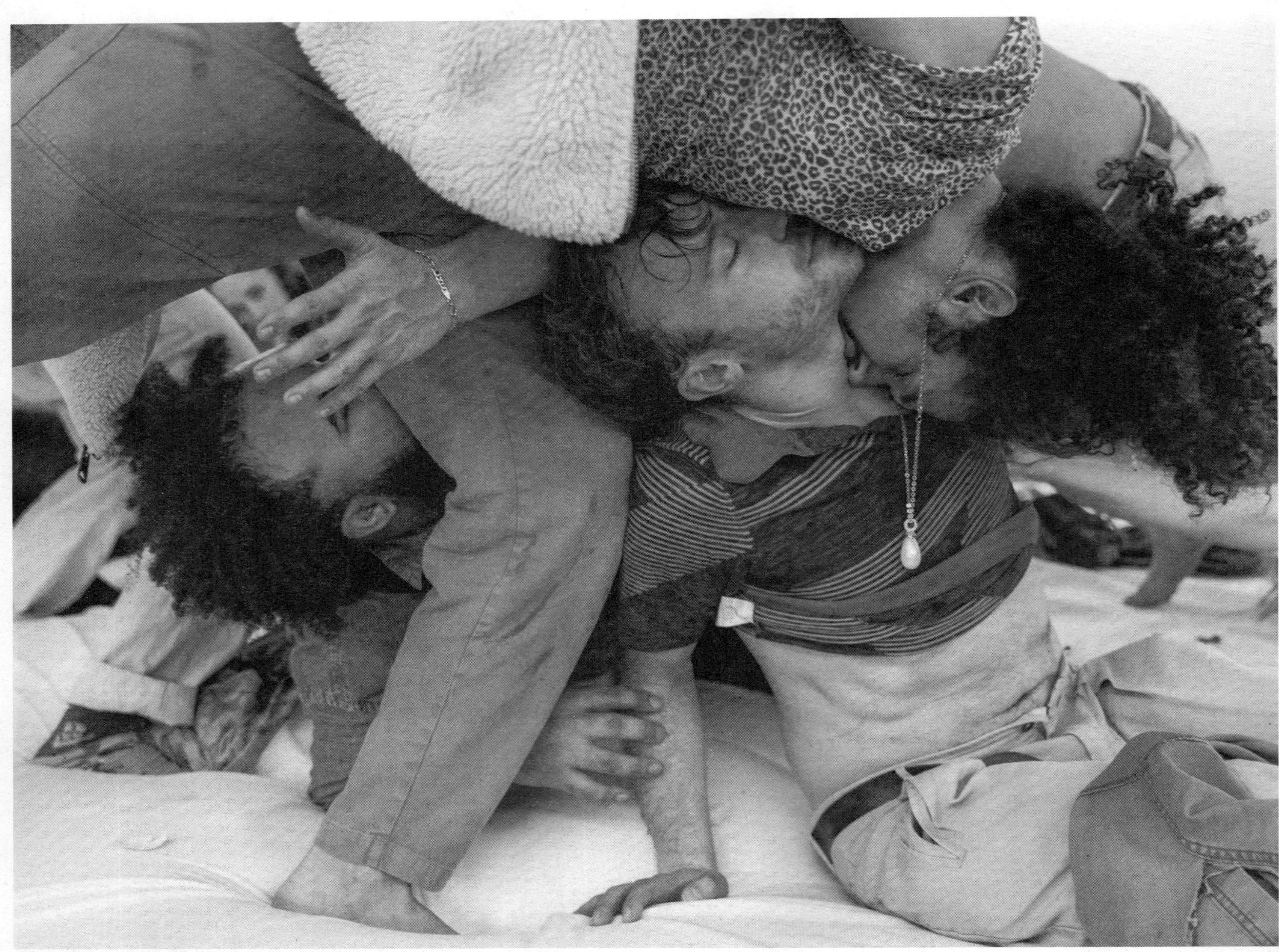

Anosmic folk may accidentally consume rancid food because they can't sniff out spoilage, and may also be unaware when they are breathing toxic or smoke-filled air. The smell of blood generates bloodlust in some, fear in others. We can smell each other's anxiety. We smell desire. We smell our way to our mother's breast shaping the fernlike unfurling of the cervical vertebrae. We literally get into each other, molecularly, materially, in ways that make matter. Its loss is meaningful.

If we cannot feel close enough for impact, we feel more alone with each other and on the planet. How much is the Anthropocene a kind of species sense loss?

We cannot shut down our sense of hearing.

We did not evolve "earlids," because audition is central to proprioception, and with it, our physical survival. We respond faster to a sound cue than to a visual one: it takes our brain a quarter of a second to process visually, but we recognize a sound in a fifth of that. We can hear the ticking of a watch twenty feet away; we endure the screaming of the subway, the jackhammer. We are, in fact, very auditorily sensitive, while navigating our way through an increasingly cacophonous world.

Our bodies evolved to hear within the range of bird song, indicating waterways, trees, food. We can hear where we can survive, where these feathered dinosaur descendents seed the earth from above. In New York City, we can no longer attune to the songs of Carolina Parakeets, Labrador Ducks, Passenger Pigeons, Eskimo Curlews. Listening is a practice of sensitization to place. We hear that we are here.

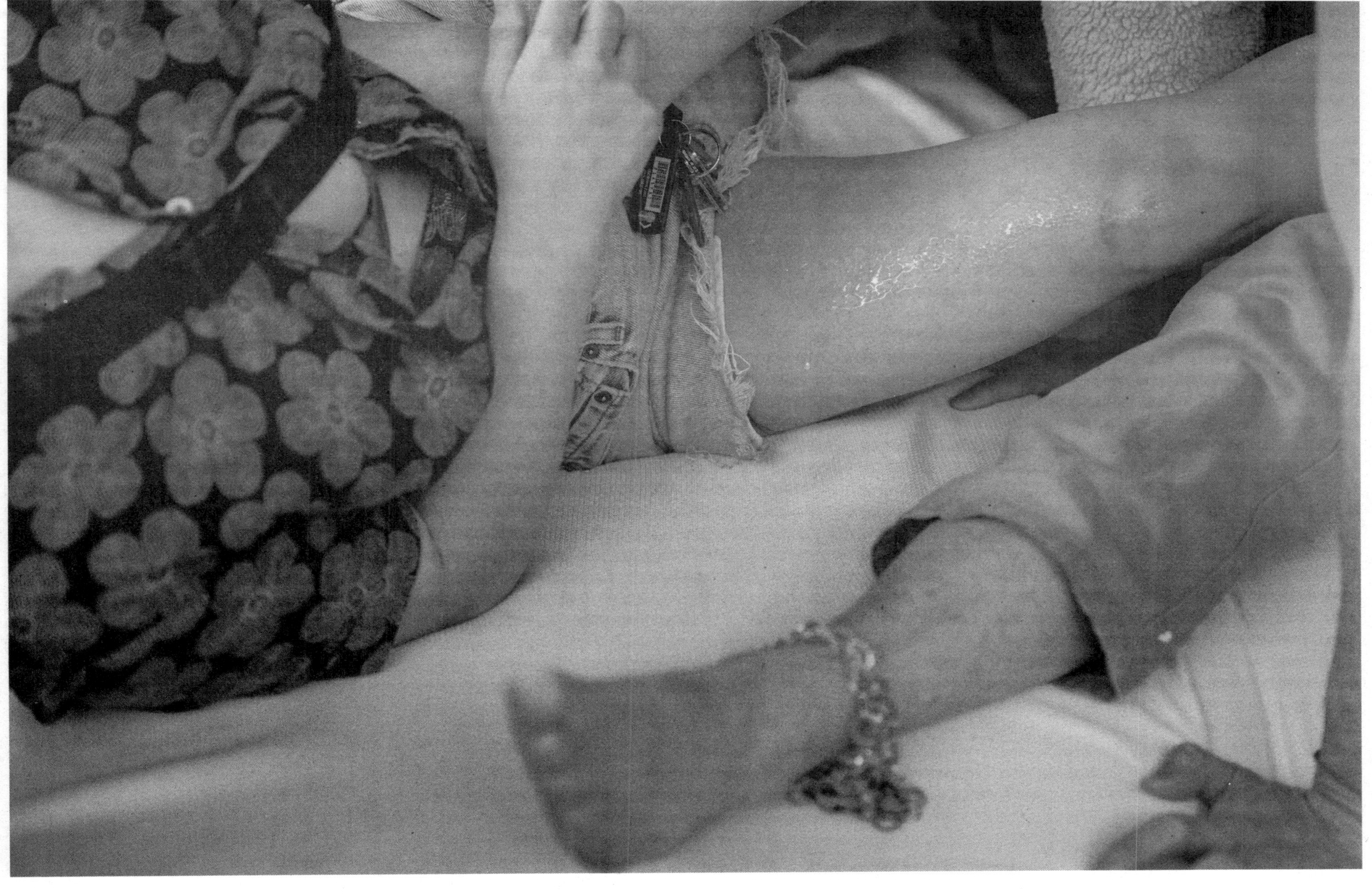

As Faye said in rehearsal, "listening is our ongoing score." In *Weathering*, sound and breath can't be sourced to just one body. We aren't sure where it comes from, where it goes, to whom it belongs, how far it extends. Whose voice is that? Whose breath? The sonic world billows within and around the entangled performers: elegiac, mantric, repetitive. It is a requiem to the lived body, the body of the beloved, the absent, the body in the act of killing itself and its context.

We are built by interspecies impact, created by a shared shape of lived experience. We are vulnerable to the complexities of this contact, feeling horror and horniness, tenderness and terror, nurture, and neglect, often simultaneously. We look inside each other for a touch, a taste, a glance of the eternal; we seek to be moved by, reborn in, and disappeared into the other. The contours of relating mold our porous ecologies the way asteroids have mottled the soft skin of the earth. *Weathering* invites us in, to take a longer, closer look; to develop a sensibility, to be in presence, to not know what's going to happen. And to be together, as transcorporeal accumulations of touch, of exchange, of wind, even—when circumstances literally take our breath away.

Dages Juvelier Keates (she/they) is an artist working with and through the materiality of their body as a somatic space for holding paradox. Their works explore performative and poetic methodologies in researching internal cartographies of somatic, psychoanalytic, and nonhuman knowledges.

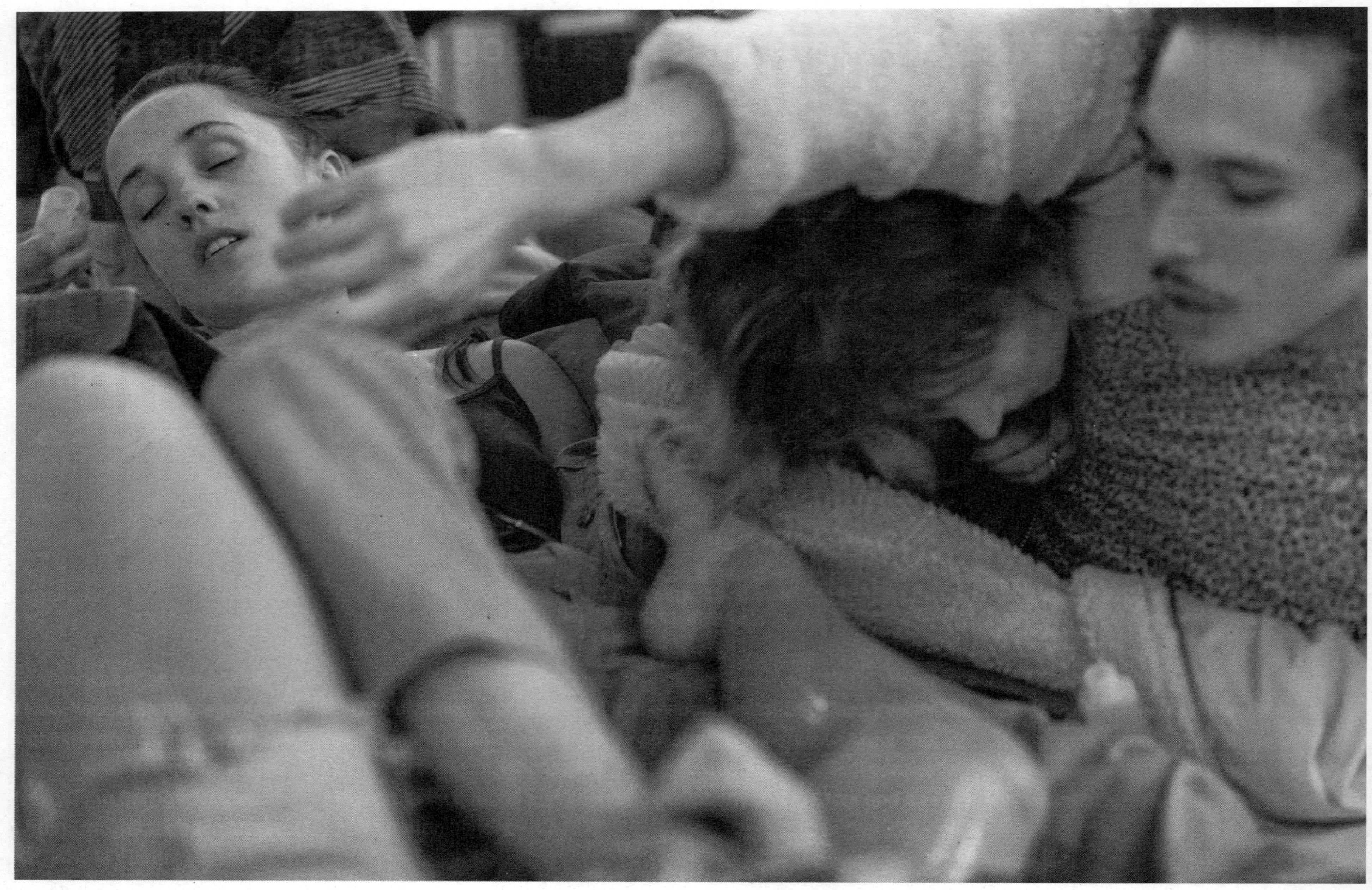

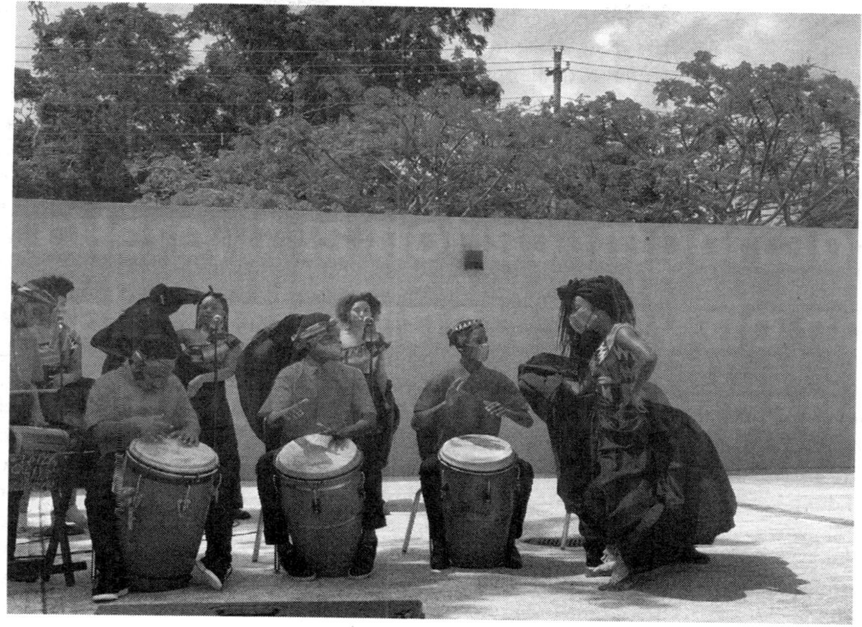

Megan Curet

Methods in En Ritmo / Praxis in Decolonizing Traditional Dance Spaces

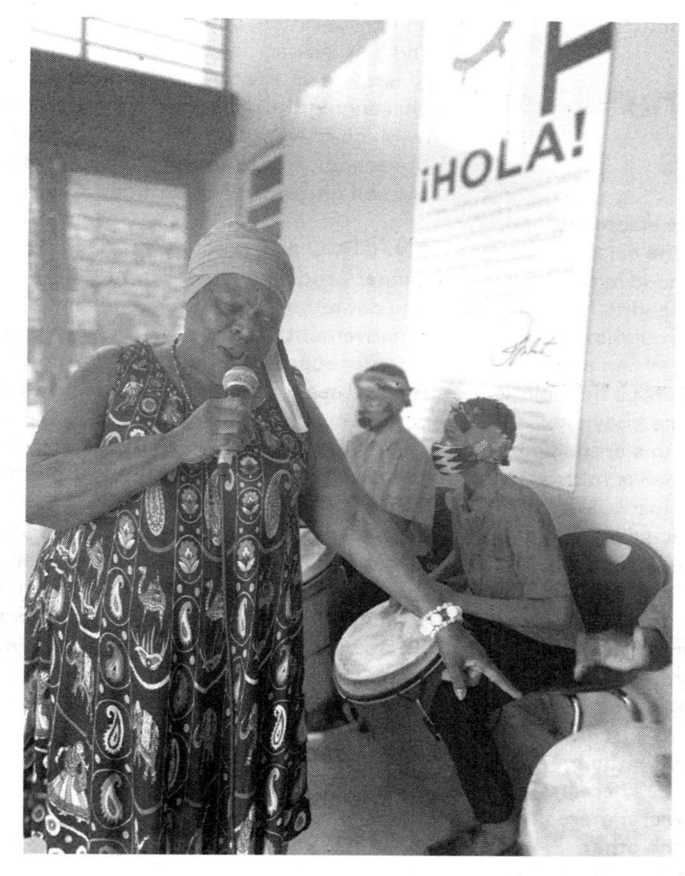

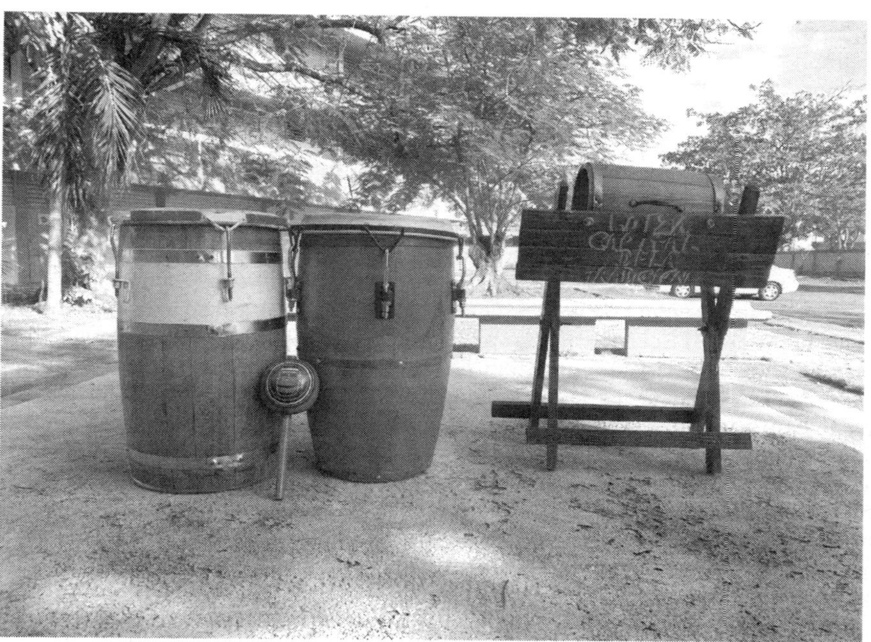

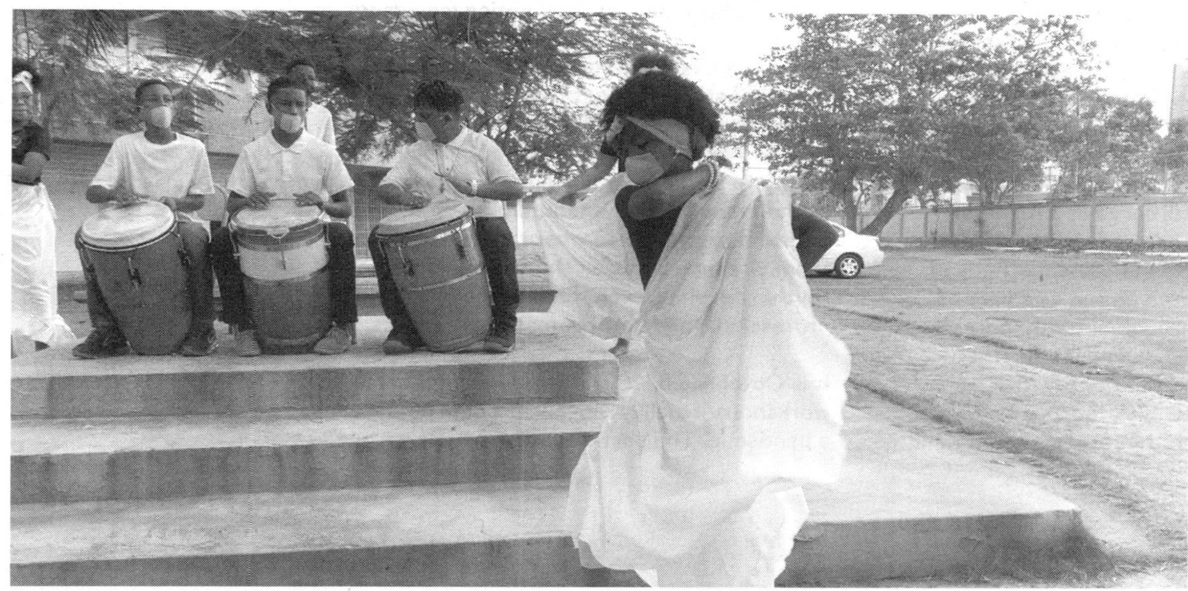

Photos: Megan Curet

EN RITMO: a practice-based framework for decolonizing the body in culturally hegemonic dance spaces, which is part of ongoing PhD research that focuses on the cultural syncretism of bomba, a Black and Indigenous movement practice that emerged in Puerto Rico and continues to reverberate in European and North American contemporary dance. Bomba: the foundation for movement investigation. With an approach to gathering, communing inside and outside of dance spaces, EN RITMO centers bomba as a movement approach for training the professional and non-professional dance body. In an attempt to decentralize classical Western approaches such as ballet and American modern dance, EN RITMO borrows elements from bomba. These elements include equal exchange, communal participation and embodiment that are born from the three distinct parts of bomba: music, song, and dance.

EN RITMO is also an attempt, through the development of a new pedagogy, to decentralize the concept of what a traditional dance space means and for whom. How can centralizing the elements of bomba through a contemporary dance vessel disrupt these existing notions? This investigation explores the value of disrupting the romanticization of a metaphorical relationship with decolonization by emphasizing actionable approaches through conscious and reflexive movement practice. EN RITMO aims to contribute to the fields of dance training and dance pedagogy—as decolonization in action, and by bridging the various worlds of European, North American and Latin American movers and thinkers.

I approach this investigation as a practitioner who has deep ties to the elements and practice of bomba, as they have aided my own practice as a choreographer. I return to bomba, not as a bomba practitioner, but as a contemporary dancer, revisiting a cultural movement language in order to expand my capacity as a mover and as a thinker, while centering the stories and approaches to knowing and thinking known and led by Black and Indigenous folks.

To ensure that this investigation does not perpetuate discursive practices of Eurocentric power relations (Parahar & Schulz, 2021) relations within Western academia, I aim to examine the following questions in order to contribute to the development of a new pedagogical approach to training the dance body: with an emphasis on Ballet and American Modern dance as currently centered colonial practices, can cultural syncretism of bomba and contemporary dance, along with reflection upon movement, be used to effect decolonization of the body? If so, how can writing decoloniality within the framework of his investigation avert becoming just another blanket academic tool?

The following is a brief outline of two of my research methodologies that aim to bring forth the rich contributions from the culture of bomba, while making sense of the methodological "mess" at hand (Law, 2003). Through practice-led research, auto-ethnography, and reflexivity, I attempt to reconcile the discrepancies that exist when locating the self within one's research while also addressing the importance for ethical ethnographic practices. Practice-led research as a methodology within this investigation will serve as a research design and provide a conceptual framework to incorporate the creative practice and methods of EN RITMO into the research design as a part of research output. Then, through autoethnography the data collected—embodied and intellectual knowledge explored during the EN RITMO workshops —can then be translated into text. As a methodological approach that bridges theory and performance, when applied, autoethnography allows the participant to name the experiences they had while inhabiting their body. Reflexivity as a qualitative approach is not only a process for examining the experience of the participant at a rigorous level, but also examining the position of the investigator/instructor as well.

Throughout this investigation I examine the data collected from EN RITMO workshops while applying methods of practice-led research, autoethnography, and Schön's method of reflective practice. I then utilize post-workshop reflective prompts to examine existing or non-existing trends experienced by participants, along with journal prompts and reflective practices collected and compiled through and from the workshops by myself, the conducting investigator. Workshops have taken place in Loiza, Puerto Rico; Choma, Zambia; virtually in Barcelona, Spain; as well as throughout North America over the span of two years, 2020–22.

Practice-led research places an equal emphasis on the artist-practitioner, the creative product and the critical process as described by Graeme Sullivan (Sullivan, 47:2009). In EN RITMO workshops, the participants engage with these three points as an approach to creating knowledge through making. Participants in EN RITMO workshops are encouraged to enter the space with as few expectations as possible. This encourages a fresh approach to movement language for new dancers and movers, while challenging returning or professional dancers to critically examine how they approach movement and dance training on and with the body.

These are the Collections

Reaching arms towards the sky, legs stretched and soles of the feet crushing into the earth. All of the energy is expanded and extended in opposite directions; participants are encouraged to hold onto this energy. The bomba is in circulation at this point, with a simpler repetition that all can comprehend—bomba sicá. As the beat drops the hold is released and all of the weight in the body moves into one massive pulse; this ends with a dropping in the torso, arms release downward, pelvis folds at the hip creases and legs fold. Participants are encouraged to hold this as the music mixes into a contemporary rhythm pattern, blending Afro house and techno.

I ask that they use the same movement language but engage differently with the rhythm pattern; I am mixing live on the decks, aiming to match the energy of the participants. Similar to a traditional bomba circle where the dancers match their percussionist, all bodies are engaged. There are no wrong answers, there are no mirrors; there is only the rhythm of the music, and the other participants. I encourage them to repeat the same movement they have begun to create, hold onto what has become familiar; I notice movement patterns taking shape, so we move into repetition. There is a heavy energy in the space; you can feel the exhaustion amongst the participants as they repeat their movement phrases. I urge them to lean into this place of exhaustion, to allow the breath to shape their movement, to become a part of their movement; I encourage them to press past the exhaustion, to see where their bodies take them. A dance between their bodies and the rhythm develops even if the space is filled with professional and non-professional dancers.

It is October 26, 2021. I am leading an EN RITMO workshop virtually from my in-home studio amidst a pandemic. The participants are in Barcelona as part of InDance International—many have never heard of the bomba, many are used to working with and in front of a mirror for their dance trainings. Participants were invited into the space we inhabited for forty-five minutes to one hour. We, as in myself the researcher, and the participants, began with a setting of intentions—this was for the individual self as well as the whole of the collective.
I introduced myself and explained a little bit about the history of this practice and the context of the investigation.

I offered participants time and space to ask any questions. I prefaced our time together by inviting all to give as much as they can in terms of movement, and to take any pauses as their bodies would feel necessary. Participants were invited to listen to their bodies' wants and needs first and foremost, and to prioritize well-being; if something does not feel good, do not do it; movement will be exhausting, but it should not be painful. Before we began, I asked them to release all that they know about dance and dance training, to begin anew in this space together. I pressed play on the decks and we began.

The practice of decolonization does not come without contradiction, often conflated with anti-colonial projects and struggles that re-inscribe the logic of settler colonialism. (Zavala, 2013:57) In the workshop spaces of EN RITMO, those contradictions are examined—from restructuring the role of teacher and student, to how the space and relationship to one another blends in with the movement at hand. EN RITMO as a space focuses on collaboration, community, and gathering, and how we can utilize the elements of bomba to reexamine an existing dance culture while challenging the strict paradigms that exist within it. Much of what autoethnography explores are the spaces of this and that through location of the self and critical reflection.

EN RITMO as a practice seeks not to unify dancers and movement practitioners under any one definition, but rather to push the boundaries of movement practice further away from any one singular approach—just as people of the Puerto Rican diaspora continue to push the boundaries of what it means to be connected to the culture of Puerto Rico. As a Puerto Rican from the diaspora myself, I come to this reflexive and ethnographic approach ready to also expand my understanding of this unique and rich music and dance culture. EN RITMO becomes not only a movement practice, but a framework for understanding dance through a multitude of lenses and experiences. To decolonize is to decentralize the binary and singular notions of knowing, which are very much associated with Western concepts.

Megan Curet is a Bronx Native Nuyorican dancer, choreographer, and educator, currently serving as Coordinator to the Artist of Color Council at Movement Research while completing a practice led research PhD in decolonial methodology within dance at Plymouth University in the UK. Former founder and artistic director of Curet Performance Project a contemporary dance company and founder/editor of online dance magazines *TiLLT Magazine*.

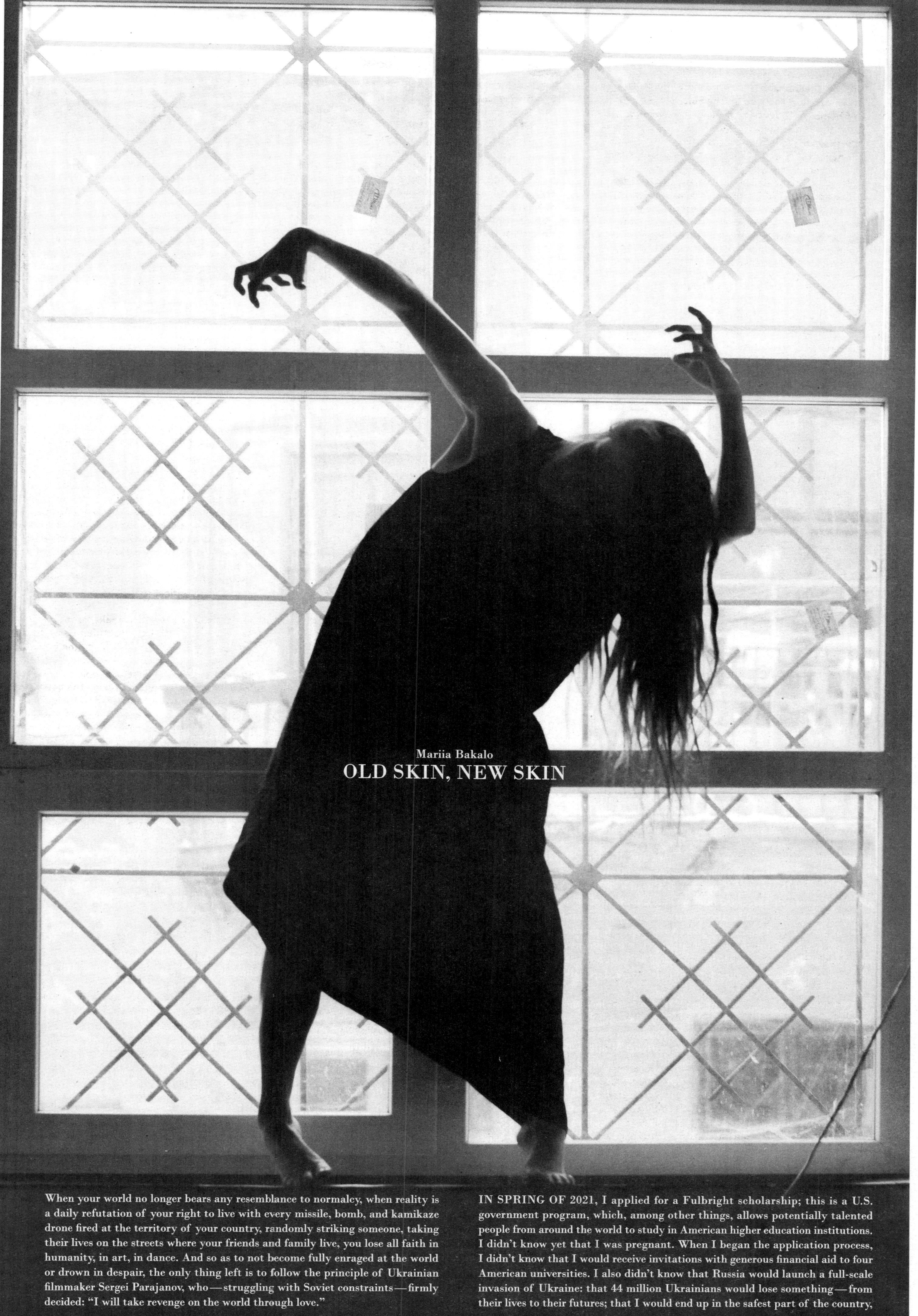

Mariia Bakalo

OLD SKIN, NEW SKIN

When your world no longer bears any resemblance to normalcy, when reality is a daily refutation of your right to live with every missile, bomb, and kamikaze drone fired at the territory of your country, randomly striking someone, taking their lives on the streets where your friends and family live, you lose all faith in humanity, in art, in dance. And so as to not become fully enraged at the world or drown in despair, the only thing left is to follow the principle of Ukrainian filmmaker Sergei Parajanov, who—struggling with Soviet constraints—firmly decided: "I will take revenge on the world through love."

IN SPRING OF 2021, I applied for a Fulbright scholarship; this is a U.S. government program, which, among other things, allows potentially talented people from around the world to study in American higher education institutions. I didn't know yet that I was pregnant. When I began the application process, I didn't know that I would receive invitations with generous financial aid to four American universities. I also didn't know that Russia would launch a full-scale invasion of Ukraine: that 44 million Ukrainians would lose something—from their lives to their futures; that I would end up in the safest part of the country,

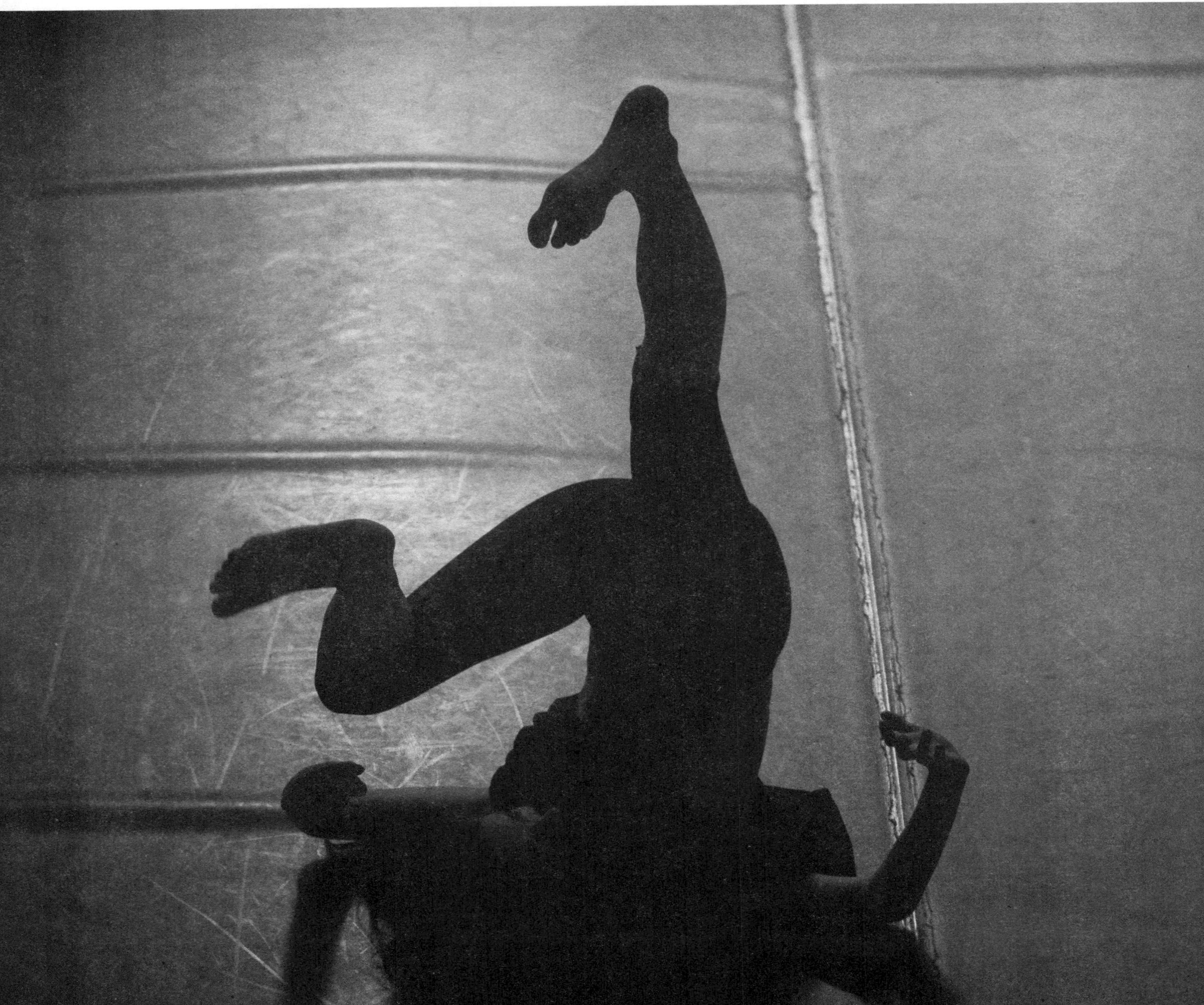

for its distance from Russia and it's proximity to the European Union; that studying abroad would be the last thing I wanted; and that my husband and I would not be able to travel there together as a family. And yet: faith in the idea of cultural diplomacy, in the beauty of art, in the transformative power of dance as something capable of forming new social patterns, and entire swathes of futures, provided the support I needed to accept the invitation and venture off to a California university to study in a Master's program in the fall of 2022.

I am truly impressed with my department and also truly devastated by the "normality" of the life and problems around me, by my uselessness and inability to exist beyond the reality of the war in Ukraine. While everyone around me is excited, enraged, concerned, and we think collectively about globalization, ecology, colonization, neoliberalism, Marxism, and other –isms from an academic point of view, I can't manage to sense these concepts as vital. Not in the way I vitally sensed through my ears and eyes, through my whole body, the shuddering from three consecutive explosions of Russian missiles that flew over my home outside Lviv, heading for a military target thirty kilometers away.

At that moment, I was holding my daughter and looking out the window. She was fast asleep. I couldn't sleep. That day, right after the explosions, I left with my children — holding one by the hand, the other in a sling — to an artist's residency I had been invited to at Hellerau in Dresden, which offered several special month-long scholarships to Ukrainian artists. This was strange, uncomfortable, and irreversible: leaving my home, my country, my husband, setting off into the unknown — more precisely, to a powerful and expensive country — with an infant and four-year-old, with my unstable profession of choreographer, not knowing whether I will have somewhere to return to. That day, we got to Dresden. That day, thirty-five people were killed by the missiles I had seen and heard.

Hellerau was the first place where I felt the irreversibility of the changes that had occurred the day that my entire world and its internationally-ratified security guarantees (at least according to the 1994 Memorandum on Security Assurances, in connection with Ukraine's accession to the Treaty on the Non-Proliferation of Nuclear Weapons) were attacked by its neighboring country — which was among those that had signed the security guarantee — with enough weapons and zeal to turn a city with a population of 100,000 into dust, targeting theaters, museums, archives, schools, universities, and nursery schools. Not far from Hellerau there is an airport, which I discovered right after arriving, since the sound of an airplane conjures immediate associations with the sound of Russian missiles in the Ukrainian sky. At Hellerau the atmosphere was diplomatic, which was refreshing to a certain degree, and after a month I found myself wanting to survive in this wildly structured world, organized according to principles foreign to me. At the same time, this diplomatic attitude deeply confounded me, as Russia's blatant aggression, its baseless mass murders and crimes against humanity are actions that demand an unequivocal position.

My journey continued: I taught dance classes in Leipzig; stayed with a German family in Bremen, who opened their doors to me as a Ukrainian woman with children who was recommended by friends in the contact improvisation community; and worked as a choreographer with the Small Drama Theater in Kaunas, Lithuania. Each of these places offered new reasons to feel surprised, thankful, and a sense of unity.

In Austria, where I received a Danceweb scholarship from the ImpulsTanz festival, I first encountered the feeling of taking revenge on the "normal" world through love. Swimming in the stream of performances, presentations, and classes, I realized that the topics of war and humans' destruction and humiliation of other humans were not considered critical issues by culture-makers in Europe. Further, broaching these themes is deemed rather lowbrow. For instance, during the ceremony honoring the festival's scholarship recipients, I took the microphone and expressed gratitude for solidarity with Ukraine, which was demonstrated by my participation in the festival. I also mentioned how I couldn't completely share in the joy of this event, with the peaceful skies of Vienna overhead, as at this moment, the people of my country were suffering under fire and violent attack. At the end of the evening, some colleagues remarked on my speech, saying, "That was inappropriate while everyone was celebrating."

That's exactly how I felt every minute of my time in Vienna — as if my presence there was spoiling everyone's celebration of dance. Even despite a certain carefulness, diplomacy, and the festival's hospitality, something elusive and strange remained in the air. For example, there was a tank gun aimed at the windows of the pavilion where classes were held: it was an inactive gun, once active during World War II, and today for Austrians is only a museum artifact. None of my program cohorts even noticed it. History and war do not exist for them in the sphere of current issues; the past exists in digested form, as something that does not compete with other contemporary issues. This amazes

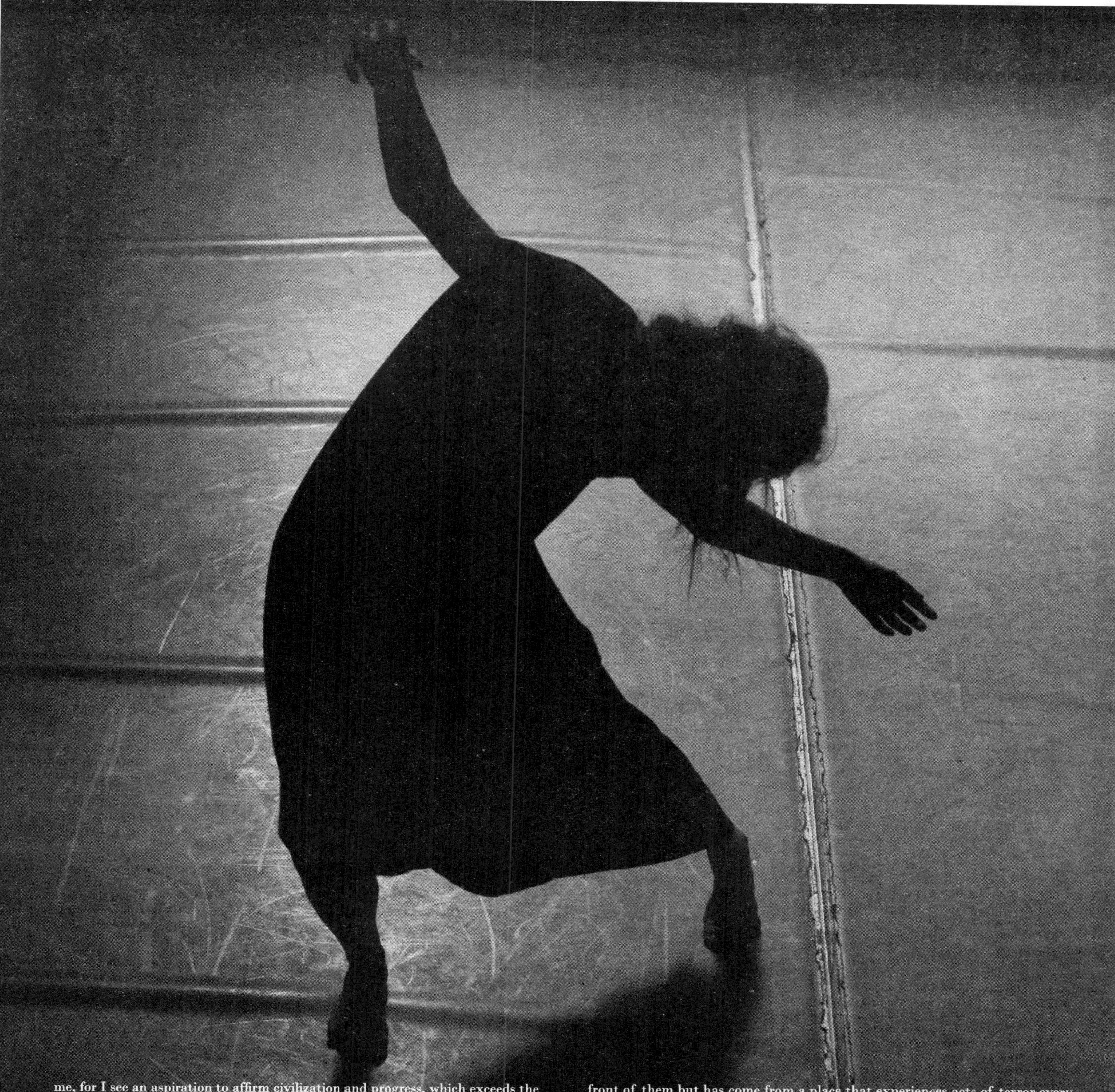

me, for I see an aspiration to affirm civilization and progress, which exceeds the wish to see and recognize truth. By the way, something similar happens here in the U.S. each time someone asks me in a light, conversational tone, "Oh, where are you from?" When they hear my reply, I notice how people around me become uncomfortable and "the party's no longer quite the same."

The topics that circulated among the dance practitioners around me in the summer of 2022 were problems like climate change, techno reality and future, globalization and age, and others. And when I, along with three other Ukrainians who were attending classes at ImpulzTanz, proposed a discussion about Ukraine and art in times of war, the event was scheduled for the last day of the festival. It was placed in the final hours of the day, in one of the last studios in the pavilion, after all the classes and events were over, when the tired festival participants were rushing to go home and finally celebrate the conclusion of a four-week festival packed with events. I sincerely thank ImpulzTanz, together with the Tanja Liedtke Foundation, for granting me access to a phenomenal chunk of professional development, contacts, and knowledge; and yet, it was poisoned by feelings that I am irrelevant, useless, and not normal. The festival, along with the more than 139,000 participants its website boasts, were breathing the same air. The air I breathed was different. And, as it was made clear to me, "that was inappropriate."

The politicized presence of Ukrainians in non-Ukrainian contexts during the war is a complexity with which I am still grappling. Those environments don't know how to respond to us. Refusing to accept us is not nice, but being with us seems to not always fit a given situation's chosen predominant position, like when that position is one of neutrality, non-interference, or the diplomatic "everything is complicated"—or its other version, "we're for peace and friendship;" in other words, "we're against war (as such)." Entire institutions and social groups large and small are confused about how to treat a person who is standing right in front of them but has come from a place that experiences acts of terror every day. Doesn't our presence as Ukrainians among you remind you of something, or compel you to do anything? The celebration is no longer that joyful, and diplomacy's straight-line buckles, if even for one uncomfortable moment. Perhaps your immunity to events for which we all bear responsibility falters in that moment, and the feeble voice of conscience breaks through the banality of your morning coffee and everyday news stream about the latest shelling of the Zaporizhzhia nuclear power plant, and mass graves in de-occupied Ukrainian cities?

My friend Sofia, a Ukrainian from Lviv, went to study at a college in Ohio in the fall of 2021. When we met in the summer, Sofia told me how her fellow students in that Ohio college reacted when Russia launched its first terrorist attacks on Ukraine. Her roommate stopped saying "Hi!" Her classmates began avoiding her. Is it because the local system of etiquette has no instructions for how to act in cases where the person next to you is suffering from genocide? Or is it the huge discrepancy between universes that I call breathing different air? Perhaps the issue is not me or Sofia?

Many of us don't dance now. For Ukrainians today, our former identification as dancers is about something other than what "dance" was during normal times. The ground that's been taken from beneath our feet, the denial of our right to live—these things have deprived us of the words and meanings we used before. I cannot dance because there is only one thing I can do right now, survive, which is a political act. Through my presence, I move toward the assertion that yes, I am from Ukraine, and that means my dance of life and kinetic experience are about the movement for freedom. Yes, this makes you uncomfortable—because the available narratives are pretty contradictory, and there is a violent struggle going on for the information sphere; because some of you have inherent sympathies toward the aggressor state; because calling it a "conflict" frees you

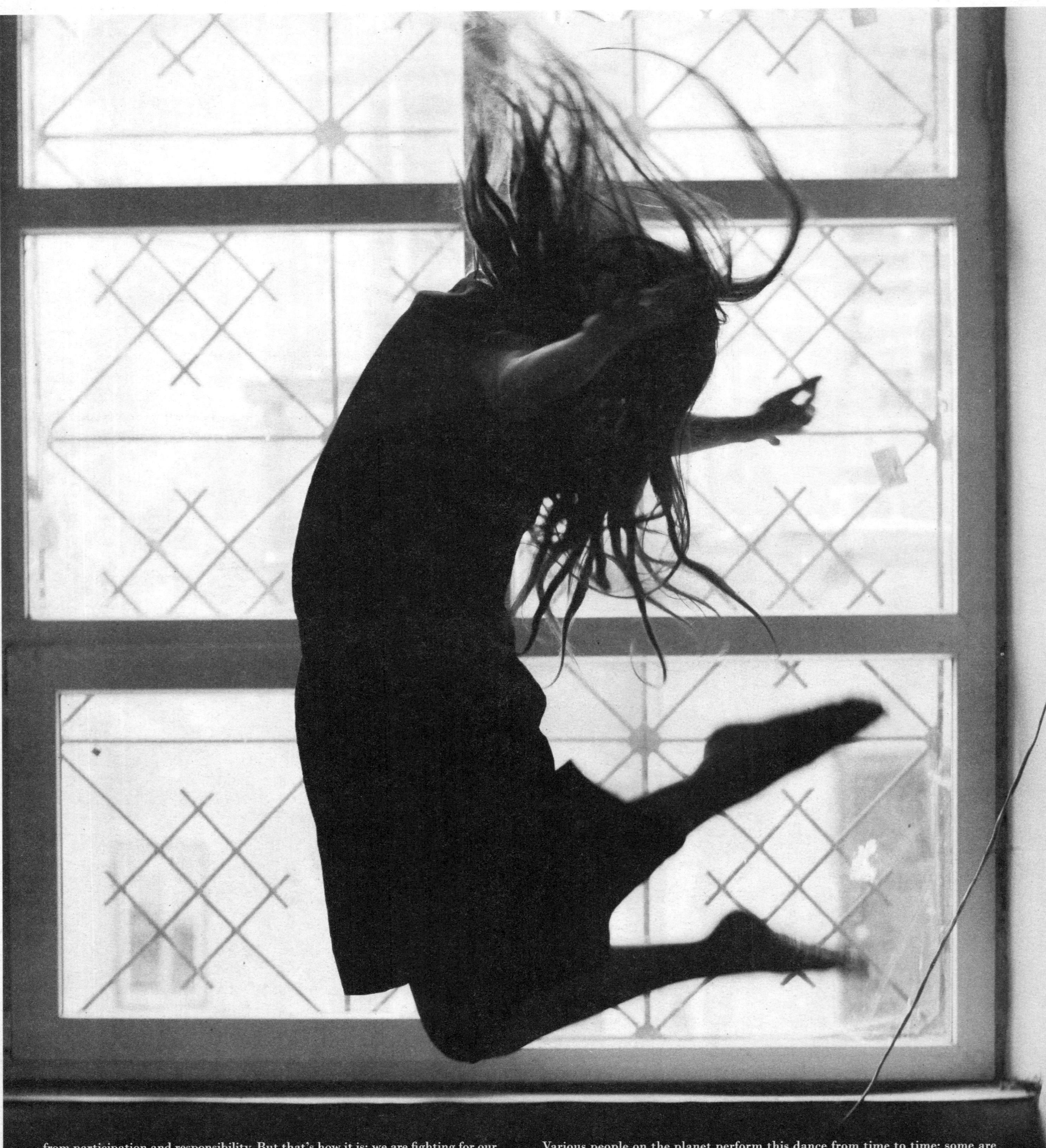

from participation and responsibility. But that's how it is: we are fighting for our right to live, and our presence in any point on the globe affirms this. I think that artists represent the time and reality in which they live, while at the same time shaping the time and reality of those who will live going forward. Therefore, I will not drag dance, which I shed like old skin on February 24, into my "revenge on the world through love." Instead, gradually and awkwardly, maybe even challenging you, I am growing new skin. Just as all Ukrainian artists today are growing new art, which perhaps is uncomfortable to see, for it exposes something the outside world wants to keep hidden.

This has become our identity: the fight for our country; our closest friends leaving behind their loved ones, sometimes young children, sometimes careers and businesses, to head for the battlefield; news of their deaths; news that after the latest explosion in a residential area, where a father witnessed the pieces of his wife and children being gathered from the roofs of the neighboring buildings; everyday blackouts and neighbors pooling funds for a generator to have at least some source of power the next time they face over 18 hours without electricity; our everyday donations to support the army; volunteering; and the persistent feeling that you are not doing enough. I am proud of this dance of freedom that we are dancing. Following André Lepecki's interpretation of Hannah Arendt's words about "moving politically" as "moving freely," movement toward freedom cannot be done just once. For when you forget to dance this dance—and every Ukrainian knows this very well now—you'll find that you don't exist.

Various people on the planet perform this dance from time to time; some are always dancing it. Excluding war and genocide from the agenda is truly fraught, for it leads to the normalization of domination, degradation, wanton violation and indignity. To those parties and festivals that were happening in the not-yet-occupied cities of Europe in September and October 1939, when everyone thought that war was about somebody far away and somewhere in the past: the price of indifference is hard to pay and easy to forget. War is not somewhere far away. War is here, each and every day. And everyone participates in it. There is nothing comfortable in that. But there is a choice: who do you support?

Translated by Larissa Babij

Photos: Anastasiia Karpenkova

pp. 43–46

Mariia Bakalo is a dance artist, choreographer, and educator in the realm of contemporary dance from Ukraine. In 2015–2017 she led regular experimental dance classes at the Ivan Franko National University of Lviv (Ukraine). Her choreographic works of 2017–2019 years were dedicated to an idea of dance as a life practice and choreography as an ongoing reality-construction process.

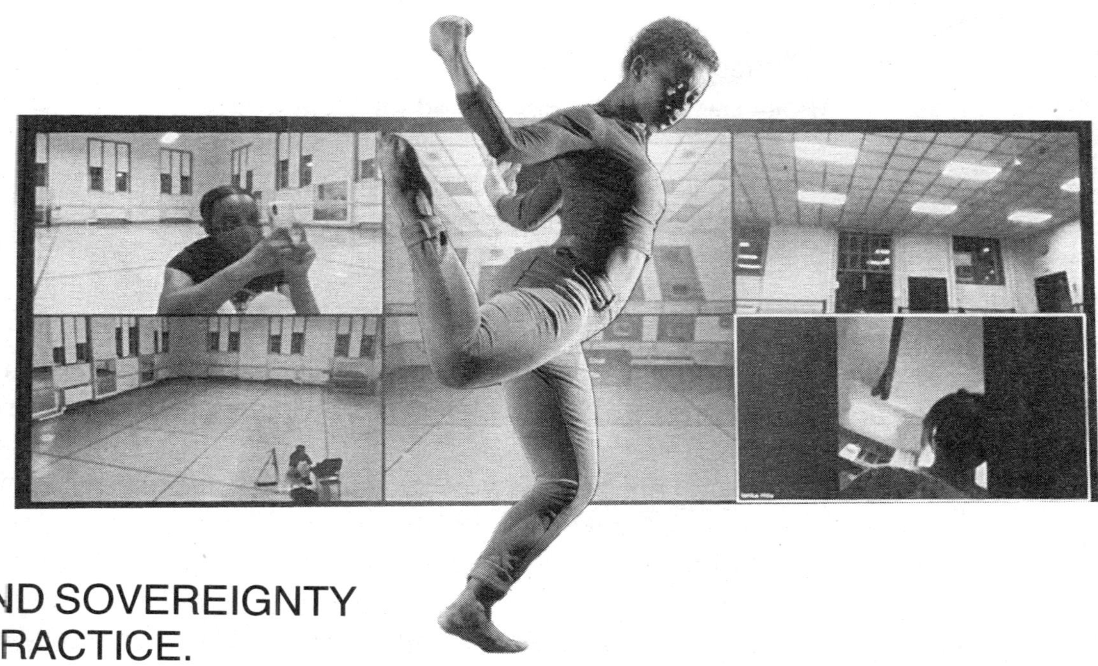

ON HEALING, JOY, AND SOVEREIGNTY AS PEDAGOGICAL PRACTICE.

Laila J. Franklin, in conversation with Tai Jimenez

This is a meta-conversation, built of quotes I remember from and my reflection on my teacher, Tai Jimenez.

[We are gazing into the screen, beaming at one another, or sharing thoughtful nods as we listen to one another. We sit in silence sometimes, to take everything in. It has been almost four years.]

I hold a BFA from The Boston Conservatory
I hold an MFA from The University of Iowa
I have taught as an adjunct professor at Salem State University
I left.

I think my early resistance to teaching arose out of a fear of repeating patterns that had instilled fear and shame in me. That seemingly undid all the affirming of my early learning experiences.

Teaching is a practice.
Teaching is ministry.

My earliest recollection of being a student is being surrounded by teachers and fellow students that looked like me.

My neighborhood school was primarily Black and my first ballet teacher was a dark-skinned Black woman who had graduated from Juilliard.

And then I was alone.

I wouldn't say that's where things "went wrong"… I was disoriented by the culture.

It wasn't that I, myself, wanted to consciously repeat those patterns, but rather the structure lent itself to those patterns producing "success"

· limited time
· required letter grading
· busy work

I was anxious. *I was moody.*
I was sad. *I was depressed.*

I left in part because I was afraid, but also because I couldn't keep churning the machine, a machine that no one in particular told me I had to churn but was ultimately rewarded for churning. I was also very alone. Again.

I remember the moment when I knew there had to be a better way.

I remember feeling invisible, wondering, "why can't he share with all of us"

I remember the moment when I experienced a better way.

Madame Darvash had a tough love, but I didn't feel invisible.

Tai's class was the first class I could push myself and not hate myself by the end of it.
The first class I felt wholly like a person and not an ethereal other.

She had a keen intellect of alignment and anatomy, from a perspective of how most skeletons actually work, and through that process, you could transform yourself, building strength for your individual body.

I can remember feeling like my body was my own, even when being pushed to challenge myself. I didn't have to fight to be seen and my presence was acknowledged as an important piece of the community we were as a class.

To teach is to give. I am thinking a lot about the ways, historically, knowledge is withheld as a means of controlling groups. I am thinking of the times I have experienced this as a student. The shame and sadness I would feel. I knew I was missing something and was not allowed to know what it was.

I shifted from academia to community-oriented teaching as a means to not only regain my sovereignty but also as a means to expand the unlearning and healing processes often so necessary after years of institutionalized learning. My students now are most often my peers, often on their own journeys of freeing themselves. I want to hold space for that.

We are an entity in a collage of influence, and sometimes our role requires us to address the influence of others. Sometimes we must facilitate unlearning, and even healing. To teach other bodies, often young bodies, how to move through the world is a heavy task, and one that requires a knowledge of and sensitivity to not just the physical, but the mental, emotional, and spiritual.

To teach, right now, is to create space for home. To create space for family. To create space to heal. To create space to listen.

you have to meet yourself
at the point of limitation
with compassion

And maybe one day I can do that in academia,
but right now that is my point of limitation.

We do all of these things for our students, and also for ourselves. By regaining our sovereignty as teachers, we are able to create spaces where students can regain theirs, and move through their (our) bodies with freedom and joy.

you don't have
to be joyous,
but you have to
allow the space
for joy.

Laila J. Franklin is a dance maker, performer, teacher, administrator, and writer. Her work extends from lineages of Black queer experimental dance makers, with a particular interest in postmodern improvisatory practices and aesthetics, and dance theater. Her performance/collaboration credits include work with Miguel Gutierrez, Melinda Jean Myers, Dr. Christopher-Rasheem McMillan, and Ruckus Dance. Laila holds an MFA in Dance from the University of Iowa and a BFA in Contemporary Dance Performance from The Boston Conservatory.

A Personal Note on Writing Before Creating: Questions on Writing and Movement in the Dance Field

• **Johnnie Cruise Mercer**

The more I recognize how tired I am, the more I am compelled to the realization that making and researching dance, at least how I am currently approaching it, may not offer me a sustainable life.

My love for researching movement came while in church, while watching local fraternities and sororities stroll, while taking part in school talent shows. I fell in love with the study of community movement and its ability to move/free people. Creating dance, for me, was tied to living in the moment—my research as a maker connected entirely to and for the communities from which it derived.

In the last four years, however, that love for digging into movements' ability to inspire community has been challenged, due to our field's fascination with writing.

Why am I required to prove myself through writing, often for free?

I've traced it back to college. I remember writing my first proposal. To prepare me for the life of an artist—a life contingent on writing all manner of grant, space, project proposals—my professors structured a process of learning to write in order to prove my ideas. Little did I know, it was a mock trial: the first of many proposals asking for "my research."

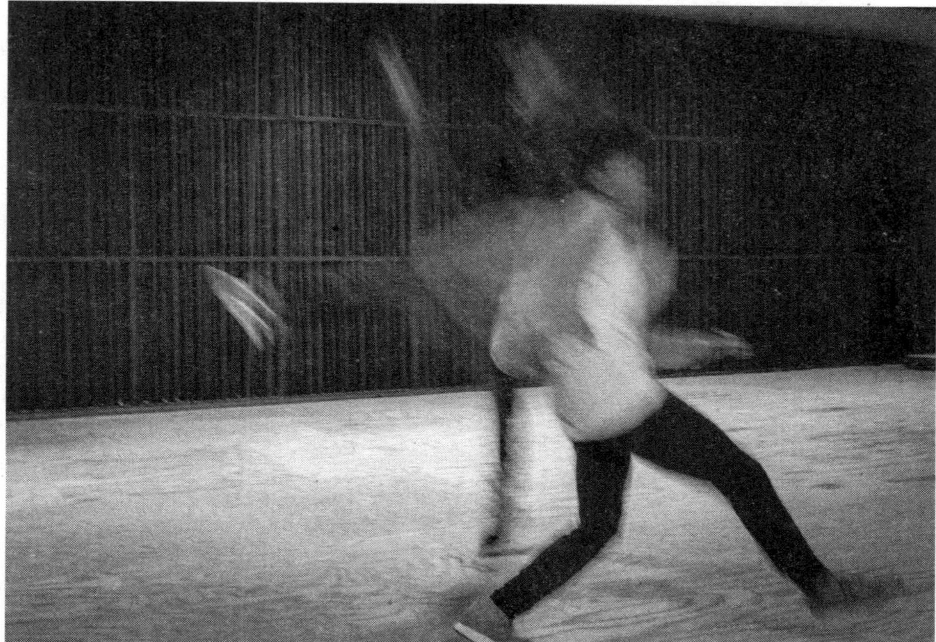

Photo: Ashima Yadava

Here are a few questions and prompts that I answered back then—and still answer, over and over again:

Please describe your dance/work.
What community does your work serve?
What is the impact you want your work to have?
How does your work touch on one of the many liberal labels that we deem important?
Write with this word count.

Today, as a movement artist who has had quite a few amazing opportunities, I feel like I am still a student attending a university everytime I submit my writing and wait for THE GATEKEEPERS (the funders, the panels) to assess the merits of my work, judging my dance in the form of my writing, a completely different art form. Writing is now the majority of my job in a never-ending cycle of proving myself to get paid.

My artistic process has become the following:

1. Take two to three years to write about my "research" in order to receive grants, residencies, and opportunities.
2. Take six months to a year to write press materials, blurbs, and more text re-explaining the work to clarify how it ties into the research topic (paying attention to key "yes" words as I write).
3. Become an editor, as I rewrite material from presenters and organizations based on my research and writings that were previously sent to them, in order to get my writing to fit into whatever format they require.
4. Finally, go into the studio, take three to six months to create said project based on said research, while attempting to explain all of the written research to collaborators in hopes that their bodies will receive it. Dance, in relation to all the writing that came before the studio work.
5. Do a show (for one weekend, sometimes for one day), then get criticized based on the performance's validity in relation to what I wrote about the work before I made it. Reviewers and others take in the work in its physical form. I count this as the "experiment" phase; the first time everything comes together! Unfortunately, to the public, to the presenters, and to everyone watching it is considered a product (gotta love capitalism).
6. Start over. Or more likely, do the same process for another project at the same time.

Importantly, I do not get compensated for five of the six points above.

Research comes in many forms. I do consider myself a writer, and I have the privilege of a college background to maneuver this complicated field. However, I write more than I dance. As someone whose research in movement is entirely inspired by people and space—writing should not be the focus of my time nor energy. I miss the days of being with people, making, and exploring without explaining what we are about to do. I miss sweating and diving into the material body first, spending actual time living in and playing with the material, not just thinking about it. Writing for me is but a tool, a vehicle of communication, used to explain and to give context to the work. I did not enter this field to write an essay, nor to present multiple research papers on what will be. Academia, it seems, has codified the process of art-making, and I am tired of following these requirements in order to make money (a small amount of money at that). I did not know when I embraced concert dance that I signed up to be an unpaid academic researcher.

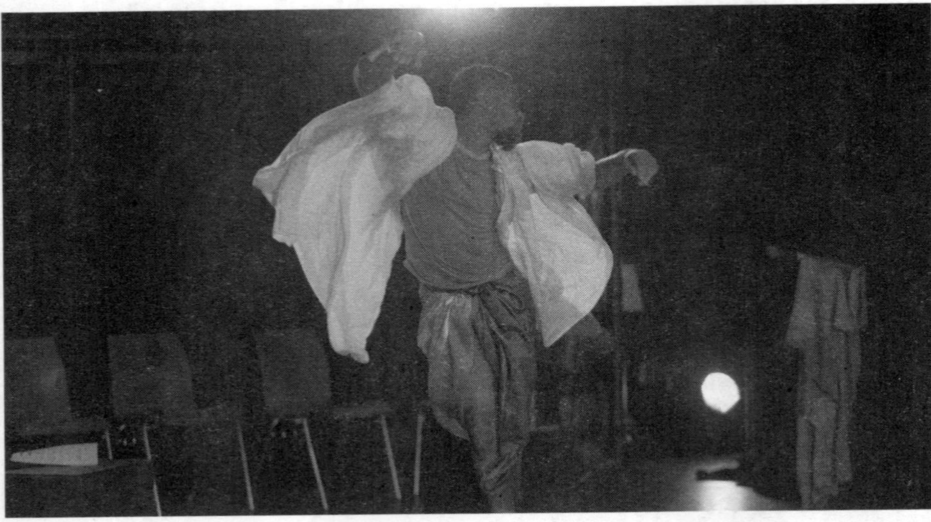

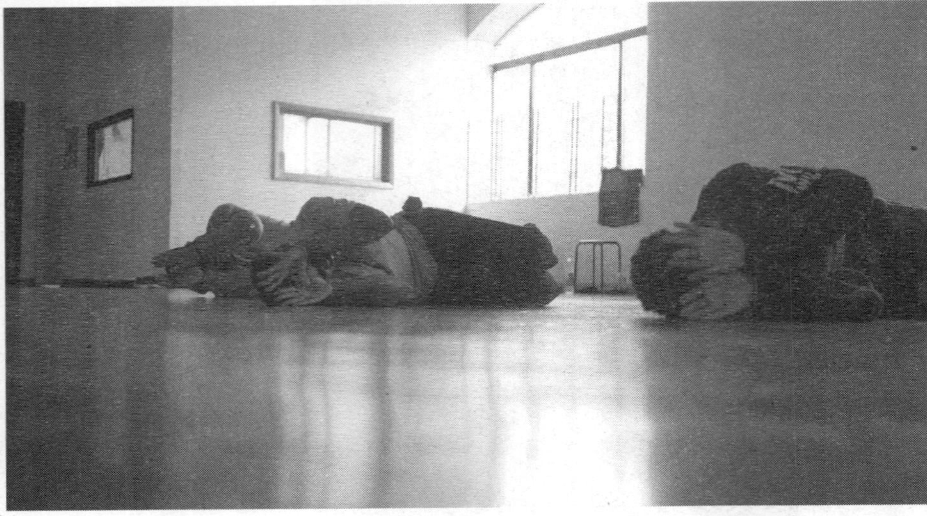

Photos: Torian Ugworji

Here are a few questions I have for the field, and for those gatekeepers who have the power to be readers instead of writers:

Aren't movement and writing two different art forms that require two different skill sets? Will we ever acknowledge the stress it takes to do both? Why do we value writing when working with a medium that lives in the body? Why am I, as an artist, required to explain something in words when there is enough proof of its effectiveness in our history, especially as an artist of color (i.e. the examples I mentioned above, at the beginning of this entry)? If there is video proof of the work, why must I also write about it? What happened to simply talking and speaking in person? Is it possible to measure an artist's capacity and a work's potential without forced writing labor? How can anyone continue to engage in a career in dance-making without being acknowledged and compensated for their time (whether it be written, or practice-based research)? Do we have the tenacity to accept the politics that go into how we view process, research, and work? Can we accept that really it's about who views it not who writes it? How does academia play a role in concert dance? How does it affect it positively and negatively? What independent artist, in the world we are slowly evolving into, will be able to take on these multiple jobs for a lifetime without true institutional support? How will our field grow if we are only listening to those who can write?

I know one thing: the formula that consists of writing, then making, then sharing is absolutely obsolete, for me and for many others. I am no longer interested in consistently taking part in this formula for free, especially under the guise of presenting research.

So what will I do? I plan to do what I can to help my own community. I am dedicated to shifting the paradigm. Maybe a solution lies in setting up my own platform, entrepreneurially setting up my own system of opportunities for my own network. It may be time to work with my community to build spaces that support the type of research I (we) believe in. There is money out there, as I see my peers in other fields spending hundreds of dollars on Beyoncé concert tickets. It's clearly time for me (us) to set new foundations and build bridges outside of what normally funds us. The time has come (or maybe it's been here) for my people to (once again) build our own, together.

No matter what I decide, I fear that we may hit a breaking point as a community (the concert dance community)—I know I have already. Something must be done, and soon, because most of us are currently putting a ton of our energy toward creating dance on paper, and what good is choreography when it's only written?

Johnnie Cruise Mercer (he/him) is a queer-black think-maker, freelance-performer, educator, and social entrepreneur based in New York City. A native of Richmond, VA, Mercer holds a BFA in Dance and Choreography from Virginia Commonwealth University. As the Company Director of Johnnie Cruise Mercer/TheREDprojectNYC, hisprocesses/work has been shared and/or hosted by 92Y Harkness Dance Center, Gibney: Agnes Varis Performing Arts Center, Dixon Place, Danspace Project Inc, Abrons Arts Center, and The Clarice Performing Arts Center's The BlackLight Summit.

INDULGENCE
COURAGE NOT TO STRUGGLE
BE GENEROUS BY BEING REAL

RECEIVE

SURRENDUR

Fragile Fall

GIVE UP

A conversation between Nora Raine Thompson (NRT) and Nacera Belaza (NB)

LISTEN LISTEN

Nacera Belaza, a French-Algerian dancer and choreographer, is concerned with authenticity. She is a choreographer in some of the most stereotypical ways you would imagine–charismatic and animated, she has a vision for what realness might look like and is unyieldingly demanding of the dancers with whom she works. She makes dances for the stage, which, although spare and darkly lit, center on the moving body. She is also a choreographer in an elemental, even spiritual way. She attempts to arrange bodies in space to enact, in her words, something real, to tap into a kind of sacred communion. In this process, she urges the conceptual innards of those dancing bodies–their motivations, fears, notions of selfhood–to fall away. She requires complete and uninhibited transformation.

I attempted this complete and uninhibited transformation for Nacera in March of 2020, days before the pandemic lockdowns began in New York City. I was part of a small cast of dancers who rehearsed for just a week to perform Nacera's U.S. Premiere of La Procession *at Danspace Project. Her process of teaching us this dance included a series of what I call (and have been writing obsessively about for three years now), impossible tasks. The score was deceivingly simple. First, be wind. Then, be circle. Then, be sound.*

This conversation, recorded in September 2022 over an outdoor dinner on the Lower East Side, betrays how I continue to be simultaneously confounded by and infatuated with Nacera's work. We talked about how to negotiate risk in dances that ask for surrender, the "human thing" of fear, and why we go onstage at all. What follows are excerpts of our meandering discussion that evening, edited for clarity and brevity.

NRT: I have been thinking about my experience with you in 2020. Being in your work felt like a strange opportunity to attempt the impossible, and it triggered a whole set of questions for me that now are beginning to impact my scholarly work. I'm thinking about all sorts of impossible tasks, especially those, like yours, that I have found simultaneously frustrating, complicated, and compelling. Do you think of your work in this way? With this sense of impossibility?

NB: It's funny you use that word, because back in 2010 I wrote something about always asking the dancer to do something impossible. I do believe that what I set up is possible, though; let's say we can't perfectly reach it. There is something interesting in the process, then. The transformation of your mind and your body while you are going from this point to another creates the work. We get to see how everything gets transformed by this action of trying to reach something impossible.

For example, I'm sure I gave you this image before, because I use it in rehearsal: if you say to a child, "Come, run and jump and touch the second-floor window!" He's not going to think about how he's going to do it, and he's going to run and jump. And he's going to believe that it's possible. So the way that he organizes his body and mind will give us the sensation that he reached the goal, even though he didn't. But the grown person, they already have a kind of plan in mind, which is: I know it's impossible, so I'm gonna pretend to do it. When they pretend, they inverse the organization. Dancers pretend a lot, and for me, when they pretend, there's nothing interesting happening.

NRT: Ah yes, the pretending. I have been creating my own impossible tasks, working with a collaborator and trying to listen to rocks. So far, though, I haven't wanted to perform these practices. I haven't wanted to do it for an audience, maybe because I fear that I will slip into that "pretending." I want to know what drives you to attempt to do the task in performance, in front of people? Even when, by performing on a stage, it almost forces you to pretend. Why take that risk?

NB: People have asked me this before: why would I go onstage if I don't want to perform? I do it because I think we can *be* differently onstage. We can share something else besides a performance. It's a bigger communion. Having the audience on my mind always makes me feel that it has to be real—as real for them as it is for me.

NRT: And putting something onstage and insisting it has nothing to do with performance is the challenge, right?

NB: The stage is that challenge, yes. The stage was made to show people what you can do. This remains in the back of our minds when we step onto stage, thinking we must hold on to something to show the audience. But take this thought away and the ten meters of the stage becomes an infinite space! The moments in my life where I have touched that space are bigger than everything… I think I still have the courage and the energy to go onstage, just because I want to touch those moments again.

NRT: Yes, those moments are so powerful. It's funny to me that you describe the stage as an infinite space because I know you've fallen off stage!

NB: I have fallen twice! *[laughs]*

NRT: Right! There is a physical danger in letting go that allows for that communion. There's risk involved in trying to get to these amazing boundless states because it is in those places, I think, that I find myself feeling like I could disintegrate into nothing. I feel like I could lose my mind, and certainly, I have felt like I could spin off stage. I have asked myself, how do I open up and let go and surrender completely, without hurting myself? I know you are here, you've made it, so how do you negotiate that risk?

NB: Yes, it's a fine line between transcendence and spiritual experience, and just taking the risk on its own. The risk is part of the experience, but it's not the goal. I'm not taking risks just to take risks. I have to take the risk in order to go further. This is how it works. Otherwise, my fear takes over. The technical elements are important for this reason, and they contributed to the falls.

The first fall was in India. The stage was very small and we didn't have time to do a run-through. And there was a scene where I turn, turn, turn, and then I open up, open up, and go. Usually in a run-through, I open my perception to gain a measure of the physical space. But we didn't have time for the run-through; so I turned and turned and turned, and just fell off the stage.

The second time I fell, it was two meters off the edge of the stage! I was working with a technician that I didn't know for that show. My usual technician knows that there is deep risk in this work, and is aware of how it can be dangerous. In *Sur le fil* (2016) there are many little pieces of light. My usual technician knows to not put those spots of light too far downstage. He knows that our perception inside of it is so blurry that when we feel the last light, we should still have one or two meters of darkness and ground beyond it. But this other technician didn't really see what kind of state we get in—so he placed the edges of the light right along the edges of the stage. So when I felt the light, of course I thought that I still had more space. And I fell right off.

Even though these were big technical mistakes, something very important happened when I fell. I wasn't hurt and I think it was because I had no resistance. No fear. I had let go, fully. So, we have been working on a piece where we just fall. The real fall. We try to extend this space of freedom, while everything in you is falling [*shrieks*]. I'm scared, but I love it.

NRT: That sounds so exciting, but so challenging to keep yourself both open and safe within it. It's fascinating to hear that the edges of light are so important, because I have noticed how much darkness and blurriness there is in your work. I almost would describe it as "edgelessness." But there are *edges, there are boundaries that are essential. Even though there's this feeling of boundlessness, infiniteness, you still have to–*

NB: You have to put a frame there, a delimitation. You have to say, *inside* this space, I will let go. By combining the fall and the infinite space, you extend your consciousness on those two levels, which will keep you from hitting a wall, or someone else. You can't just close your eyes and let go. Your consciousness can throw an invisible thread into the space, a measure. That's how, even though I make pieces where performers could hurt themselves, they usually don't. Because they have this–

NRT: Frame.

NB: This question of frame and what the dancers share is important. They have to have a sense of solidarity between them and knowing that they're all going to take the risk, that they won't avoid it, but also that they'll be very aware and conscious about the whole thing. The dancers often say the hardest part is to be conscious while you let go. Because the letting go makes you go deep inside of yourself, and the consciousness keeps you aware of what's going on around you. I always say that it's a horizontal line and a vertical line. You have to work with both.

NRT: It seems so precise. Such a delicate balance. Have you ever felt yourself go to an extreme? Let go too far or start to pretend?

NB: Well, even after thirty years, I still don't trust myself. But I keep myself in this place that is deeply human. And I have so much vigilance with myself.

NRT: How do you get that sense of vigilance?

NB: This is a bit more personal, but I have faith. So I know there is something bigger than me: I am not the center; I am not the end of the thing. And I know that in this work, you may touch it today, and it may be gone the next day. That is why you must be vigilant, and how you become humble. There is humility. You can never master this. I know there are dancers who dream of mastering it, but even after many years, they are beside the thing.

NRT: But will they ever reach it, do you think?

NB: No. I have to accept that. Actually, it's my sister who has told me this a few times. She says, "Nacera, you have to accept that there will be different levels of communion. Everybody can't be at the same level of consciousness." That makes me feel a bit sad, though, and lonely on this earth.

NRT: But I wonder if there's something valuable about its impossibility too, about the way it can't be reached... Or the way you can't really set out to reach it, but you circle around it?

NB: I did not set out to work on transcendence. I just decided to try something, and it grew from there. It doesn't work if you want it too much.

For instance, I worked with this dancer who wanted the transcendence and freedom so badly, and she wasn't getting it. But one week before the performance, she got the bad news that her father-in-law died. So, she asked to leave for a couple days and then return before the performance. I don't fight against life, so I said of course. Just go. When she came back, I knew before we even performed that she was going to be right in it. I knew it. It's like a frequency that you catch. Mastering is probably something like that in my work, looking for a frequency. How do you say that, looking for a frequency? You have to tune yourself and find that precise place. And with my work, it is always hard to understand why it's happening now and not before.

This reminds me of a journalist who used to write about my work a lot, but would say he couldn't really connect to the work and didn't understand what I was looking for. That journalist came to the performance of *Le Cri* on the same day that a very famous French singer died–Alain Bashoung. The journalist wrote an article the next day, where he seemed to get the work. He was mixing his experience of the death of the singer and his experience of the piece. He was a big fan, you see. So, when this kind of event happens in life, bad or good, it hits you in a place that you don't usually touch when you go onstage, because you are performing—you are enacting a fake life. This is a place that doesn't resonate most of the time. But, because he had been hit in this deep place and came to see my work that same day, he found the right angle to see it.

So, similarly, when the dancer experienced the death of her father-in-law, it brought her to a new place where the performance part gets kind of pushed back. It's not the primary goal anymore, not the first thing on your mind because you have just gone through a very intense and real human experience. So, then she was in it as a human.

NRT: It makes sense to me that sometimes it takes death or grief to tap into that kind of vastness, that letting go... And I am still not sure if I let go fully in your work, in the way you wanted me to. But I do know what it took for me to get to a different level.

You remember probably, I was struggling to get to where you wanted us to be. I kept feeling and thinking that I was letting go, and you would say, "No, you're not letting go, Nora." [laughs] Where it changed for me was just before the performance itself. I had reached this moment where I knew I could ruin it. You couldn't say anything else, or tell me what to do, or that I was doing it wrong. I had to find my own way of getting there. The realization that I had to figure out how to be wind and be the circle by myself, that was an important step. It took this refusal, or kind of acceptance. I had to throw up my hands and say "Fine, I'm not doing it right, I guess."

NB: Yeah, I often tell my dancers, if someone pushed me every day to let go, I wouldn't let go either! [*laughs*] I'm the first to not let go. The only way that I can do it is through a process of talking to myself; saying, "okay, go, go, go, go, you're gonna go. You have to go, go go, go, go."

NRT: But also, the performance was special because we could immerse ourselves in that world of fog and dappled light and endless sound, which helped. I want to go back to how you work with light and sound, since they feel essential to the whole environment of your work. Do you work with a composer?

NB: No, I just connect sounds. While I'm working on a piece–it's like when you buy a car and you start to see the same car everywhere–any sound that brings me to that sensation or resonates with it, I just collect it, and I hear it everywhere. And then, I ask my technician to mix the sounds with another, taking away all the normal context. I make it more blurry. I work this way on the lights, on the sound, and on the body.

But I would say that it's much easier to work on the light and sound than with humans. I think when I get older, I will just do light and sound. Light doesn't have any ego. And then you have a human stepping onstage with his huge ego. The human has so many limitations. What's the point?

NRT: Well, maybe the point is that we can be light and sound. Maybe humans can be as malleable as light and sound, or at least attempt it.

NB: We can be! You can be infinite space! You have to relate yourself to the infinite space, relate yourself to the sound, relate to the darkness. If you try to *just* be yourself and perform in the middle of that, you become little. It is so easy to become little.

In 2006, I did a piece where for the first thirty minutes there was just light and sound, no dancers. I did not know how to enter, how to step in. Because when you have emptiness, the audience is looking at the whole space confidently and someone stepping in can reduce all that. But I had a video projection. We added light from the back and light inside the video itself, and you would start to see something–and it was my picture in the video. Once this picture appeared, I would appear alongside it, on the other side of the screen, and meet myself. Eventually the picture disappeared, and that was my entrance. This was the only way.

NRT: It allowed you to be more than one! It feels like one is more the opposite of empty than many is the opposite of empty. You coming in as one would have been more disruptive than you coming in as many versions of yourself.

NB: You're right. And that's why being alone onstage contains a big responsibility of staying wholly open. But for me, it's still easier to be alone than to connect myself to people who are closed. When I feel them close, I feel like someone is knocking at the door beside me. Someone knocking on the door of the cosmos! It can ruin the whole piece. But I can't make it easier, and I can't make it alone. It has to be human, and so it has to be fragile. But for some, the fear is so strong.

NRT: Right, the fear. I think what can cause resistance is the way fear has often been cultivated for good reason. Resistance exists because resistance has been necessary for survival in this world. This world is not infinite space, it is not hospitable. So, if we're living in that world where the fear is vital and trained, it feels endlessly complex to try to even look at that fear.

NB: I think that is why each person must take on the responsibility of it, instead of wondering how someone else will push the fear out of you. You have to know you'll have the strength or energy.

NRT: They each have to find their own way.

NB: Yeah, it's a human thing.

Nora Raine Thompson is a performance writer, dance-maker, and performer. She dances and writes to experiment with ways of gently dismantling constructions of selfhood. She is beginning a Ph.D. in Performance Studies at NYU in fall 2023.

Nacera Belaza was born in Medea, Algeria. Self-taught, she entered dance driven by the necessity to express herself and unravel the complexity of a dual cultural background. Her language emerged from her confined body, somehow imprisoned by cultural constraints during childhood and adolescence, drawing first from inner material, and later from literature.

Image: Nora Raine Thompson

I have never done fine art; what I would like to do is bad art.

What's the opposite of fine art? Bad art? Awful art? Gross art? Hateful art? Cheap art? Et cetera.
I did not study at the *Beaux-Arts* in Paris, but I studied at the Moches-Arts (Ugly-Arts) in Paris.
It is from this imaginary school that my artistic practices, and my emancipatory thoughts, result.

A real goddess is the witch of a stolen land

Sorour Darabi

Watching you,
from thorax to throat,
wave of your eyes in the sea-blood.
Sky dreams,
sulfate blue,
because it's not true:
a real goddess has no blood.
Like a witch,
the ocean knows
how deep it goes.
Fake goddesses for the fake world,
nowhere witch land,
sulfate blue ground,
the fluid extension
of your toxic body in the toxic land,
a fake goddess for the fake world.
Witches are from a stolen land.
Poison troubles your gaze,
black is the color of this haze.
Ocean knows
how deep it goes,
night

for *Natural Drama*, 2021

For several years, I have been developing work between dance, theater, visual art, song, and writing—giving special place to poetry and spoken word in my latest creations.

In these creations, I look for a liminal space, an in-between, where artistic expression can be free from the dominant social and political order. Being constantly manipulated by propaganda and dominant ideologies, how can we possibly transform this pressure of having to perceive the world in a certain way into a form of authentic presence? How can we accept "darkness" or obscurity as a bias in and towards life, consider darkness as an emancipatory aesthetic, instead of allowing ourselves to melt into normative thoughts?

Translated by ava ansari

At first, *Dance* appeared to be an inaccessible topic to me in a normalized sense. Before anything else, I am an underground dancer and choreographer, even before being a lonely eastern in the middle of the turbulent ocean of religious discrimination and racism in white Europe. Being an artist from the underground is a privilege to me because the blade of censorship cannot sever my freedom of expression and right to artistic choice. I have always approached dance in a certain way since the very beginning, even during my time in Iran, with the same aesthetics and styles evident in my recent productions.

At times, artistic directions taken by *us*—refugee artists exposed to Europe's relative freedoms—are perceived to deviate from—what might have been—back home, under the influence of the new environment. While the living conditions of an artist inevitably impact their artistic choices, we mustn't disregard personal subjectivity. Even in Iran, I harbored no desire to conform to classic elitist fundamentalist and constructive approaches to movement and dance. The principal questions of "who can dance?" and "which body is suitable?" have always struck me as inherently fascist. Since I was 18 or 19 and first began to explore dance as a topic, I have never felt influenced by famous dancers such as Forsythe or Charmatz. The first choreographer who gave me hope with my work was Meg Stuart. I believe that many of the issues in dance stem from an elitist perspective that places an undue emphasis on virtuosity. Elitism is like the bourgeoisie, a value that even those on the extreme left consider superior and aspire to but ultimately hate because they can't attain it and pretend to conflict with it. The slip happens when the hate caused by the "the lack of access" turns into our driving force and moves us into a collective counterpoint. It shouldn't. It creates a dangerous cycle where our desire to attain virtuosity becomes a source of conflict and division.

Instead, we have to build another culture, a culture inherently liberated from the "inaccessibility" complex that plagues the majority of dance. We must work to cultivate the courage within ourselves to stand proudly next to others, with our own values, without underestimating their values. Virtuosity can take on many forms, and we must not limit ourselves to the elitist's idea of what it is. As a choreographer, perhaps my ultimate goal is to prove that everyone has access to their own virtuosity; we just need to become familiar with it and trust it. It is ironic that in the progressive world of Europe, we claim to be aware of the diversities and capabilities of different humans and the differences in pedagogical systems that can contain those values, yet expect the same conservative feedback that has been the norm for the past thousand years. We continue to admire the rotten virtuoso approach; isn't this a sign that we didn't come to be anything new? We pretend to be more advanced than those in other parts of the world, deserving of more power and wealth, when in reality, we are no different from those who lack access to educational resources and welfare.

For me, research in movement involves developing variable dimensions unique to each project, encompassing intellectual, physical, musical, and sensual modes. The body that generates movement is rich with sensual, mental, and visual experiences delivered within a specific position and shared through one cohesive physical experience. This physical experience includes

رقص در ابتدا برای من یک مقوله‌ی غیر قابل دسترسی بود. غیر قابل دسترسی از منظر نرم (norm) ، نرم آنچه رقص در جامعه‌ی نرماتیو –کانسروتیو رقص اروپا تلقی می‌شود.
من قبل از هر چیز یک رقصنده و طراح حرکت زیرزمینی هستم، حتی قبل از اینکه یک شرقی تنها در میان دریای پرتلاطم تبعیض و نژادپرستی مذهب گرایانه در اروپای سفید باشم.
برای من زیرزمینی بودن یک انتخاب و یک حسن بود، چرا که به عنوان یک آرتیست نمی‌خواستم تیغ سانسور، آزادی بیان و حق انتخاب هنریم را سلاخی کند.
از همان ایران به مقوله‌ی رقص به شکلی می اندیشمندم که جهت‌گیری هنری و زیبایی‌شناسی امروزم را می‌شود در آن ردگیری کرد.
گاهی قضاوت می‌شود که جهت‌گیری هنری ما (هنرمندان پناهنده ی بهره مند از آزادی‌های نسبی در اروپا) تحت تاثیر شرایط ، به وجود آمده و ممکن بود در کشور خودمان متفاوت باشد. نمی شود شرایط زندگی یک هنرمند را در انتخاب های هنریش نادیده گرفت اما نباید سابجکتیویتی و عامل بودن او را منکر شد.
من حتا در ایران هرگز نخواستم وامدار زیبایی شناسی الیتیست، کلاسیک و تحت تاثیر نگاه بنیادگرایانه و ساختاری به رقص و حرکت باشم.
برای من اساس ایده‌ی این سوال که «چه کسی می‌تواند برقصد؟» و یا «چه بدنی؟» فاشیستی بود و هست.
من به طور واضح از همان ۱۸، ۱۹ سالگی که توانستم به رقص به گونه‌ای دسترسی پیدا کنم هرگز تحت تاثیر آرتیست‌های مطرحی چون فورساید، شارماتز و .. نبودم.
اولین طراح رقصی که مرا به کاری که می کنم امیدوار کرد: مگ استوارت بود.

به نظرم همه مشکل به ایده‌ی بیش از اندازه بزرگ شده‌ی «ویرتوئوزیته» از یک نقطه نظر الیتیست برمیگرده.
الیتیسم مثل بورژوازی می‌مونه، ارزشی که ناخودآگاه جمعی همه‌ی ما، حتا چپی‌های افراطی اون را والا و برتر طلقی می‌کند و نهایت آرزومون اینه که اونجا سوق پیدا کنیم. اما ازش متنفریم چون بهش دسترسی نداریم پس وانمود می‌کنیم که باهاش در تضاد هستیم.
من فکر می‌کنم اشتباه همین‌جاست، تنفر ناشی از عدم دسترسی به چیزی، نباید تبدیل به نیروی محرکه ی جمعی ما بشه که باهاش در جهت متضاد این ایده سوق پیدا کنیم یا در مقابل هم قرار گیریم.
ما باید فرهنگی دیگر بسازیم، فرهنگی که نیروی بلقوه‌ای داره و ذاتش به شکل مطلق از عقده‌ی حقارت «عدم دسترسی» به آنچه اکثریت به آن دسترسی دارد، سرچشمه نمی‌گیره.
ما باید باور داشته باشیم که ارزش‌های متفاوتی داریم بدون اینکه بقیه‌ی ارزش‌های انسان‌های دیگه رو نادیده بگیریم، ما باید با ارزش‌های خودمون در کنار بقیه با سرفرازی قرار بگیریم و برای این کار قاعدتن جسارت زیادی رو در خودمون باید تقویت کنیم.
«ویرتوئوزیته» ممکنه اپروچ‌های متفاوتی داشته باشه، تمام ویرتوئوزیته‌ای که ما می‌شناسیم نباید تنها ایده‌ی الیتیست ویرتوئوزیته باشد. شاید دلیل اینکه من کرئوگرافر هستم همینه، اینکه ثابت کنم که همه‌ی ما یا شاید بیشتر ما قدرت دسترسی به ویرتوئوزیته‌های شخصی خودمون رو داریم، فقط نیاز داریم که بهشون آشنا بشیم و بهشون اعتماد کنیم.
توی دنیای پروگرسیو اروپا خیلی ضد و نقیضه که ما به گوناگونی قابلیت آدم‌های مختلف و گوناگونی سیستم‌های آموزشی در خور آن اعتقاد پیدا کردیم اما هنوز انتظار همون بازخورد کهنه‌ی کنسرواتیو چنده هزار ساله قدیمی رو داریم. و هنوز تنها رویکردی رو که می‌تونیم تحسین کنیم همون رویکرد ویرتوئوز پوسیده است. معنی این تضاد آیا این نیست که ما به چیز جدیدی باور پیدا نکردیم بلکه وانمود می‌کنیم که انسان‌های پیشرفته‌ای هستیم؟
وانمود می‌کنیم انسان‌های پیشرفته‌تری از بقیه‌ی دنیا هستیم برای اینکه خودمان را شایسته‌ی قدرت و ثروت بیشتری جلوه دهیم در حالی که در اصل با بقیه‌ی دنیا که حتی شاید یک هزارم ما از دسترسی به این همه منابع آموزشی، رفاهی برخوردار نیستند هیچ تفاوتی نداریم.

ریسرچ برای حرکت برای من مقوله‌ایه که بسته به نوع پروژه، ابعاد مختلفی پیدا می کند.
یعنی در چندین بعد؛ انتلکتوئل، فیزیکی، موسیقایی، احساسی توسعه پیدا می‌کند.
بدنی که حرکت را تولید می‌کند بدنی مملوء از تجربه‌های احساسی، ذهنی و بصری متفاوت است که در وضعیتی خاص این تجربه‌ها را در خلال یک تجربه‌ی یکپارچه‌ی فیزیکی به اشتراک می گذارد. این «تجربه‌ی فیزیکی» همان طور که از انتخاب کلمه مشخص است می‌تواند جنبه‌های مختلف داشته باشد. تجربه‌ی فیزیکی یک احساس، تجربه‌ی فیزیکی یک نور، تجربه‌ی فیزیکی

Trans bodies, a diversity of gender expression, trans life experiences, trans voices, trans beauty aesthetics, the social and political place of trans people, trans sexualities…are and have been excluded from the majority of society's standards and norms since the dawn of time. As a trans artist, it is critical for me to open a space within my work that gives access to what has been made invisible, and to offer the contemporary artistic landscape multiple ways of glimpsing minorized bodies.

various facets, such as the physical experience of light and sound. I intend to focus on the physical experience itself rather than an interpretation of it. I hesitate to use the term translation. In the same way that transformation is different from translation, I see dance to be different from the translation of something such as sound in the language of the body. Similar to how it is impossible to translate a poem from one language to the other. Instead, we transform poems into different languages, like pouring water from one chalice to another!

Conservative approaches persistently separate dance from choreography. I don't insist on this division. Many, from and before my generation, have tried and continue to break this traditional belief. To me, choreography and dance are woven into one another and appear at once. This is the only way to escape the tiring dances, especially those designed with the dominating European contemporary dance aesthetics endorsed by all for an admiring beauty that bores me. I have never been able to watch Anne Teresa De Keersmaeker's to the end, I must confess, and she will probably never be a good viewer for my work. Her aesthetics are boring to me. She has worked hard to change the artistic heritage she is standing on; still, from the perspective of a human empty of bias towards this particular heritage, the traces are clearly visible in her work. These types of work are too obligated to receive and prove virtuosity and elitism so much so that they become empty of everything else.

Usually, all those who endorse these values and want to promote them are mesmerized by the capitals of the European micro bourgeois. Humans are either a part of that culture or terrified of being humiliated by it. I may sound like a leftist or an anarchist, but I'm just a free thinker who thinks freedom of speech is a populist illusion that won't be handed to us. So, we should be courageous to express ourselves freely and accept unexpected consequences. As I said, I do not separate dance from choreography, and for ease in work, I call both movement for the reader to understand without confusion. Movement is a process on the stage, and stages of practice, in manifestation.

In *Natural Drama*, I tackled the over-fetishized ideas of "nature" and "natural." The idea has always existed in a fundamental form in dance. We are aware of its highly exaggerated contrast in the cases where forms are inherently at odds with the idea of nature and natural forms. I am referring specifically to Isadora Duncan, as contemporary ideas of dance in Europe, and especially in Europe, are still secretly, deeply internalized values of what is more historically rooted in the classical, modern, and other related dance cultures. What is our understanding of nature today? When we refer to nature and naturalness, do we include the transformations caused by the definitions of nature in the last hundred years? Does something as *nature*, in the virgin sense of it that we seek, exist today? For instance, as trans bodies, we are considered by the majority to be basically unnatural; where does our existence fit into this idea of naturalism? Is it not that social and political mechanisms violently reject us? Is it not that we are not a part of the idea of what is truly natural in the pretending eyes and virtues of the powerful?

Movement is a constant tension and conflict between something intensely personal and something extremely public, between the inside and the outside. The gradual destruction caused by human encroachment and dominance over the environment and bodies of *us*, the non-white, female, trans, non-binary, and nonconforming gender human beings, is systematically denied by the powerful. Art, perhaps, should reflect the current world with a more genuine and liberated expression. Why does an artist like Jerome Bel, a white cisgender male, on the one hand, get to perform as a defender of the environment and, on the other hand, reenacts Isadora Duncan with big budgets, without the slightest responsibility

یک صدا.. منظور من از تجربه‌ی فیزیکی، ترجمه نیست. من از استفاده‌ی لغت «ترجمه» پرهیز می‌کنم. من فکر نمی‌کنم که رقص ترجمه‌ی مثلن یک صدا یا هرچیز دیگری به زبان بدن نیست.
همان قدر که ترنسفورمیشن با ترنسلیشن متفاوت است.
برای همین است که مثلن شعر را نمی‌شود در حقیقت از زبانی به زبان دیگر ترجمه کرد، بلکه ما شعر را در زبان های مختلف ترانسفورم می کنیم! مثل ریختن آب از ظرفی به ظرف دیگر.

در یک رویکرد کانسروتیو به کورئوگرافی، اصرار بر تفکیک رقص از کورئوگرافی پررنگ‌تر است.
من اصراری به تفکیک این دو ندارم، فکر می کنم خیلی از هم‌نسل‌های من و قبل‌تر از من هم سعی به در هم شکستن این باور سنتی داشته و دارند.
برای من کورئوگرافی و رقص در هم تنیده‌اند و با هم آشکار می‌شوند. این تنها راهی است برای فرار از رقص‌های کسل کننده‌ی طراحی شده‌ی بعضی از آرتیست‌های به خصوص.
زیبایی‌شناسی غالب (همه پسند) معاصر اروپا در زمینه‌ی رقص برای همه زیبایی ای تحسین کننده ولی برای من کسل کننده دارد. باید اعتراف کنم که هرگز نتوانستم هیچ کاری از آن ترزا دی-کریس می‌کر را به طور کامل ببینم و احتمالن او نیز هرگز نمی‌تواند تماشاگر خوبی برای کار من باشد. زیبایی‌شناسی او برای من بیش از حد کسل کننده و استوار بر میراث هنری ای است که هرچند او برای تغییرش زحمت زیادی کشیده است، اما از نقطه نظر انسانی که هیچ تعصبی به این میراث ندارد آن را در کارهایش به شکل کسل کننده ای آشکار می بینم. این گونه کارها بیش از حد پایبند و در تلاش اثبات ویرتوئوزیته و الیتیسم است تا جایی که از هر چیز دیگری خالی می شوند. معمولا تمام کسانی که این قسم ارزش‌ها را می‌پسندند و می‌خواهند رواج دهند بیش از اندازه مسحور جلب توجه سرمایه‌های خرده بورژواهای اروپایی هستند.
انسان‌هایی که یا جزئی از آن فرهنگ هستند یا از مورد تحقیر قرار گرفتن از سمت آن بی‌نهایت ترس دارند.
شاید به نظر برسد من چپ‌گرا یا آنارشیست هستم، من تنها آزاداندیش هستم و فکر می‌کنم آزادی بیان قاعدتن تنها یک توهم پوپولیست است و نباید منتظر باشیم که به ما پیشنهاد داده شود، باید برای بیانی آزاد جسارت داشته باشیم و بتوانیم عواقب غیرقابل منتظره‌ی آن را قبول کنیم.

همان طور که گفتم من رقص و کورئوگرافی را تفکیک نمی‌کنم. و برای سهولت کار به هر دوی اینها اسم حرکت را می‌دهم که خواننده گیج نشود.
حرکت یک پروسه است، چه بر روی صحنه و چه در زمان پیدایش‌های اولیه‌اش در روند کار.

در پروژه‌ی نچرال دراما، به ایده‌ی بیش از اندازه فتیشایز شده‌ی طبیعت و طبیعی پرداختم.
این ایده به شکل بنیادین همیشه در رقص وجود داشته، و ما آگاهی به تضاد به شدت مبالغه آمیزش در مواردی که فرم‌ها به شکل ذاتی به شدت با ایده‌ی آنچه طبیعت و فرم طبیعی است در تضاد بودند را داریم.
من به طور مشخص ایزادورا دانکن را مد نظر دارم، چرا که فکر می‌کنم ایده‌های معاصر رقص در اروپا (به خصوص در اروپا) هنوز به طور مخفیانه‌ای عمیقن ارزش‌های درونی شده‌ای از آنچه ریشه‌ای تاریخی‌تر در فرهنگ رقص کلاسیک، مدرن و الا آخر است را دارند.
استدلال ما امروز از طبیعت چیست؟ آیا وقتی به طبیعت و طبیعی بودن دلالت می‌کنیم دگرگونی‌های ناشی شده طی صده‌های اخیر را در تعریف «طبیعت» لحاظ می‌کنیم؟ آیا امروزه چیزی به اسم طبیعت، در معنای اصیلی از باکرگی آن دنبال می‌کنیم وجود دارد؟
به عنوان بدن‌های ترنس، که اساسن طبیعی تلقی نمی‌شویم، وجود ما در کجای این ایده قرار می‌گیرد؟ آیا برای این نیست که ما از جامعه و سازوکارهای سیاسی با خشونت تمام ترد می‌شویم این نیست که جزئی از ایده‌ای از آنچه طبیعی و یا نرمی که قدرتمندان وانمود می‌کنند هنوز صحت دارد تلقی نمی‌شویم. نابودی تدریجی ناشی از تجاوز و سلطه ی انسان بر روی محیط زیست به مثابه بدن‌های ما (غیر سفیدپوست‌ها، زن‌ها، ترنس‌ها، نون-باینری‌ها، انسان‌های جندر نون کامفورمینگ..) چیزی است که به شکلی سیستماتیک از سمت قدرتمداران انکار می‌شود. هنر شاید باید با بیانی آزادتر واقعیت کنونی دنیا را انعکاس دهد.
چرا آرتیستی مثل ژروم بل به شکل ملغطه‌واری به عنوان یک مرد سیس جندر سفید پوست از طرفی از طرفداران مدافع محیط زیست است و از طرف دیگر کارهای ایزادورا دانکن را با بودجه‌های کلان بازاجرا می‌کند بدون آنکه کوچک‌ترین مسئولیت‌پذیری در بازاندیشی آن‌ها داشته باشد. در واقع هنرمندی مثل ژروم با ایده‌های عامه‌پسندانه‌اش هم از توبره می‌خورد و هم از آخور.
هم مدافع محیط زیست است هم ایده‌های هنریش انکار واقعیت کنونی آن را ترویج می‌دهد؟
مثال‌هایی از این دست در جامه‌ی هنری اروپا کم نیستند.

A real and possible space could emerge beyond all binaries—binaries that are imposed on us and that we accept out of the fear of being excluded, of being sidelined. This binary is present in multiple political strata (right–left, man–woman, beautiful–ugly, them–us…). For some people, life is a constant negotiation between two extremes.

toward rethinking them? With his popular ideas, an artist like Jerome licks both ends of the sugarcane. How does he get to publicly defend the environment while his artistic ideas promote denial of its current reality? Examples of such are not few in the European art scene.

I recently worked on a project titled *From the Throat to the Dawn*, which was first performed at Palais de Tokyo and recently at Traumabar in Berlin. We may all know about the *House of The Pelvic Truth*, how inspiring Graham's technique has been for women, empowering their gender and sexuality by putting a lot of emphasis on incorporating the potential force of vagina. Since 2020, I have intended to use my technique to center the potential power of the anus in dance. Of course, anus has been a source of inspiration for many artists before and during my time. The anus is a common organ that we all have. It is beyond culture and sexuality; this mode of communication is very different. However, since the anus has been widely condemned in many cultures for hygiene reasons, majorly internalized through religions, we usually carry with it our shame and all of the heavy social and political baggage that comes with it in dance techniques, especially in Europe.

The extent of shame we sometimes carry toward our anus leads to our complete unconscious forgetting of it. The anus can be imagined as a potent force of creativity of which we are unaware. People who have a different relationship with their anus, due to their sexuality or culture or else, have their anus consistently more active in their conscious relationship with their body, of course. The anus is a part of the body that is neither entirely from the outside nor from the inside. It is something in between. Coagulated sphincters bring it closer to the inside, and expanded sphincters bring it closer to the outside. Just like the throat, and with sound quality, of course! Now, how can dance turn with this awareness? Sometimes movement is like superhuman fluid energy to me, a cyborg born from our physical struggles that appears momentarily and then remains in space for eternity. It is like desire, movement. Perhaps that is why it should not be irrigated, as it will be lost. That is why I do not understand the elitists' efforts to gain Dance, as it is not something to gain but to let go of to emerge, to release to appear, to be.

* * *

حرکت برای من یک تنش و درگیری مستمر بین چیزی به شدت شخصی و چیزی به شدت عمومی است. بین درون و بیرون. من به تازگی بر روی پروژه ای کار کردم که «From the Throat to the Dawn» نام دارد. این اجرا برای اولین بار در Palais de Tokyo و اخیرا در Traumabar در برلین بازاجرا شد. ما شاید همه در مورد «house of the Pelvic Truth» شنیده باشیم و تکنیک گراهام که چقدر به نوعی در توانمندسازی زنان از نقطه نظر جنسی و جنسیتی الهام‌بخش بوده است چرا که تاکید زیادی بر به کارگیری نیروی بلقوه‌ی واژن در تکنیکش تاکید داشته است. من از ۲۰۲۰ در صدد به کارگیری تکنیک شخصی مبنی بر چگونگی بکارگیری نیروی بلغوه‌ی مقعدی در رقص هستم. قاعدتن قبل از من و همزمان با من آرتیست‌های زیادی مقعد برایشان الهام بخش بوده است.

مقعد عضو مشترکی است که همه‌ی ما از آن برخوردار هستیم. فراخور فرهنگ، سکچوالیتیو..

نوع این ارتباط بسیار متفاوت است. اما از آنجا که مقعد اصولن در بسیاری از فرهنگ‌ها به دلایل نظافتی که تا حد زیادی از طریق مذهب‌ها در ما درونی شده‌اند و همچنین تمام بار سنگین اجتماعی و سیاسی که با خود به همراه دارد، معمولن در تکنیک رقص به خصوص در اروپا تا حد زیادی مورد نکوهش قرار می‌گیرد. اینکه تا چه حد ما از مقعد خود گاهی شرم داریم باعث می‌شود که ناخودآگاه آن را کاملن فراموش کنیم. این در حالی است که مقعد می‌تواند نیروی و خلاقیت بلقوه‌ای باشد که ما از آن آگاه نیستیم. انسان‌های که به دلیل سکچوالیتی و یا فرهنگی یا خر چیز دیگر با مقعد خود رابطه‌ی متفاوتی دارند، قاعدتن مقعدشان به طور مداوم در رابطه‌ی خودآگاهشان با بدنشان بیشتر فعال است.

رقصیدن با وجود این آگاهی چه تغییری می‌تواند داشته باشد.

به علاوه مقعد یک عضو از بدن است که نه به طور کامل به بیرون و نه به طور کامل به درون تعلق دارد.

چیزی بینابینی است.

اسفنکترهای منعقد آن را بیشتر به درون و اسفنکترهای منبسط آن را به گونه‌ای به بیرون بیشتر نزدیک می‌کنند.

درست مثل گلو و البته خاصیت صدا !

حرکت گاهی برای من یک انرژی فرا-بشری سیال است. یک سایبورگ که از تقلاهای فیزیکی ما زاده می شود و برای لحظه‌ای پدیدار و بعد در فضا برای ابدیت باقی می‌ماند.

حرکت مثل اشتیاق (désire) است، برای همین است شاید که نباید سیراب شود چون از دست می‌رود. برای همین است که الیتیسم را نمی‌فهمم چون سعی به دست آوردنش را دارد، حرکت به دست آوردنی نیست، باید رهایش کرد که ظهور کند، که باشد.

Sorour Darabi (Iran) is a self-taught artist living and working in Paris. Working actively in Iran, s/he was a part of the underground organisation ICCD, whose festival Untimely (Teheran) hosted their work before their departure for France.

Ava Ansari is a Farsi interpreter, transmedia poet, transcultural curator, and yogi working with the sensual, institutional, and digital bodies. Their practice lives at the intersections of choreographic, linguistic, musical, and spatial composition; heterotopic healing and radical cyber celebration; and translingual embodiment and bodies' free navigation.

It is important to me to believe that things can be porous and fluid.

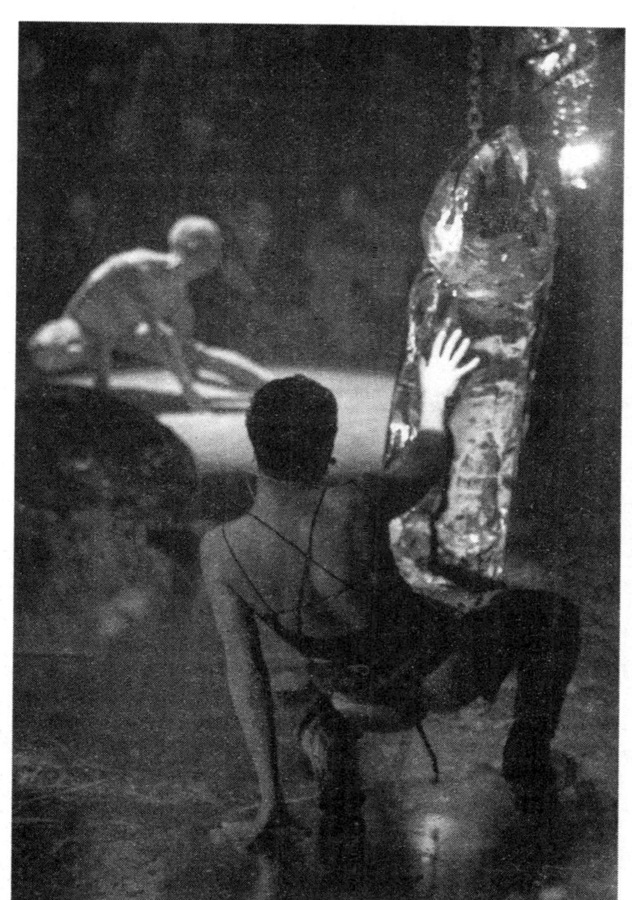

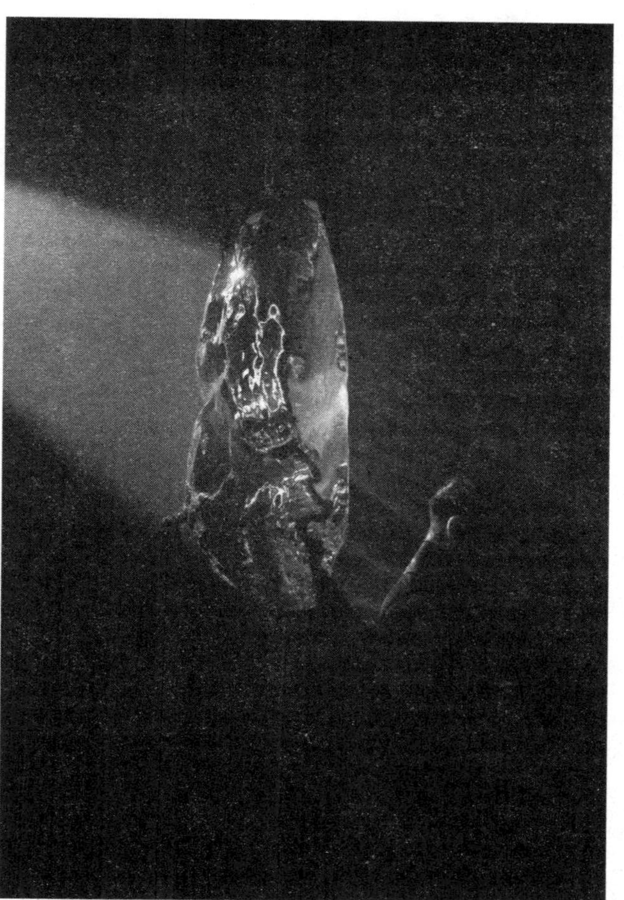

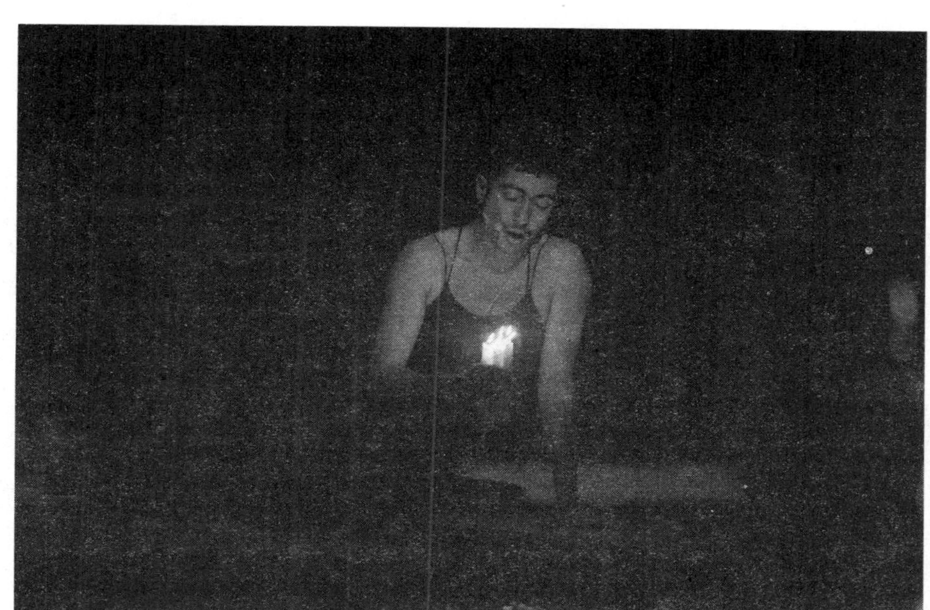

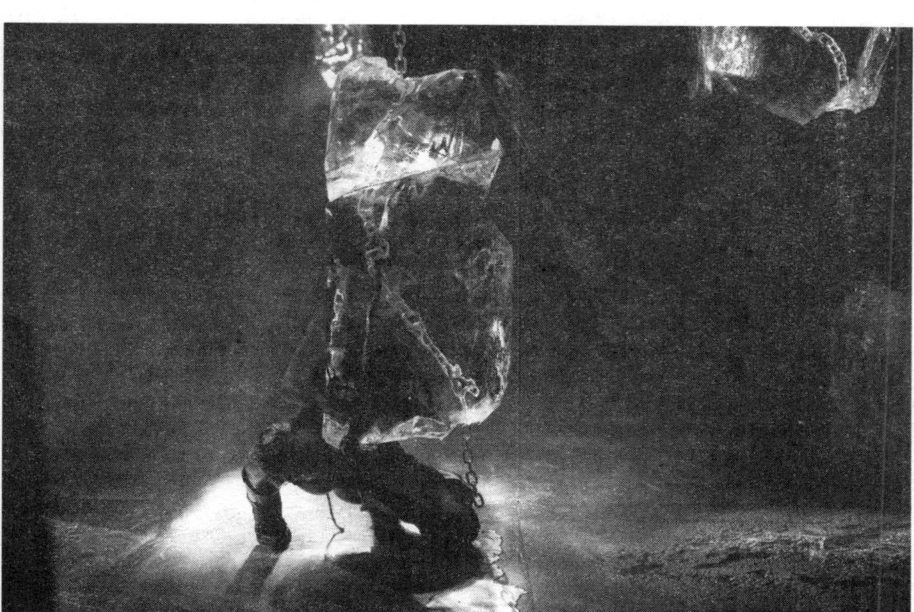

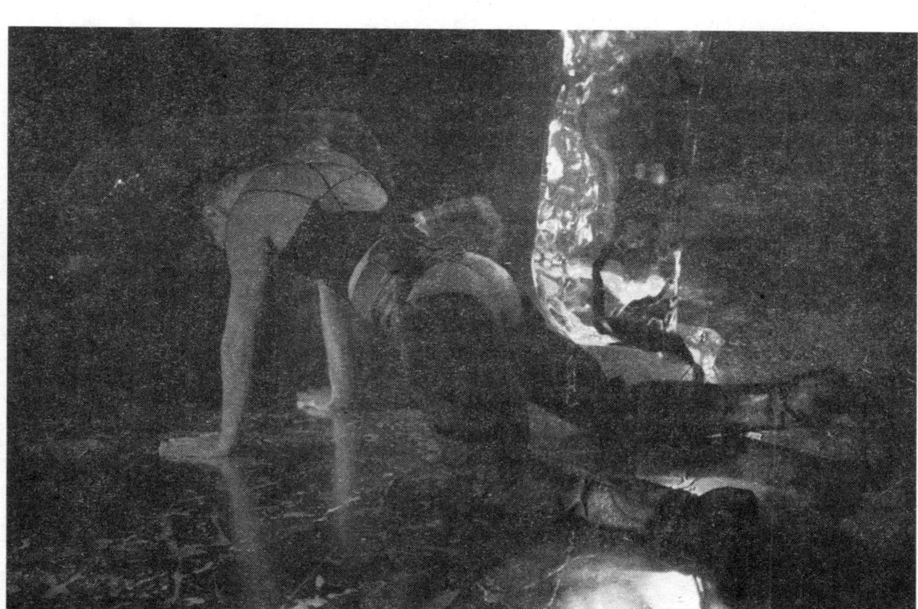

From The Throat To The Dawn
at Trauma Bar und Kino. January 20–21, 2023.

Photos: Camille Blake

From a purely somatic point of view, my body was attacked by an external agent that knew, very well, how to creep inside and settle for some time. That time has been twenty-seven months and counting…

This invasion came after a seven-year journey of observing the body every single day, following the movement wherever it would take me. The bare gist of your many transformations being realized through the simplicity of a body in movement. The manifestation of your distillment. Timelessly present.

Yes, one day it all came to a very abrupt end, and only because someone else had the malice and audacity to make that happen.
To bring movement into stillness. But it wasn't only stillness — for nothing could be calm, nor uninterrupted, after this moment of movement's arrest.

The first observation of the body in this situation came up later in this literal nightmare, long after the severe pain had settled into the body and the spirit, deeply. Pain, pain, and more pain: coming, gathering, accumulating, perpetuating. Stillness, in the sense of stagnancy, and death had enclosed the body inside a dark and eternal abyss. Never-ending, no thought of movement; no desire to breathe, let alone move. Expression faded out. Constriction multiplied.

Six, seven months of constant physical therapy, running to alleviate the angst, yoga to stabilize the body-mind apparatus, and tons of reflection together with an always-present frustration about the (im)possibility of a return to the moving body. Years passed: one, two… the body/spirit enslaved by hatred, fear, and darkness; devoid of dance, deprived of self.

The subject of this attack was the body itself; it had to be erased, for it posed great danger to those who feared it dance. Somewhere throughout this unfortunate petrification, a question presented itself — what happens to a dancing body when dance is taken away? Trauma is differently experienced and processed through the psyche and the soma. Could I not have been able to just move the body and live through the experience and thrive like the phoenix from the ashes, gently shaking away the remains of every cell of the body scorched and reduced to ash?

Perhaps someone else might have been able to live up to that choice. My truth, though, was mostly that of pain and the utter inhibition of the body. The mind finds ways, despite the body, to break free from this darkest tunnel. The wisdom of the body is ancient and futuristic, beyond time and space. It has a desire to awaken and a willingness to dance.

Abisa Serin
Tehran, Iran
February 24, 2023

Breaking Away

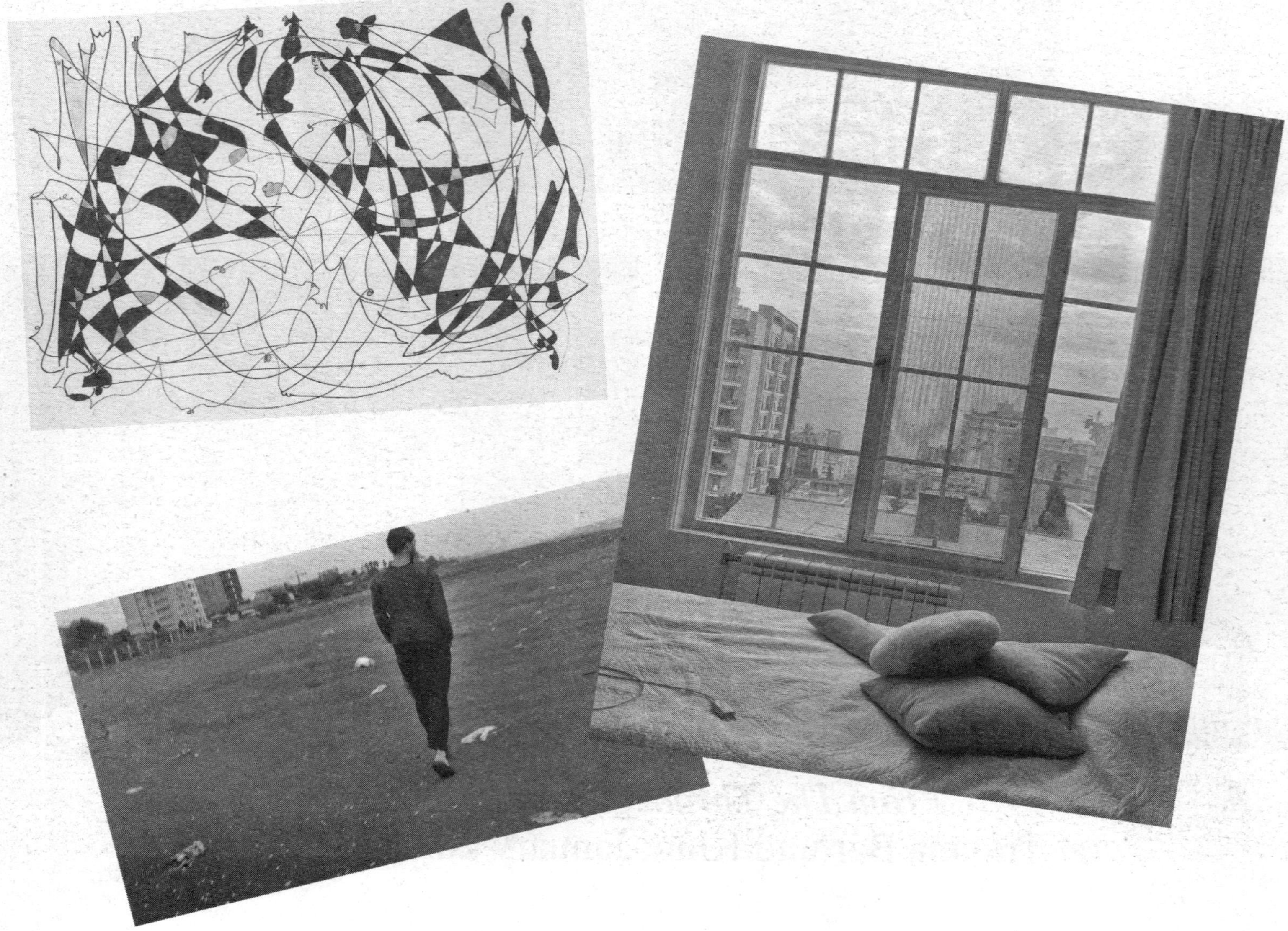

Abisa Serin is a pseudonym.

aeroplanes, fake flowers, and meditation soundtrack

Tiran Willemse

sidewalk, pathways, pavement, roadside, traffic light, boulevard, highway, drive through, Texas, street corner, pedestrian, in between, me and you, back of car, Mulholland Drive, basement, interval ticket office, stairs to his bedroom, standing at the back of the concert, dancing at the side of the dance floor, mourning in private. Uncomfortable with a group of closest friends, a handsome piece of deformity and perfect state of distortion, "fuck coca cola, sprite for life."

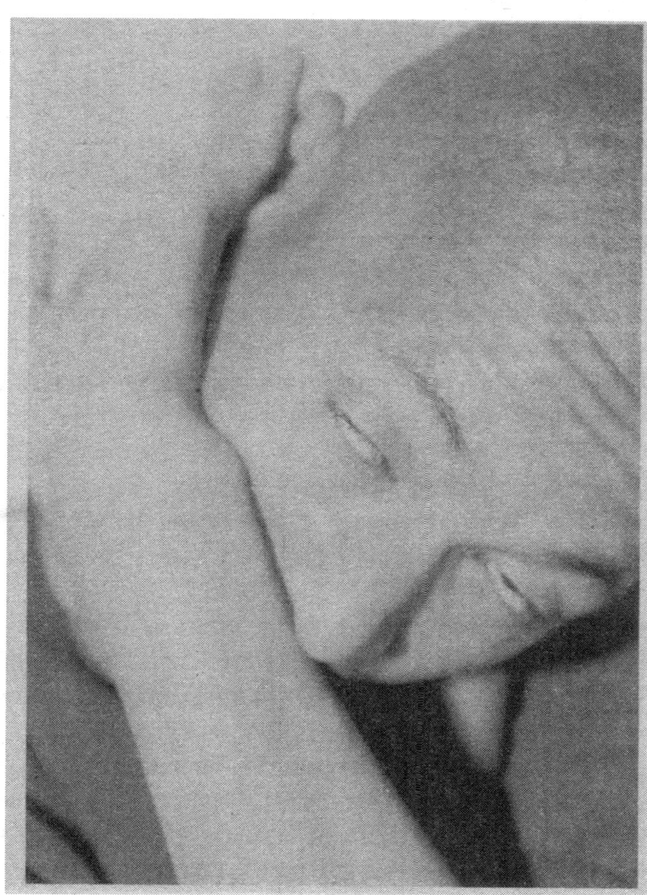

Lights on, audience, full-on script, real Shakespearean shit. Fully embodied delicacy. We are, we are not. Feeling beyond revolution, material desire, pain, love, love, pain. Rivers flowing, sea breeze, compressing, compressing thin air into no air. Speed, trains, prayer, movement, three hundred kilometers per hour, standing in front of a mountain. Total freedom. Don't try to understand it, just feel it. At peace with paper planes landing in space. Fake flowers and meditation soundtrack. Doctor's office, no infection, just politics numbing my senses.

I wonder if I was in reality or outside it.

An extension of me, physical absence, thirteen-hour flight from Cape Town to London, thrown off balance, sitting, moving, disembodied, not fully present, alienation. Crossed lines, situations, people, and borders. The pressure, depression, air pressure, scream. Agonizing tenderness flying in the air, long distances of torture that I've been carrying through generations.

Monuments, smoke machines, strobe lights, empty fields with nothing but beautiful flashing lights. Red, orange, yellow states affairs. Grey zones. Amsterdam to Los Angeles, São Paulo to Dakar, Helsinki to Moscow, Toronto to Istanbul, Mumbai to Bangkok. It's all so small you can't really see anything, microscopic time traveling, time machine, machine man, man, voices, voices whispering, sounds turning into zero seasons, fall, winter, winter, fall. No spring, no summer. Unpredictable anthropomorphism. Phone bills. Calling my mother from Rio to Cape Town. Best friend from Toronto to Berlin. Boyfriend from Seattle to Paris. Long-distance relationships, strange conditions, feelings in Marrakech but stuck in Stockholm, bad weather, war thunder, grey desires, ongoing challenges, cobble stones, early appointments which I'm always too late for. Wish I could have stayed longer.

"I can't tell you what it really is, I can only tell you what it feels like."

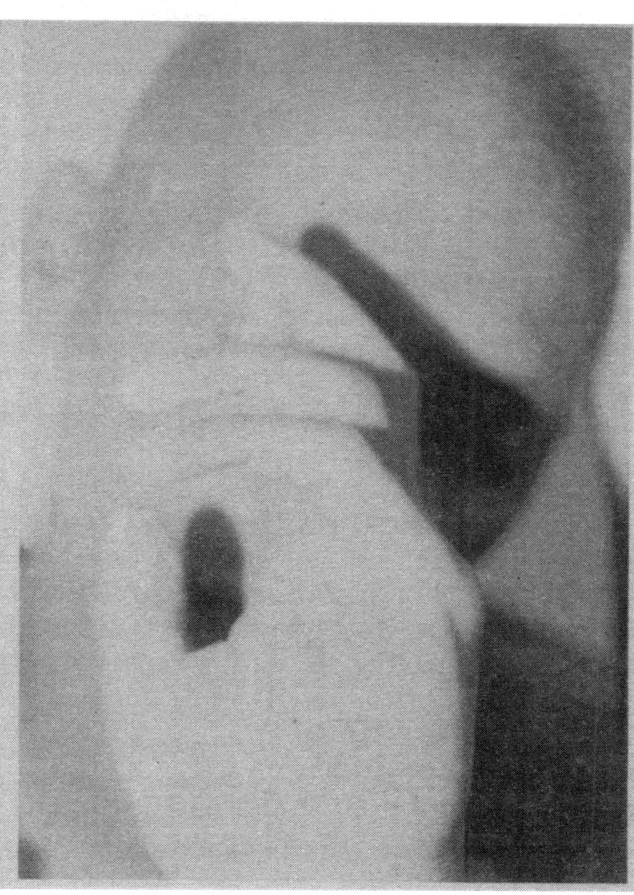

Left to suffer in virtual isolation with a feeling I don't understand. Feelings faster than an algorithm. The kind of feeling one can't describe, that makes your knees weak just thinking of it. Eyes wide open, falling into it so deep. You won't go but I'll go. What matters is the one thing I really wanted. This thing, something, only things. The only satisfaction. The beginning and end of everything. My house, my body, yours? Reincarnate yourself in me. Inhabit me, live in me, don't leave, hold on, dirty, stay in me. Forever and ever. Everything good is always somewhere else, even when you look the part. Closer please come home.

Stand there. Stand there. Stand there. Repeat the cues over and over, till it's perfect.

think: brain
see: eyes
face: me

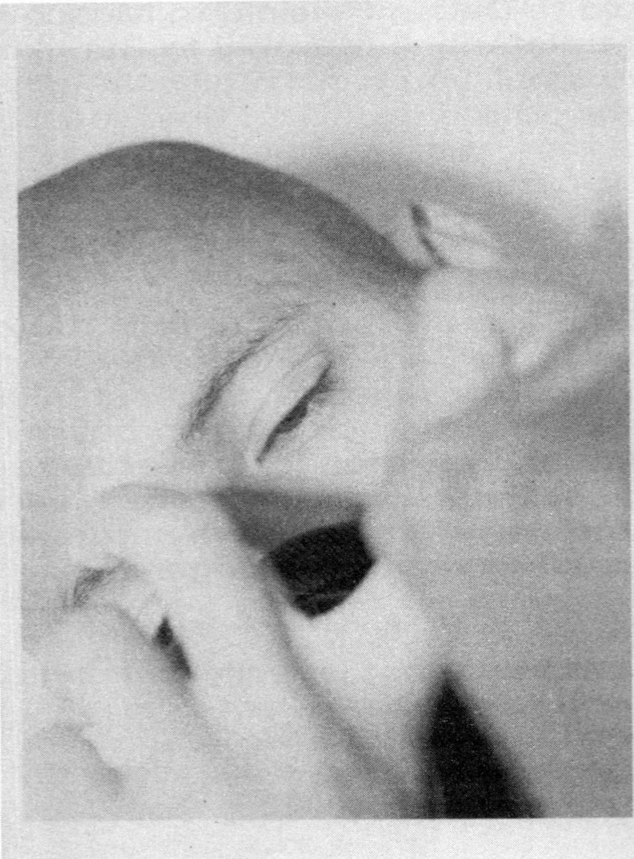

confusion: headache
A strange alliance of blindness and madness
upside - down inside - out
bringing the underground to the main floor
the sides to the centre, look out, there's also something over there.
when the smoke clears, we open the roof

we move on so quick to the next part Cause it's an experiment
It's like trial and error All measurable values
That will make you feel in a very specific way.
And if it's cut directly, it will probably feel violent
It's gonna feel sacrificial
It's gonna feel Fleeting
It's gonna feel like it's in danger or something.

When it's this close, like
OH,
I remember
I remember what my mind was
Before the thing happened that ruined it
I remember who I am not
And I don't need to sleep on the sidewalk
If this is a dream then make it come true
Let me step back into my body and start dancing
Dancing to be more, more of who I am,
More black, more queer, more fem
There is conflict and a desire to keep things together when I dance. A driving force that recognizes two tendencies and sees them as ways to make things happen
BlackWhite
MascFEM
KanyeWestLanaDelRey
VirginiaWoolfJamesBaldwin
SoftHard
BoringEntertainment
awkwardlygenuine
skillfullyunfit
LameMagic
LowQuality
Now you see me Now you don't
he loves me he loves me not
The space of them has never been can also be as close as when they're all inside my brain
Penetrating organs, blood and guts everywhere. Inhabiting the fragility of obscurity, not understanding and accepting a non-binary state
Open borders, let's not get too used to this place. Inhabit practice or craft with a strong motivation but with a distance what I create can disappear at any moment, how movement happens. It is not about inhabiting form but feeling for imagination and potentiality which allows the lines to crack and reveal what lies beyond, beyond what we know — welcome these unknown wonders.
contradiction to critique and simultaneously celebrate
futurehistory: forever time traveling.
I genuinely feel and see so much my instincts just react to what is at play; I even become unfamiliar to myself when I dance.
Connecting to them who have been and those who are coming, you might not see it but you will feel it, that's my offering to you, to myself and my craft. Once I am in front of you ill fuckin go for it.
You can't ghost a ghost but you can try.

Tiran Willemse is a dancer, choreographer, and researcher from South Africa based in Zurich and Berlin. Their performance practice is rooted in a careful attention to space, imagination, gesture, and sound, focusing on how they relate to the ways in which constructions of race and gender are performed, communicated, and challenged. They're interested creating experiences that communicate somatic and psychological landscapes beyond the human condition. Since 2022, he is house artists at Gessnerallee in Zurich, and their work continues touring internationally.

Since 2006, I have taught intensive studio courses titled *Delicious Movement: Time is Not Even, Space is Not Empty* at Wesleyan University, New York University, Colorado College, and the University of Tokyo. Accommodating my performing schedule, I teach in different lengths at each school with an average of two, eight-week courses per year. All are with similar content and the same style, though I always adjust to what is happening in the world and with each particular group of students.

Commissioned to be included in the book *Art That Inspires and Communicates*, soon to be published in Japan, I first wrote this text in Japanese. One of the book's editors hosted my course at the University of Tokyo and asked me to write how I teach as practically as possible. He is one of three professors who took my course as full participants.

Encouraged by such curious, open-minded teachers, I decided to offer its English version to teachers, students, and movement practitioners in my community here. After Shingo Umehara translated the original Japanese text into English, I revised it. I hope you find an idea or two to ponder.

Eiko Otake

Memo on Teaching Delicious Movement: Time is Not Even, Space is Not Empty

[1]

Why I teach

We reside in our bodies. My work as a performing artist is physical as well as mental. I am interested in observing and feeling many kinds of movement, not limited to that of human bodies.

As an artist, I resist any label, particularly Butoh, since it happens to be the one people want to use for me the most. When I was 19, I lived in Tatsumi Hijikata's studio for three months and left it with Koma. Later we went to Kazuo Ohno's improvisation class twice a week. They were differently amazing artists and their oddness was liberating, but we left both of them quickly, to their puzzlement. Practicing autonomy has been more important for me than being a good student.

My partner Koma and I left Japan in 1972 when I was 20. While we studied with Manja Chmiel in Germany for about nine months, we began performing in Europe. We moved to New York in 1976 and immediately presented our own works and kept making new pieces. I am in the New York downtown dance community, but I do not use techniques from American modern dance, because I hardly took classes in the U.S.

[2]

The only exceptions were Anna Halprin's one-day workshops and Elaine Summers' Kinetic Awareness classes.

When I experienced 9/11 in New York, I was about to turn 50. We had a studio throughout the year 2000 on the 91st floor of the North Tower of the Trade Center. Seeing the towers fall from my apartment window, I was shaken. I realized that by disregarding the terrorists' attack eight years prior, my guard to the world was completely down. I shivered thinking I had put my assistants' lives in danger. The sense of regret pushed me to go to graduate school to study the history of massive violence, in particular artistic representation of the human experiences of the atomic bombings. My thesis was on writer Kyoko Hayashi, a Nagasaki A-bomb survivor. I translated her short novel *From Trinity to Trinity* and published it along with my essay. The same year, I started teaching a course that combines learning about the atomic bombings with the study of body and movement. Though I had often taught dance workshops since the early 1980s, teaching an interdisciplinary, graded course at a university brought me a different sense of responsibility and gravity.

[3]

In every class, my students moved me to tears. I have so much to learn from a generation as many as fifty years younger than I. And they make me feel that I, as an analogue generation, have something to offer them, and that I cannot afford to be nihilistic. To my delight, I often find my former students when I perform. Some students become young friends and collaborators, not by my choice but by theirs. Loving them makes me want to die before them. I do not want to break the order. Having students in my life has changed my sense of positionality to the larger society and brought different notions to why and how I create and perform.

[4]

How I teach

- Teachers do not choose students; students choose teachers. I am interested in knowing why and how each individual student comes to my class and chooses to stay. I want to be useful to them.
- No one can or should trust others at their first meeting. I say so to my students in my first class. Deep learning happens when students and teachers work hard toward gaining trust from each other. I want my class to be where my students discover longtime friends.
- I ask my students to learn voraciously, using their bodies, brains, and all their senses. I want their learning to be radical, physical, and memorable.
- I think a lot about how I can help students to acquire knowledge and thoughts that they will remember. If easily forgotten, it is not learning. I want students to choose what to remember and how to use what they remember. We forget easily what we are told and what we read, but we remember strong physical and/or emotional experiences. We also remember our own discoveries and thoughts we worked hard on. Hence, I try to create time and space

[5]

in which the students use their bodies to think, rejoice at their "Aha!" moments, and actively linger at their "whmmmm" moments.
- I teach in a studio without chairs, desks, or shoes. We also work a lot outside. We do not avoid undesirable conditions. We have to learn how to expose our bodies to heat, cold, wind, noise, and strangers' gazes. We work on uneven and dirty surfaces. However, I am mindful of my students' safety.
- Students move feeling their own bodies. One, two, or three people perform in front of others. Watchers feel their own bodies and those of the movers. Being watched and watching others are often challenging but profound experiences.
- Through hard-to-swallow reading, intimate discussion, journal writing, and movement work, students also uncover what has been stored in their bodies. The body is conservative. There are times when the brain knows but the body does not, and other times when the brain forgets but the body remembers. Past traumas or unsolved nuances may be stored somewhere in the body.
- I dissect my working-artist-self and share my sources and influences. I show my videos and perform in class. We eat together, and they read books and articles I am enthusiastic about.

[6]

- Students can learn not only from studying with academic scholars, but also from working with field professionals and artists, who have particular, practical experiences and layers of episodic knowledge. Being with these practitioners, students hear their voices, sense their tones, and see their bodies in action. Those are valuable, personal experiences.
- I do not teach art-making, choreography or dancing. No previous movement work is required. I say so clearly in my course description. This is not that I discourage art-making. Whether my students become professional artists or not is not important to me. I want to help them in becoming whom they wish to become. I ask students whether they have been moved by art, and if so, why and how. What were their physical and emotional states when they were moved? What do they remember? I think when we are moved by an artwork, we tend to feel positive about ourselves. It is hard to hate oneself when one is being moved by beauty in art or by strength in an artist. Seeing, hearing, and experiencing art is a process of discovering and nurturing one's own sensibilities.
- I actively seek diverse participants and students from various majors, so we can learn from each other. Moving together, students

[7]

get to know their classmates. Observing each other, they learn to respect plural bodies. By sharing journals and conversing, students learn different experiences, voices, backgrounds, and sensitivities. In the process we find and challenge our assumptions. Society will not change just because some people become smarter. How can we help each other so we all learn but differently?
- The class is a place to practice democracy that does not rely solely on majority rule. For democracy to function, there must be a mechanism that listens to the voices excluded by majority rule. The laws and restrictions that win majority votes should not be automatically imposed. Before doing so, we need to imagine and debate who is hurt and what is lost. Only after that, we vote again or find alternative ways of decision-making. Students and I learn that democracy requires many steps and efforts.
- Nonviolence does not mean to not fight; it is to fight while forbidding ourselves from harming lives of others. It requires our commitment and effortful communication. Debate, movement work, just being with and getting to know "others" can be effective training.
- Rules can and should be broken when necessary, but carefully. We should avoid being overtly restricted by rules. However,

 [8]

we cannot break too many rules at once. We must consider the consequences of ignoring rules. We practice physical sympathy through movement work in the studio where we must be mindful of everyone's safety and hurtful consequences.

- I create my syllabus in a way where I lead the class activities at the onset, but as the course progresses, the students are expected to contribute more to the class. By the end, students should own the course and their learning. I adjust my online syllabus before and after each class, so I tell my students to never print it.
- Students read and discuss time, distance, history, the environment, nuclear issues, war, other massive violence, democracy, and fragility of life. My syllabus focuses on nuclear issues: human experiences and environmental damage of atomic bombings, the Manhattan Project, and nuclear meltdowns. This is not because I am Japanese, but because I think nuclear issues are universally, existentially threatening.
- By collapsing our sense of distance to people far away from difficult subject matters, we can alter our chronic indifference.

[9]

Movement Instructions

- Lie on the floor, eyes closed, and move slowly. Observe your body. Allow yourself to not be productive. Actively forget your name and your plans.
- Move your body without a need to express yourself. Rest and sabotage are also movements.
- Move on the floor for a very long time. Let your perspective, from which you observe society and other beings, change.
- Move on the floor. Free yourself from the assumed notions that dance requires healthy, able-bodied, and rhythmic movement.
- Explore animals, plants, minerals, things, and the environment through the body. Move closer to them and discover similarities and differences between yourself and other beings. Experience limits and boundaries of being human.
- Do not move in symmetry. The body is not symmetrical. Free the body from appearance and form. Think of it from the inside.
- Move to think, move to know. Feel movement even in the midst of what seems to be stillness. There is no stillness in the living body.

[10]

- Move to grasp the different movements of time. Feel the unevenness of time.
- Think of the body as a place and a landscape. Places and landscapes are also bodies.
- Work in pairs and trios. Support each other's body and movement. Afterwards, just as important: work alone. That aloneness is rich with memories.
- Do not use music. To move in silence is to leave one's reliance on music. Free movements from the so-called "dance." Take in movements of society, leaves, rivers, clouds, time, et cetera.
- Move in front of others, be seen, and be aware of being seen. Learn to observe yourself from the outside and to understand your own relativity to others.
- See how each classmate moves differently with the same prompt.
- When seeing others move, imagine what's happening inside them. Feel involved but not to the whole person. Observe body parts and particular segments of time. When feeling involved, you might experience some discomfort or disappointment. That is okay. That person who is moving is not you. Involved seeing helps you notice and nurture your own aesthetics.

[11]

- Say or show "No" when necessary. People can be differently hesitant about being seen, being touched, or touching other bodies. It is possible for you to not want to participate immediately but feel more comfortable doing so after you observe others do the work.
- I do not teach existing dance techniques nor choreography. What I teach is largely what I made up, so I can say to my students: Please take what you want and reinvent it. Please do not credit me. I do not want to be responsible to your invention. Students are accountable in elaborating their learning.
- Dance alone in a safe place to review movement prompts and create new ones for yourself and to share with others.

[12]

Talking and Listening

- I often ask students to talk in small groups about their experience of moving, without me joining their conversation. I just observe the atmosphere of the room and the expressions of students during their small group discussions. I want them to notice without my guidance that after movement work, conversation becomes nuanced and wording more precise. That is profound. How to communicate in words what we have learned without language?
- It is always okay to talk or to not talk. Talking is not obligatory. We all have to learn how to enjoy silence in discussion and use it for our own reflections.
- At times, they talk to each other immediately after the movement. At other times, I ask them to take time alone before talking to each other. Every routine should have variations.
- When we shift from small groups to a whole class discussion, I ask students to share with the class what they have heard and what has stayed with them, not what they have said or thought. This is to avoid only a handful students dominating the discussion. We learn

[13]

to listen more actively and intently when we are tasked to report back to the whole class. To become a conduit and effectively introduce the thoughts and opinions of others is a powerful skill that supports democracy.

- Students individually and collectively find possible connections between the assigned readings and movement work. I do not make that explicit or clear. I ask them to not pay overt attention to the particular reading assignment and particular movement work of the week. Instead, I ask them to connect among all accumulated readings and movement experiences. And without a particular "answer" to connect parts, they could learn a lot from each part.

[14]

Homework

- Students read assigned literature (Kyoko Hayashi, Kenzaburo Oe, Michiko Ishimure, et cetera.) and watch films (*Atomic Café*, my *A Body in Fukushima* et cetera)
- Reading is an experience. I also assign a particular task to each reading to select and read aloud, handwrite, or memorize passages; point out some details that connect or reveal the core of the work, and draw scene(s) of their choice. Why and what do you choose to remember? These tasks are shared in class.
- Students will reflect on what they learn in class by writing a journal entry between each class. The journal is freeform. There is no set format or word limit. I ask them to write their journals until they find themselves writing something they have not planned to write.
- Students share their journals as much as they are comfortable to share. They learn from each other by reading classmates' journals. People notice different things.
- I ask students to not end their journals with a question. Doing so might feel stylish, but I want them to put some effort into answering their own questions with their own words, even though

[15]

doing so might feel clumsy and less smart.

- I read through all journal entries and respond. It is quite a task, but I feel it is important for students to know I read them.
- All students write one Op-Ed during the course. They develop opinions from what they have written in their journals. Working with a small group, they revise and rewrite, making sure opinions are clear and persuasive. How to be persuasive to others yet open to new possibilities?
- All students write a letter to one of the authors of the assigned readings. I encourage students to write to an author who is no longer alive.

[16]

Final Projects

- All students will work on their own final project to deepen and expand the syllabus, and contribute to the learning of their classmates. The subject matter should be relevant to the syllabus; students set up their own questions, research, and plan how to use/place their bodies.
- Deciding on a title creates direction, though one can always change the title. A title works as a compass and an anchor in pursuing one's own project.
- I ask students to share their research questions and present findings in creative and captivating ways. They have to learn how to advocate for their projects and raise interest from others.
- Presentations should be low-cost and low-tech.
- They must prepare and practice their presentations.
- Everyone must be present for everyone else's presentations.
- Everyone shares individual responses to each presenter by talking and/or writing. That is not to make any work better, but for self-expression and mutual discoveries.

[17]

Miscellaneous

- I do not allow students to call me a professor. I instruct them to address me by my first name, Eiko.
- I ask my students not to use "interesting," "cool," and "I can't (even) imagine" in class discussion or in their journals. The first two are so overused. The last expression is usually used in sympathy but allows little effort in knowing and imagining others. Students and I bang the floor whenever we hear these words in class, and the speaker has to rephrase them, which sometimes takes some time to ponder. Over the course, students become aware of how often these words are used to spare us the effort of articulation and imagination.
- I avoid having too many dancers in my class. People who have learned to move like "dancers" could discourage others to move on their own terms.
- My classes are open to visitors—past students, their family members, and guests.
- I give all students my cell phone number and encourage them to call me without an appointment. I try to pick up whenever possible. I am aware I can do this because I teach for only part of the year.
- After the last class, I hand out my movement manifesto below.

Born and raised in Japan and a resident of New York since 1976, **Eiko Otake** is a movement–based, interdisciplinary artist. After working for more than 40 years as Eiko & Koma, she now performs as a soloist and directs her own projects collaborating with a diverse range of artists. Eiko regularly teaches at Wesleyan University, NYU, and Colorado College. She received an honorary degree from Colorado College in 2020.

Shingo Umehara's interest lies in education, art, and words. He lives and works in Tokyo, Japan. Over the last few years, he has committed to providing support for Japanese high school students who wish to study in America. He is passionate about demystifying how we interact with words, facts and understandings on a social level.

[18] [19]

DELICIOUS MOVEMENT MANIFESTO

Move to linger, rest, sleep, and dream.
Move to taste and share.
Move to forget and remember.
Look at dance as a flower that grows, blooms, wilts, to be noticed, and be savored.
Appreciate life as movement (even in relative stillness).
Feel everyone's life as an unrecoverable, transient, precious process.
Nurture kinetic imagination to others living or dead.
Be with others (present or lost), find a way to enjoy conflicts.
Be sensual. Be beautiful and inviting in ways that are not necessarily sexual.
Dance a solo as a duet with a shadow. Dance a duet as a solo remembering a shadow.
Enjoy the flow of life but also enjoy being stuck. There is always something that can move even when one is stuck.
Do necessary things well, but more importantly do unnecessary things passionately.
Think about what dead people might want from us.
Honor silence.
Distance is malleable.
Time is not even, and space is not empty.

Please add your own.

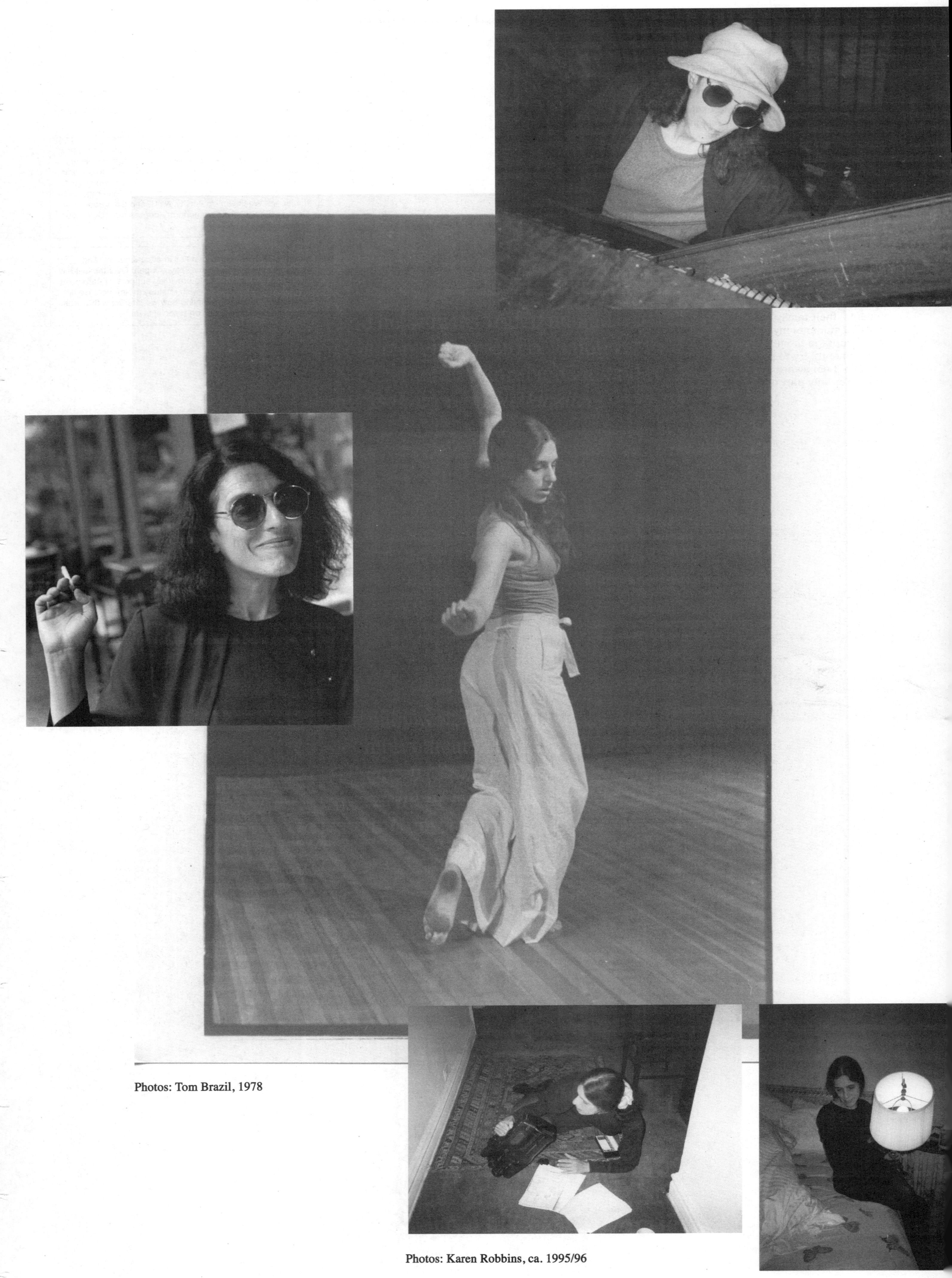

Photos: Tom Brazil, 1978

Photos: Karen Robbins, ca. 1995/96

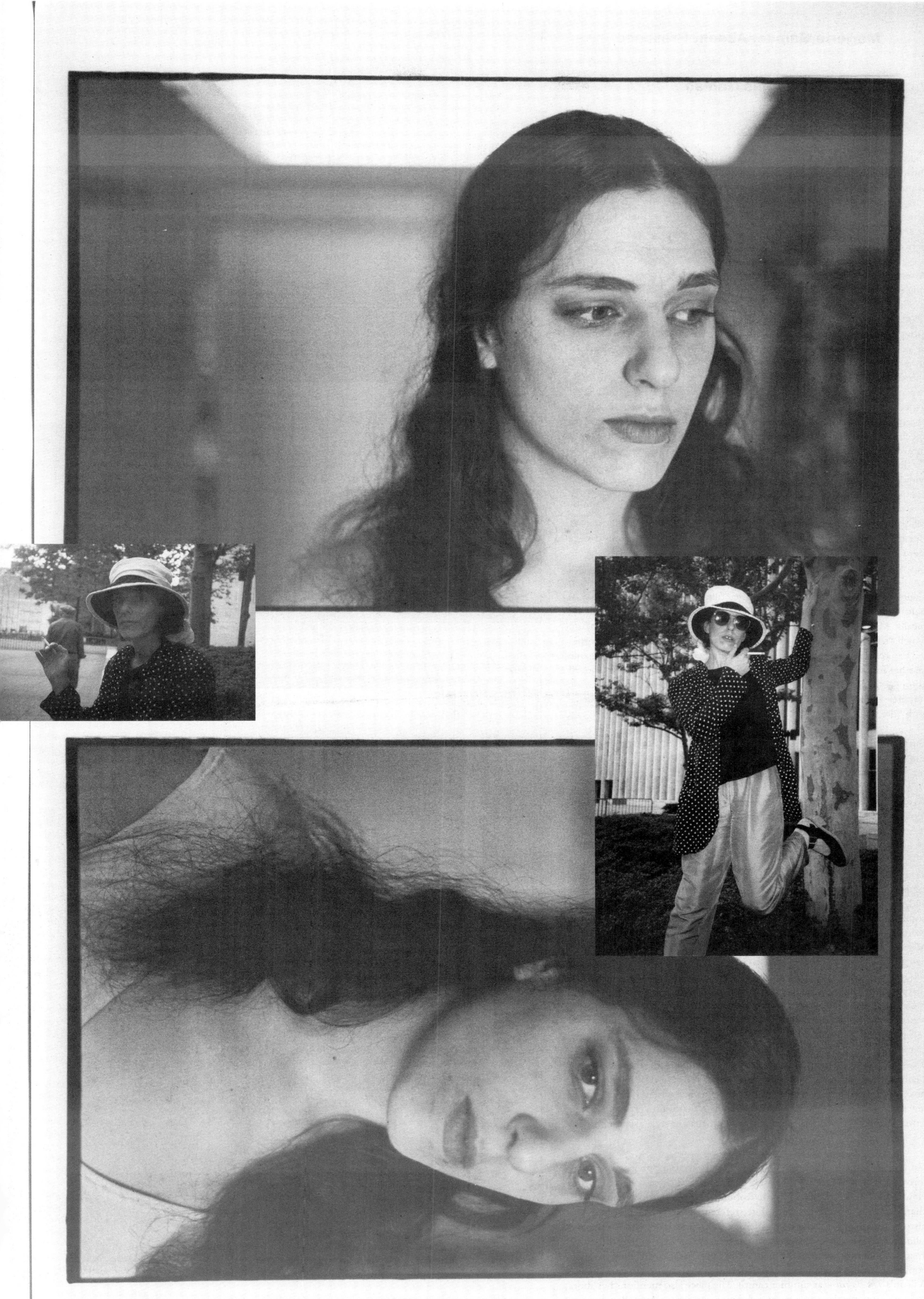

Marjorie Gamso: Absent Presence

Nicholas Gamso

Choreographer Marjorie Gamso (1944–2011) created dozens of dances throughout her life, as well as film and video pieces, published and unpublished essays, and poems. Her work was performed at PS1 (at the para-narrative "Dance/Text" festival in 1980), The Kitchen, the New Museum, and the Cunningham studio at Westbeth; she often performed at The Construction Company, a small dance theater on East 18th Street, between 1980 and her death.[1]

Although she took ballet classes at the 92nd Street Y, and organized a single student performance at Skidmore College (before transferring to Columbia), Marjorie only began to produce dances in earnest after relocating to Los Angeles in 1968. She became active in happenings and group improvisations, appearing in two Steve Paxton pieces at Ace Gallery in Venice, while at the same time studying ballet with Carmelita Maracci. It was in LA, too, that she presented her first work of professional choreography: *Octopus City* (1970), at the University of Southern California, part of a festival sponsored by Experiments in Art and Technology. Eight dancers stood on individual plexiglass platforms, each over a bay of colored lights. As the lights switched on and off, the dancers executed specific movement combinations—a conceit that anticipated Marjorie's future interests in chance and variability, in addition to her complicated production designs. When she returned to New York in 1971, she studied with James Waring and Merce Cunningham and in 1973 founded her own company, Marjorie Gamso and the Energy Crisis.

Marjorie's choreography was inventive, difficult, and, above all, precise. But it sometimes had the illusion of disorganization. Her group dances were full of repeated gestures that moved at different speeds, falling out of sync and creating a sense of dissonance and plurality. She liked to inject chaotic elements—in *Fugitive Furniture* (1983), she threw wooden chairs from a balcony onto the stage, filling it with obstructions just before a dancer's entrance. Bryan Hayes, who appeared in the piece, recalls Marjorie's preference for a "choreography of indirection" in which "some element was left out of the equation that the dancer would have to resolve."[2] Dancer and choreographer were conspiring, driving one another forward. Perhaps this approach explains the devotion she enjoyed among a small circle of collaborators—writing in *The New York Times*, critic Jennifer Dunning described Marjorie's dancers moving about the stage with "dreamy reverence."[3]

But it was never just dance. She used tape recorders, silent film reels, a polaroid camera, live video projection—components that weren't always part of the performance, but enabled a kind of research into the moving body. In a study for her unfinished cycle *The Enlightenment* (1989–92), she made a video of herself dancing, scanned the tape with an optical printer, and replicated individuals frames; she could examine her movements, learn them in reverse. The process would, in turn, distort the final product, giving the impression of faint "ghost images" haunting her figure.

Technical experiments like these were often alibis for more philosophical explorations. Marjorie was fascinated by the discourse of self and other and, in later pieces, cast fellow performers to play her double—including a cousin, Sophia Orlow, in her final dance *After You* (2011). As the dancer and writer Kenneth King remarked in a tribute to Marjorie published in *Dance Magazine*, "[h]er dance always confronted and celebrated otherness."[4] She had, in fact, studied anthropology in college (reputedly soliciting a graduate school recommendation from Margaret Mead) and was versed in critical theory, psychoanalysis, and modern literature, which she read for hours each day, cigarette in hand. Her eccentric tastes and preoccupations had a way of appearing in her performance work, sometimes as a kind of veiled self-portraiture. She identified strongly with Lucia Joyce, for example, channeling the famous dancer and schizophrenic during a segment of *After You.* Later she conceived a piece around the life and death of Charlotte Temple, the doomed protagonist of Susanna Rowson's so-titled 1791 novel—part of an unfinished collaboration with Andrew Gurian. These few examples (of many) evince an aestheticism that was everywhere in her work, and which set it apart from the more austere style associated with live art since the 1960s.

"In the Continuous Present . . ." is one of several unpublished writings recovered from Marjorie's files after her death, and since collected by the New York Public Library's Jerome Robbins Dance Division. The essay is characteristically Marjorie: deliberate; referential; drawing from personal history (disclosing a "mad love" for a "genuine madman"); reflexive (alluding to her own "skewed romanticism"); dosed with portentous imagery (a hunter wearing the pelts of his prey) and confrontations with popular culture (experiencing her first period as she prepared to star in Sandy Wilson's *The Boyfriend* at summer camp). The piece also mentions her short and unhappy marriage to a theater director and writer, Jerry Benjamin—an experience that is not addressed in any of Marjorie's other work.

In the Continuous Present . . .
Marjorie Gamso

1. A Party Dress. It is pink, of course, and it is organdy. It itches and makes me feel special, desirable. No subsequent garment has ever produced such sensations. Yet sometimes, when I dress up for a performance (a ritual dressing up always precedes the act of performing), I am reminded of the garment that had the power to transform the one it clothed, and I feel special and desirable. I wonder how hunters feel when they put on the skins of animals they have killed.

2. The Poor Little Match Girl. Every telling of this story moves me to tears. I learn that the tears produced by tear-jerkers are permissible tears while those produced by mishaps and misbehavior are mere self-indulgences. Later, when I learn to read for myself, I read everything as a tear-jerker. Like Don Quixote and Madame Bovary, I have learned to misread. An eternal curse on Hans Christian Anderson who deceived me for so long! When there are tears in your eyes, you are apt to miss the tears in things -- yes, "the tears in things."

3. A Secret Club. There are three of us. We collect colored pencils (actually, we steal them from 5&10¢ stores) and sharpen them down to nothing, saving the sacred shavings and glueing them on to cigar boxes. Sometimes, we paint and shellac the fetish objects we have created; other times, we leave them raw, unfinished; ultimately, it is their fate to be destroyed. We are, after all, a secret club, a band of robbers; we have to erase our tracks. Is it an accident that the career I eventually choose, dancing, consists of tracing gestures in time and space and erasing them? No, it isn't an accident: I still love the forbiddenness of the activity, the sense of adventure into a realm both sacred and profane. I admit, however, that the impermanence of the work troubles and saddens me with increasing frequency.

4. The Grey Goose. I play the role of the grey goose in an enactment of the folk song that begins, "O my daddy went a-hunting, lord, lord, lord. . ." I do not realize, at the time, that this inconsequential grade school sketch marks the beginning of my life as a dancer and of the skewed romanticism that will come to characterize my subsequent work in dance -- a dying goose as opposed to a swan.

5. The Boy Friend. All in one summer, I get to play Polly Brown in "The Boy Friend," have my first menstrual period and my first adolescent romance. I'm at a summer camp where boys and girls are separated except for 15 minute meetings after dinner and closely chaperoned "socials" on Friday nights. My boy friend only does the "slow dances," so at the socials we sit primly on the sidelines, looking on a bit disdainfully at the awkward lindy-hopping of our peers. It is cool to disdain rock 'n roll, it is cool to disdain adolescence, it is cool to disdain. . . .

1

6. Bridge. I pick up this compulsive card game at HUNTER COLLEGE HIGH SCHOOL. There are enough of us who have learned the basic rules of the game that a foursome can usually be found in any given class at any given hour. Sometimes, it is even possible to play during class -- during those classes in which the teacher looks at her lesson plan instead of the students in the room. I am the only one of the bridge players who isn't clever enough to do well at schoolwork without paying attention to it, but I absolutely refuse to degrade myself by giving my attention to the kind of education being offered in school. School -- a place where the (supposedly) knowing pass on the (supposedly) known to the unknowing -- seems to me to have very little to do with learning. It still seems to me (5/28/86) that what's interesting to learn about is what's unknown, and that only when teacher and student, master and apprentice, adept and beginner grope towards it, together, unknowing, does significant learning take place.

7. Class Consciousness. During orientation, they give out maps of the town where the college is located and warn you about the streets you must avoid. It's a "town and gown" town, they say. Help! I'm a prisoner in an ivy tower. I read the daily newspaper assiduously as if the smell of ink could somehow put me in touch with the reality from which I am so far removed.

8. L'Année Dernière à Marienbad. I'm enthralled. Nothing is predictable and everything is inevitable. The characters (including that central character, the camera) glide back and forth between the present tense and the past one with such slippery grace -- experience I've been writing for. After Marienbad, it recurs with other works of art that I encounter. One day it occurs with a man in whom nothing is predictable and everything is inevitable, a genuine madman.

9. Mad Love. The encounter with the man becomes an affair, later a marriage; still later, a memory -- no, a whole memory theatre filled with images of pain, grief, anger, pity, love and delirium. (On memory theatre, see Frances Yates' The Art of Memory.)

10. California. I hitchhike every day to ballet lessons, to rehearsals, to workshops in invisible theatre, to the university where I'm enrolled as a graduate student in a department of anthropology (my feelings about school remaining unchanged, I finally do quit). I make close friends, friends who risk poverty and danger in order to dance. I've never known such close friendships before: we go late at night to brightly lit delis where the waiters and waitresses have been trained to refill coffee cups every quarter hour; we talk faster and faster as the clock ticks on, switching back and forth between standard English and hip-talk, never quite finding the words for what we have to say to each other. The whole State of California is laid back except us; we're energized, we love to dance.

2

11. The Work. I am invited to make a piece for an "Experiments in Art and Technology" festival. I think about nothing else but the piece 24 hours a day for days and days. I am both thrilled and disappointed with the resulting work, but I realize that the work itself has become more important than the friendly milieu in which it takes place. To develop the work, I return to New York. I sublet a filmmaker's loft on Chambers Street. I am practicing hard and studying hard and going to office jobs (best of all are the ones that are totally routine, where I can daydream and contemplate The Work while typing, etc.). I am always working when I am awake and always I am awake until exhaustion overcomes me late at night. I am now the opposite of the sluggard I was at HUNTER COLLEGE HIGH SCHOOL.

12. Ambition. Now that I am always working, I find myself wanting recognition. How to get myself recognized as a choreographer? Well, there is one older and respected choreographer who believes in what I do and tries to help. He dies prematurely. I miss his sage sad eyes and his mordant wit and his good intentions for me. Curiously, however, within weeks following his death, opportunities begin to come my way: a teaching gig in England, a sizable grant from the government. Strange to feel that Jimmy's death was somehow connected to my sudden good fortune; sobering to realize how short-lived good fortune can be. No invitations to appear at important European festivals following my trip to England, no big grants the following season – only a few invitations to work as artist-in-residence at a few unexceptional colleges with, by and large, unexceptional student bodies. I accept the invitations. I continue working and wanting the recognition that one is always wanting.

13. Ennobling Blood. Every month now, I bleed excessively and undergo severe bouts of nausea and fatigue, violent upheavals of the digestive system. No doctor that I consult has any miracle cure to offer. Will I at least be ennobled by suffering? Will it make me wiser? A better artist? Will it prepare me for sainthood?

3

The origin of the text remains a mystery. Many of her essays and commentaries began as grant applications, for example her unfinished "Proposal for a Seminar on Chance," dated 2004, which relates the experience of undergoing an MRI. Other writings, like a twelve-page single-spaced letter to the audience of her *Enlightenment* cycle, were written to "supplement" her dances. "In the Continuous Present…" is more autobiographical than either of these, and considerably shorter—thirteen vignettes, written as a list, perhaps with a larger project in mind. Clearly it was worked, edited; in the archive, there is a copy with some hand-written corrections (the list numbered, as it is here). I think of the text as an accidental counterpoint to Marjorie's essay "Apartment" (1999), which accompanied a video piece of the same name, reflecting on what she saw as a cloistered childhood—growing up on West 93rd Street in Manhattan—and a difficult relationship with her mother: "It was for that brief period after my mother's death my privilege (indeed, it was my duty as 'executor' of her 'will') to transgress the law to which I was subject as a child … 'DO NOT TOUCH,' and all the variants."[5]

Reading "In the Continuous Present … ," I find a whole "memory theater" (Marjorie's phrase, borrowed from the historian Frances Yates) of the artist in her youth. There are early encounters with stage and screen, adolescent embarrassments, intellectual rites of passage. She is bored with LA, uninterested in the "friendly milieu" of artists she meets. She's captivated by her own mind and hungry for rigorous, meaningful work ("I am now the opposite of the sluggard I was at Hunter College High School"). Signs of distress are there, too. She admits to "wanting the recognition one is always wanting" and betrays specific disappointments: "No invitations to appear at important European festivals following my trip to England, no big grants the following season." There are other, more personal hardships. The essay is dated, parenthetically, May 28, 1986; within a few months, she would visit my family in Lubbock, Texas to undergo a hysterectomy—she suffered horribly from endometriosis—traveling 2,000 miles from New York to spare herself the stress of convalescing on 93rd Street. The last lines of the text refer to her illness and intimate a succession of crises to come.

Marjorie's essay is noteworthy for another reason. The Jimmy she references is James Waring, the celebrated avant-garde choreographer with whom Marjorie studied some time after her return to New York in 1971 and before Waring's death, from cancer in 1975, at the age of 53. Marjorie shared Jimmy's idiosyncrasies, his sense of humor, his radical commitments.[6] The two seemed to move in similar circles, even before she became his student. (He almost certainly knew her husband, who reviewed one of Jimmy's productions in the *Floating Bear,* in 1962.) But the substance of their friendship remains unknowable to outsiders, and was, in any case, cut short by fate. "Strange to feel that Jimmy's death was somehow connected to my sudden good fortune," she writes, describing a grant she received shortly after he died, "sobering to realize how short-lived good fortune can be."

***

1 Thanks to Sally Bowden, Andrew Gurian, Leslie Satin, Elena Alexander, Kenneth King, Ellen Kastel, Philip Beitchman, and especially Jeff Gamso for help in researching this. Much of the information came from Marjorie Gamso's performance chronology, assembled by Bowden and Gurian, for the NYPL's Jerome Robbins Dance Division. Thanks also to Ammiel Alcalay and Lost & Found: The CUNY Poetics Documentation Initiative for supporting my inquiry into Marjorie's unpublished writings several years ago. Special thanks to Karen Robbins and Tim Armstrong, partner of the late Tom Brazil, for providing photographs of Marjorie.

2 Bryan Hayes, "Marjorie (His One Thousand and One Memories)," unpublished manuscript, 2012.

3 Jennifer Dunning, "Dance: Marjorie Gamso," *The New York Times*, March 6, 1979.

4 Kenneth King, "Marjorie Gamso: Dancing the Enigma," *Dance Magazine*, January 12, 2012.

5 Marjorie Gamso, "Apartment," *Women & Performance* 10 (1999), nos. 1–2 ('Performing Autobiography,' ed. Leslie Satin), 59–68.

6 For more on Waring's work and teaching, see Leslie Satin, "The Philosophy of Art History, Dance, and the Sixties," in *Reinventing Dance in the 1960s: Everything Was Possible*, eds. by Sally Banes and Andrea Harris (Madison: University of Wisconsin Press, 2003).

Nicholas Gamso teaches in the History of Art and Visual Culture program at California College of the Arts.

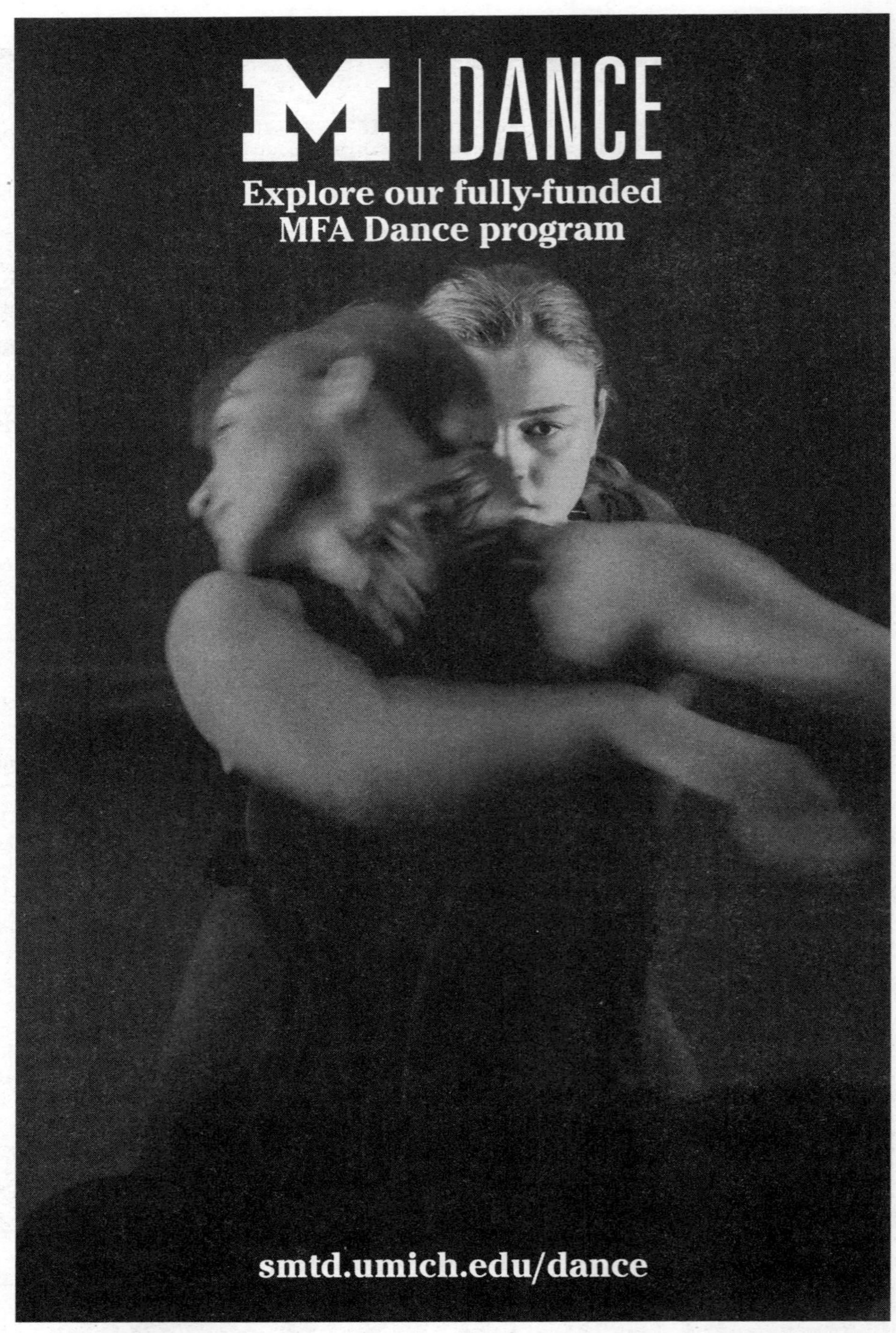
M | DANCE
Explore our fully-funded
MFA Dance program
smtd.umich.edu/dance

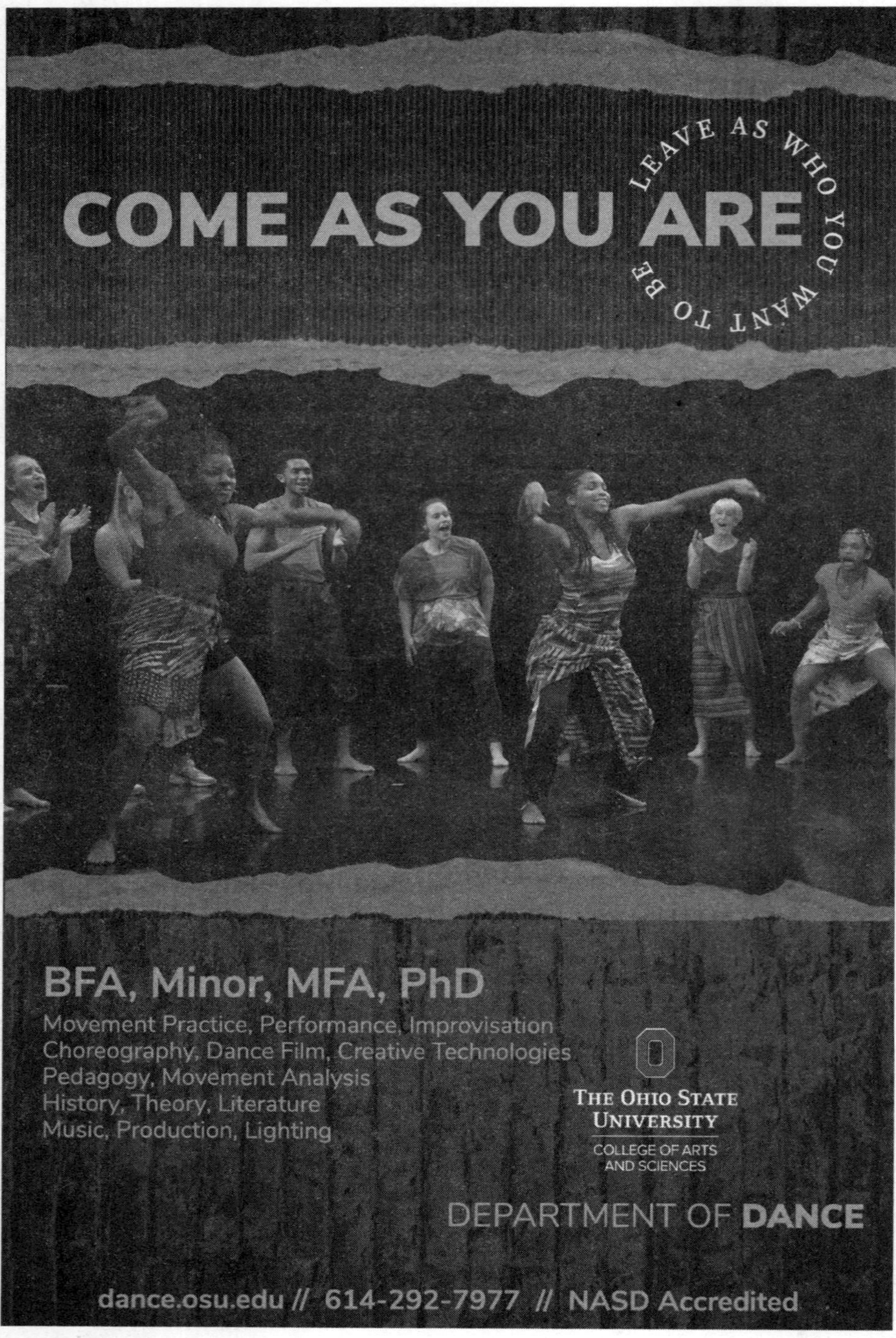
COME AS YOU ARE
LEAVE AS WHO YOU WANT TO BE
BFA, Minor, MFA, PhD
Movement Practice, Performance, Improvisation
Choreography, Dance Film, Creative Technologies
Pedagogy, Movement Analysis
History, Theory, Literature
Music, Production, Lighting
THE OHIO STATE UNIVERSITY
COLLEGE OF ARTS AND SCIENCES
DEPARTMENT OF DANCE
dance.osu.edu // 614-292-7977 // NASD Accredited

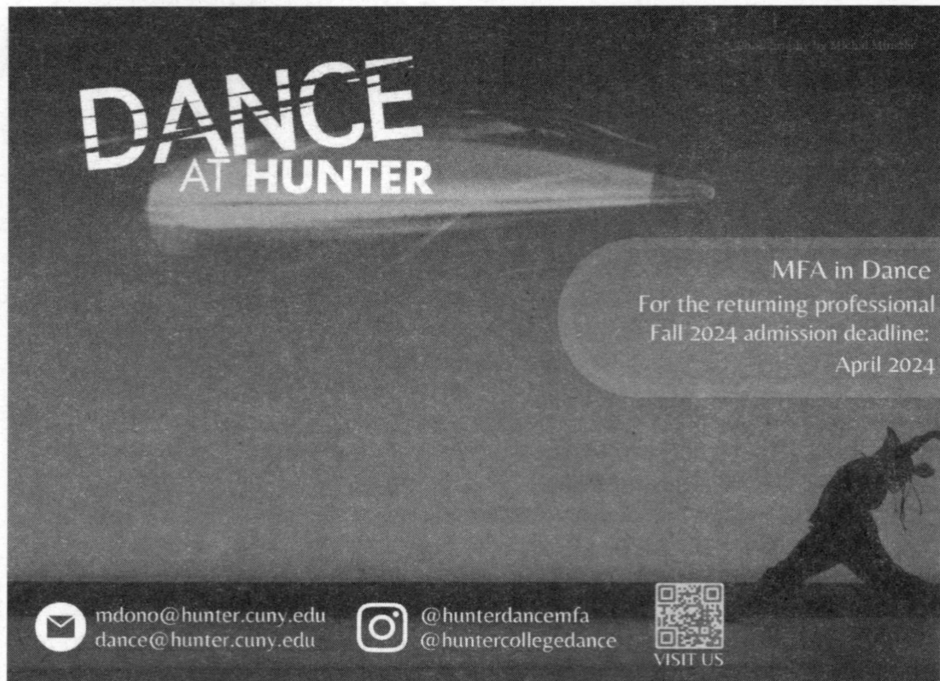
DANCE
AT HUNTER
MFA in Dance
For the returning professional
Fall 2024 admission deadline:
April 2024
mdono@hunter.cuny.edu
dance@hunter.cuny.edu
@hunterdancemfa
@huntercollegedance
VISIT US

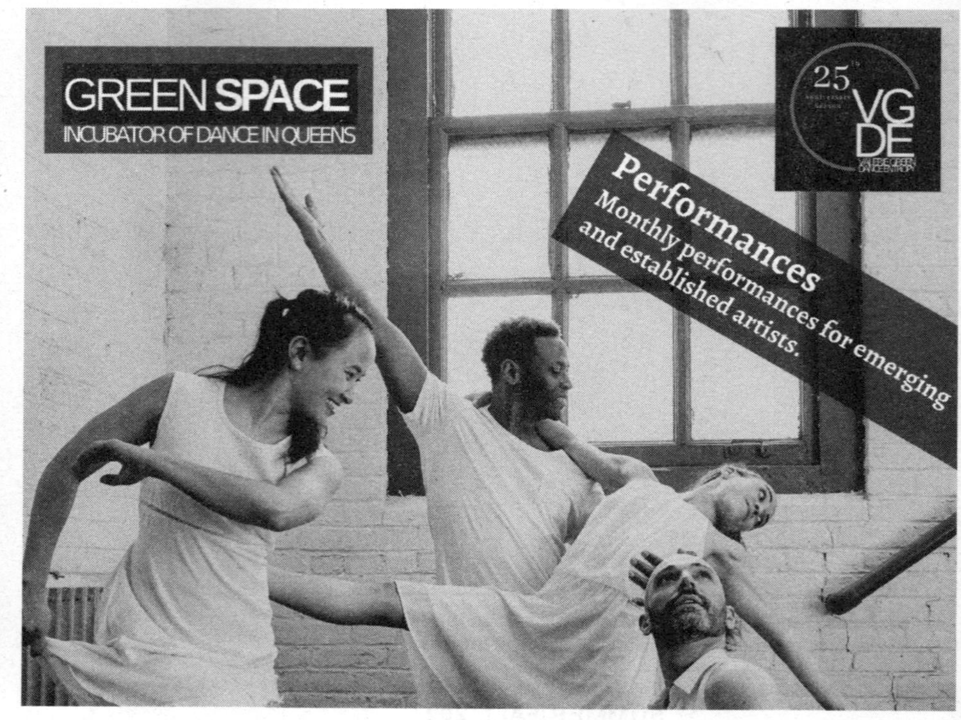
GREEN SPACE
INCUBATOR OF DANCE IN QUEENS
25
VGDE
Performances
Monthly performances for emerging
and established artists.

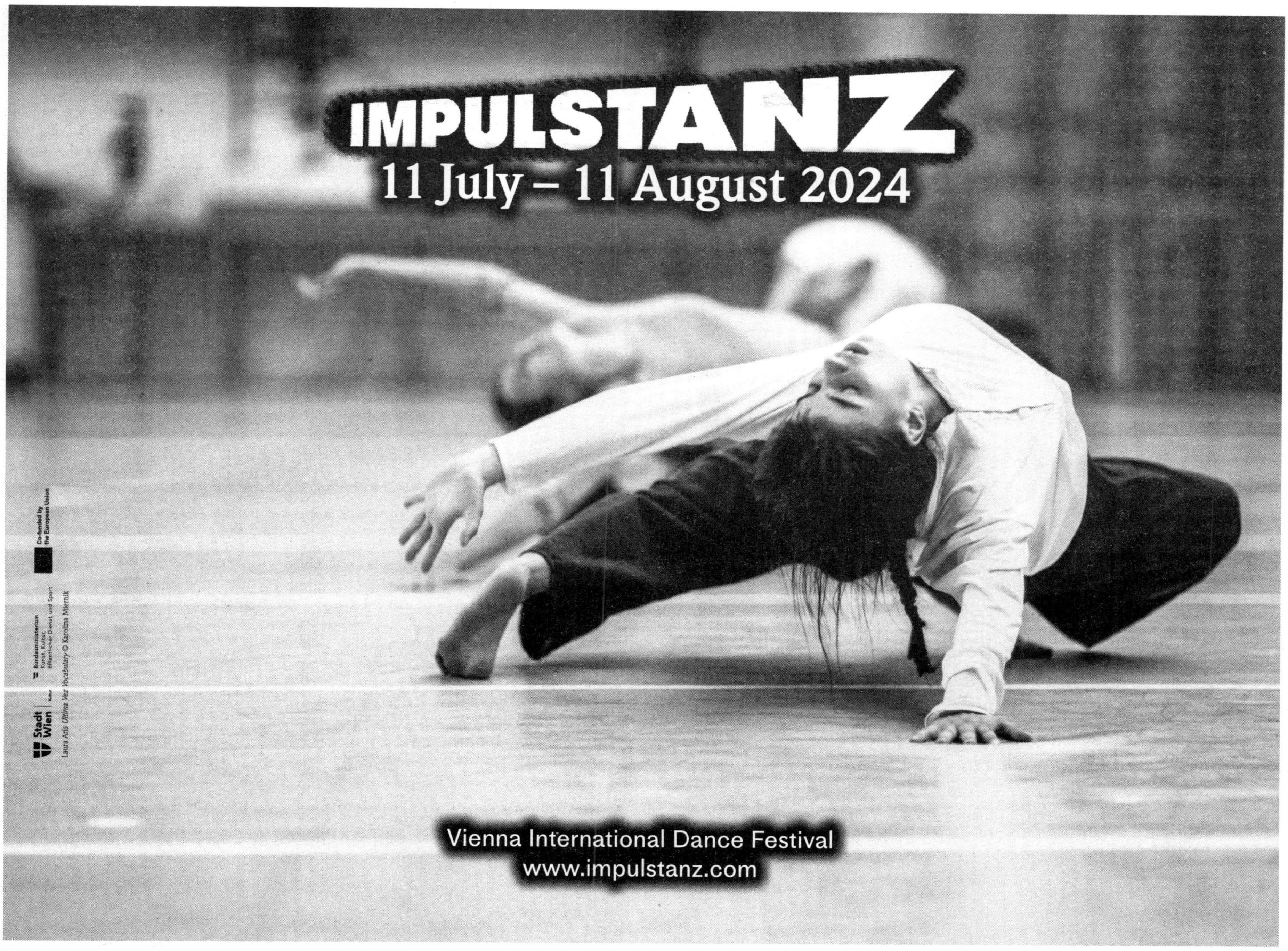

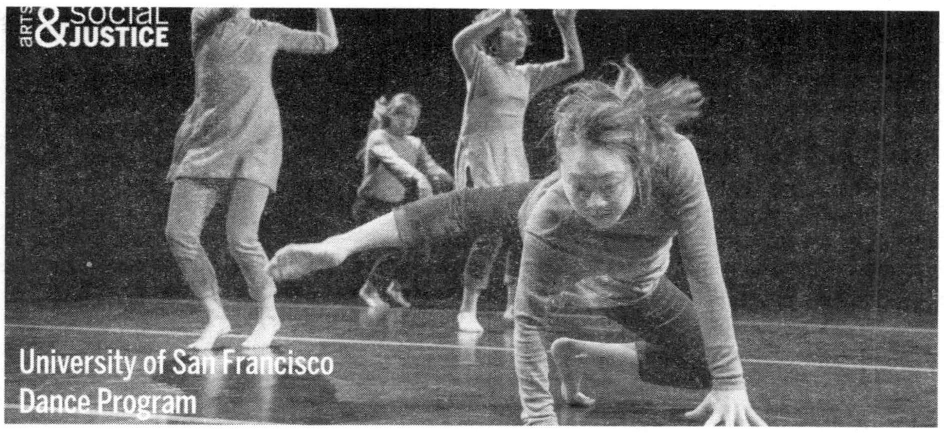

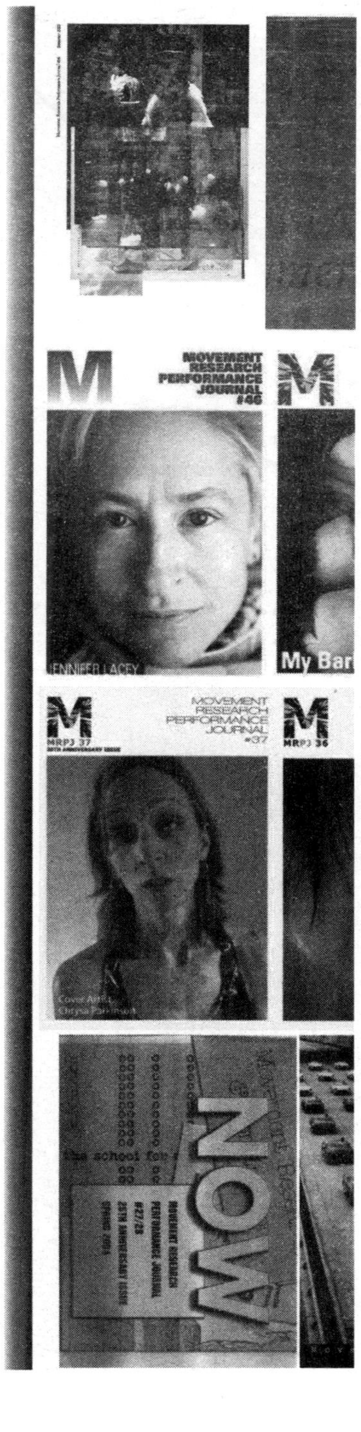

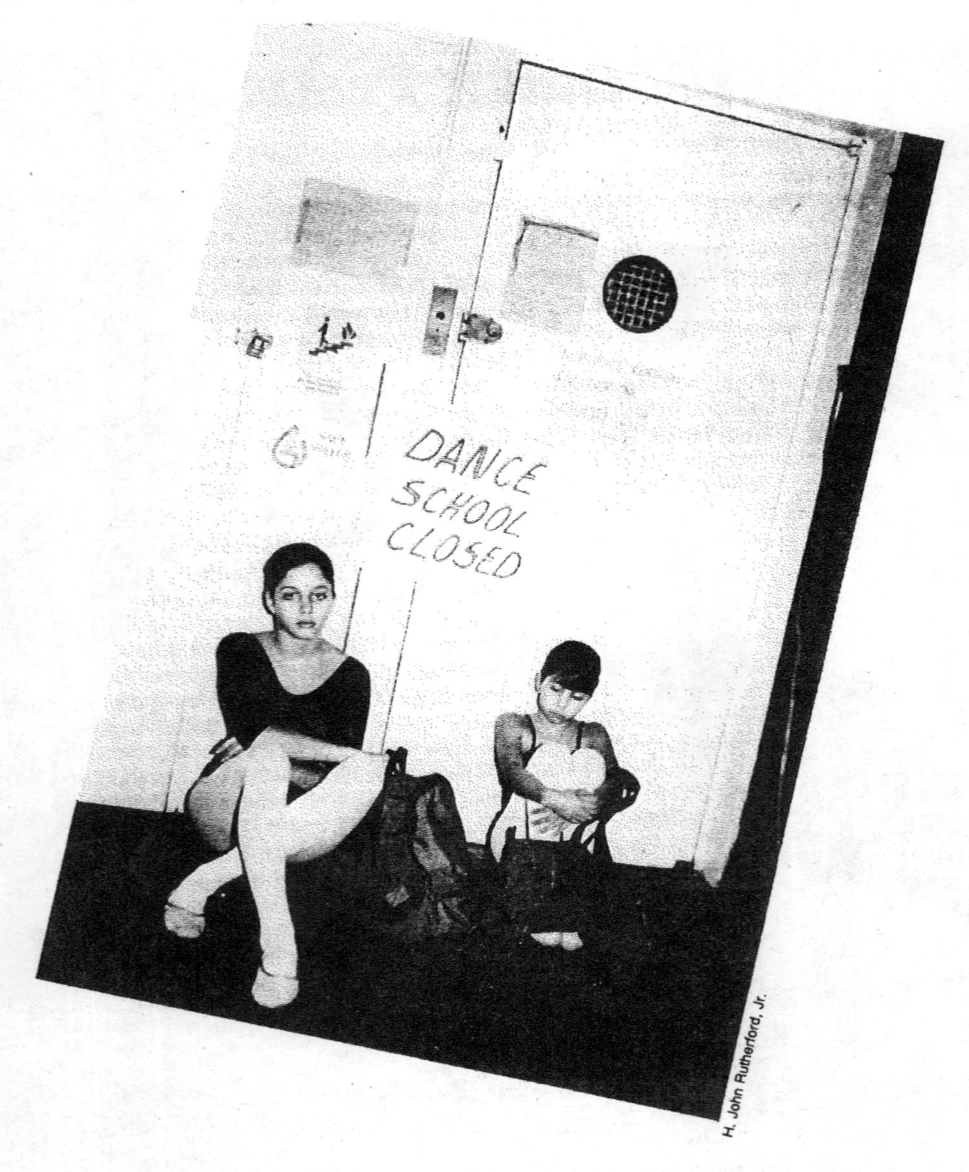

H. John Rutherford, Jr.

01	02	03	04	05	06	07	08	09	10
11	12	13	14	15	16	17	18	19	20
21	22	23	24	25	26	27	28	29	30
31	32	33	34	35	36	37	38	39	40
41	42	43	44	45	46	47	48	49	50
51	52	53	54	55	56	57	**58**	**59**	

Summer/Fall 2023